Desiccated Land
An American in Kashmir

David Lepeska

Desiccated Land

1st Edition published in India by Vishwakarma Publications in May 2023
© David Lepeska

ISBN - 978-93-95481-20-5

Disclaimer

The views and opinions expressed in this book are the author's own and the facts are as reported by her, and the publisher are not in any way liable for the same.

Published by:
Vishwakarma Publications
34A/1, Suyog Center, 7th Floor, Gultekadi Marketyard Road, Giridhar Bhavan Chowk, Pune-411037, Maharashtra, India.
Mob. : +91 9168682200
Email: info@vpindia.co.in
Website: www.vishwakarmapublications.com

Cover Painting: Masood Hussain
Cover: Muntazir Yaseen, Chaitali Nachnekar
Typeset and Layout: Vishwakarma Publications
Printed at: Square Digital, Pune

Contents

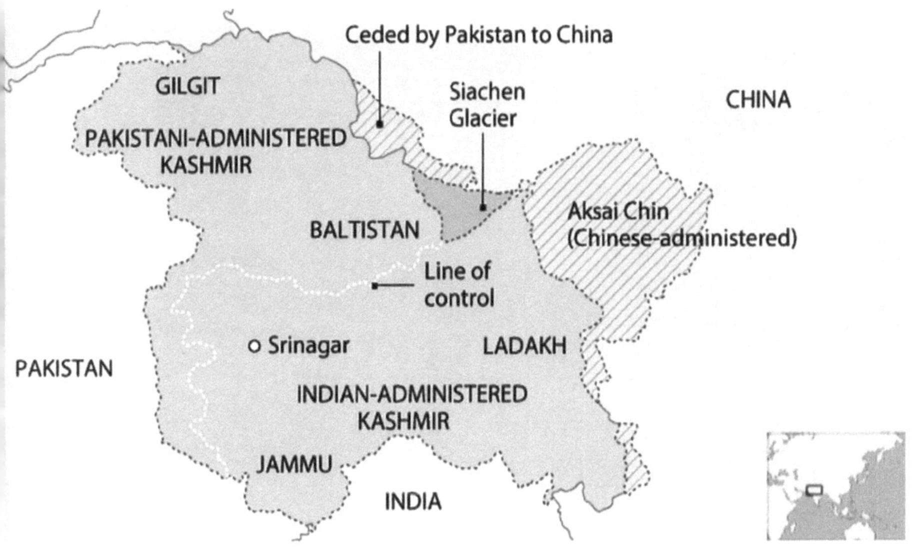

Political Maps of Jammu & Kashmir

"Where could this place be? Grand mountain peaks covered with snow, full of ice, abounding in cold. I am there. I am an eagle. I am flying over the mountainous terrain...There is no ocean in sight. From all ends, the territory is completely dry." [1]

Steering a Better Course in Kashmir

By Wajahat Habibullah[2] — November 2022

What a small world. I've been friends for years with Sajjad Haider, his former boss at *Kashmir Observer*, but I've never met David Lepeska, the author of this book. In fact, we hail from different generations, countries, continents and cultures. Yet much of *Desiccated Land*, published as part of *Kashmir Observer's* Silver Jubilee, resonates with my own experiences.

I've known the family of Agha Ashraf Ali, the renowned Kashmiri educator and intellectual who plays a key role in the book, for decades. Around 1980, I worked with his cousin Agha Muzaffar when he served as Kashmir's Chief Secretary. I was once a suitor for Agha Ashraf's radiant daughter, and while serving in India's US embassy I became friendly with his poet son Agha Shahid Ali. Years before at New York's Hamilton College, Agha Shahid had taught my niece, Pakistani novelist Kamila Shamsie, who credits him with shaping her feel for language. Agha Ashraf's wife Sufia came, like me, from Lucknow. I suspect this is why she was so cordial, though I never received the sumptuous meals David recalls at their Rajbagh home.

But beyond social ties, it's clear that David and I share a deep and abiding love for Kashmir and its people. His book is a tribute to a community in crisis, and it has confronted me with a pointed question: must I also shoulder some blame for Kashmir's enduring trauma?

I grew up near Pune, as my father was helping establish the National Defense Academy, and studied at The Doon School, near Dehradun. My first visit to Kashmir was on family holiday as a teenager. My memories of that trip are hazy, but they do bring to mind something like the vision of Kashmir-as-paradise David describes in his Introduction. In 1969 I returned as a civil servant with the goal of completing the Valley's integration with the rest of the country. At the time, this seemed a real possibility. Jammu & Kashmir had been denied full democratic functioning since its inception, but the air was alive with hope. I soon came to share the aspirations of the local people, and worked to address their discontent. By the time David arrived in the late 1990s, my time in Kashmir was coming to an end. I had served in every Kashmir district and in Jammu's frontier district of Poonch and by then it was cruelly obvious that full integration would remain an elusive dream.

David's book, unsurprisingly, touches on many of the key figures and events of this failure. In an interview, Islamist leader Asiya Andrabi tells him, "Yasin Malik is also I think somewhere engaged (by the intelligence services)." Indeed, from 1991, when I was Divisional Commissioner Kashmir, I was Malik's handler — a situation that led to mutual respect and an abiding friendship. Agha Ashraf, who served as host for several of my meetings with Malik, tells David that among separatist leaders, Yasin "is the only one who's remained uncorrupt" — and although Yasin is today facing trial for terrorism, this view aligns with my experience.

David mentions, almost in passing, the devastating impact on young Kashmiri minds of the firing by security forces on protesting civilians in Bijbehara in 1993. Nearly 30 unarmed citizens, including women and children, were killed, and more than 60 injured. I was in my second term as Kashmir's Commissioner at the time, and my report on the incident became the first case taken up by the Centre's new National Human Rights Commission. After thorough investigation, I found that the firing was entirely unprovoked — a view contested by the Border Security Force responsible for the firing. My report detailed a panicked response by a frightened paramilitary, mostly made up of striplings. On the basis of its own examination, the Commission recommended that 11 BSF troops be dismissed from service and brought to criminal trial. These young men were court-martialed, but the proceedings were kept secret on the grounds of maintaining troop morale, and nothing more came of it.

The tragedy is that Bijbehara was by no means the worst such incident. The first of these, before my posting as Commissioner, was the 1990 Gawkadal massacre. But as with the Bijbehara shooting and subsequent events I investigated, this made no impact on the government's position or approach, putting India's failures in Kashmir in sharp relief and ultimately warping the minds of a generation of Kashmiris. From then on, Kashmiris were all too well aware that the state did not support them and would be unlikely to deliver anything resembling justice.

In the book, David highlights a 2016 report by Doctors Without Borders finding that nearly half of adult Kashmiris had some form of mental disorder, while an incredible 9 out of 10 had experienced some sort of conflict-related trauma. Count me among them, after suffering a near fatal accident on a Srinagar street in 1993 that left me in the hospital with a split skull. It took me decades to recover, and to this day I work with the Healing Minds Foundation to improve the lives of the countless Kashmiris who have been 'collateral damage' of this unending conflict.

What is remarkable about this book is David's complete identification with Kashmiris, so that even his view of the Valley's history is through the prism of a Kashmiri eye. For the foreign correspondent, he argues, "the fears and concerns of the local population become your own." His view is that from Mughal times Kashmiris have been under "one or another oppressive yoke."

At one point he even faults Kashmiris for having made mourning and victimhood a defining trait, thus rendering legitimate liberation antithetical to their way of life. At another he places the blame elsewhere. "Count Pakistan, Great Britain, the United States and the UN among the guilty as well," David writes, also pointing to Hindu and Muslim extremists and the international media. I agree entirely with this assessment, and would go one further. During an interview

Kashmir's spiritual head, the young *Mirwaiz* Umer Farooq, tells David: "The problem from Delhi is that they don't have a consistent policy on Kashmir." Having served in Kashmir more than a dozen years and advised several prime ministers on Kashmir policy over several decades, I confirm this assertion.

David also laments being inadequately critical of Kashmiri, Pakistani and Indian politicians during his time in Kashmir, and lacking the determination and conviction to report more conflict-related stories against his editor's wishes. Reading this book has helped me reflect on whether I too could have helped the state steer a different course.

I take solace in the thought that, as Kashmir Commissioner for two interludes between 1990 and 1993, I provided Kashmiris with perhaps their only ear within government at a time of complete administrative breakdown. And I'm proud that I never ordered my charges to fire on their fellow countrymen, even when confronted with hostile mobs hurling abuse at me personally. Even so, the Indian administration of that period — like that of today — has never been held to account. As a result, most Kashmiris now view India as merely one in a long line of oppressive rulers. Perhaps this book, in identifying and detailing so much that has been lost, will begin a movement toward Truth and Reconciliation in Kashmir.

The India of Mohandas K. Gandhi deserves nothing less.

■

Introduction

The seventh of eight children, I was born outside Chicago and grew up in the most wholesome of suburban family homes as the United States licked its Vietnam wounds and discoed into the go-go 80's. While their kids mercilessly pricked, chased and teased each other, my parents never fought, or even argued, really, and never seemed anything but in love. My father had studied engineering before becoming an entrepreneur, and did well enough: our Wisconsin lake house surely qualified us as upper middle class. My mother liked to wake her children with a song — "Good morning to you, Good morning to you. We're all in our places, with bright shining faces…" — after rising early to whip up great vats of pancakes or scrambled eggs. She'd make sandwiches and place them, with an apple and dessert, in brown paper bags that stood neatly folded on the counter, a child's name on each, by the time we'd cleared our plates. About once a week my father donned an apron to dabble in the kitchen, doctoring his beloved marinara or making a happy show of grilling a large hunk of meat. Our family touchstone, our talisman, to which we returned every Christmas, reciting lines aloud and coming away teary-eyed, was Frank Capra's *It's a Wonderful Life* — a heartwarming 1940's classic that places friends, family, and goodness before personal achievement. It was all very Norman Rockwell: childhood as blissful blur. As Ronald Reagan stared down the evil Soviet empire, the outside world failed to intrude on our *Leave It To Beaver* redoubt.[5]

Until it did. I was 10 when the eldest of us children, my brother Bill, who'd taught me how to tie my shoes, came home from college with fire in his eyes. Decades later I still feel the shock as I watched him rage at my parents for misleading us, as he put it, and failing to prepare us for a cold, dark world. The idyll had been shattered. Bill dropped out of the University of Chicago and was soon diagnosed as bipolar, then, years later, schizophrenic. My father's business failed and he was forced to downsize, selling one car, then another — one house, then another. For my senior year of high school, when only my younger brother and I remained, our family rented out a drafty farmhouse on the vast property of a wealthy friend.

Even so, my head remained in the clouds. My father's career downturn failed to encourage in me any discipline or focus. My life had always been charmed and there was little reason to think that might change. As I arrived at university, the Soviet Union had just been vanquished, history had supposedly ended and the good guys had won. Knighted by the double-edged sword of American entitlement, I felt certain whichever route I chose would be right. In Madison I started drinking beer and smoking weed, took literature and psychology classes and got top marks at socializing, but not at settling on a career path.

I had dabbled in writing for years — short stories I'd share with friends; articles for my high school newspaper — but it seemed an unlikely future. My interest seemed less about word smithery than about escaping into the protagonist's shoes or enjoying the unbridled life of writers like Ernest Hemingway, Jack Kerouac, Norman Mailer.

I felt a connection to famed WWII correspondent Ernie Pyle, but I was no Robert Fisk, who writes of being obsessed with becoming a foreign correspondent as an adolescent. I tended toward the flippant and superior: did one really need to study the craft to become a writer? I thought it was more about the daily doing of it, putting pen to paper. Though, of course, I wasn't doing it. I was mostly enjoying newfound freedoms, worry-free about the future. When a friend suggested an acting class, I dove in. I wasn't half bad, and within a year I'd convinced myself I was destined to be a movie star — a vision that rendered classes unnecessary.

In the middle of my third year of college I dropped out and moved to New York City. By the spring of 1998 I'd gotten as far as nabbing a few supporting roles in little-seen Downtown plays, which is to say not very far. Yet I had found relatively lucrative work as a writer-researcher for a small consulting firm.[6] I saved up for summer travel and settled on India after a friend's slideshow of his around-the-world journey spotlighted monkeys in the sub-continent. I was a big fan of monkeys. Not that I'd seen any outside a zoo. I'd never crossed an ocean. Apart from a few childhood hours strolling a Matamoros market with my family just across the Texas border — I can still hear the gum sellers' call: "Chiclets! Chiclets!" — I'd never stepped foot outside the US. But I dreamed of international escapades, a la James Bond, of tackling a life-defining challenge, as in *The Old Man and the Sea*, or cracking the confounding case, like Hercule Poirot.

On the eve of my departure an Indian immigrant friend offered some advice. "Enjoy yourself. Have an adventure," he said. "Just promise you won't go to Kashmir." Even back then I knew India and Pakistan had fought bitterly for this patch of land for ages. I was dimly aware of the insurgency and Kashmir's mountains and purported beauty. Thanks to an impulsive decision, I have since learned a great deal more.

The story of Kashmir begins with a glorious body of water.[7] Early in the *Nilamata Purana*, a folkloric Hindu history of Kashmir likely written in the 7th century, the goddess Sati creates a lake, Satisar, in the center of a Himalayan valley. "Enjoyable, heart-enrapturing, and the sporting place of the gods," the *Nilamata* says of Satisar, echoing modern-day rhapsodies of Srinagar's mountain-ringed Dal Lake. "Deep like the sky, bright with lotuses, containing cool and clear water, it is the most charming on the whole earth." [8]

Visiting the lake one day, a chief named Sanghra spies the stunning wife of the deity Indra and attempts to kidnap her. Indra intervenes and kills Sanghra — but not before the latter discharges himself into Satisar. His seed spawns a half-demon child known as Jalodbhava, or "water-born", who is granted immortality in the water. He begins destroying local villages, and when the gods come to kill him he hides in the lake. Frustrated, the gods urge Balarama, the brother of Krishna known for his skill with a plough, to knock down a mountain and clear a path for the water to flow out and expose Jalodbhava. "He broke forth Himalaya, the best of the mountains on earth, with plough," says the *Nilamata*. "This country will be called Kashmira. Because water, called *Ka*, was taken out by Balarama from this country."

Little is known with any certainty of Kashmir's pre-history, and an alternative etymology is that the word is derived from a lake ("mira") named for the Vedic sage Kashyapa. But in addition to touching on some possible geological history, the *Nilamata* version foreshadows modern-day Kashmir. In Sanskrit "*ka*" does mean water and "shimeer" means to dry out or desiccate, and geologists generally agree that the Kashmir Valley was in prehistoric times dominated by a lake, which may have drained through the Baramulla gap.[9] Hinduism, of course, advocates well-being through purity and prizes water for its ability to heal and purify. This is why the Ganges is so revered, and why the *Nilamata*, a Vedic Hindu text, is mainly a paeon to various bodies of water. In Hindu myth, to call a land "desiccated" is to describe it as unholy or irredeemable — particularly so when what dried out had been a heart-enrapturing playground of the gods. In life, as in lore, Kashmir is both heaven and hell.

It would be hard to find a more inapt physical description of this place than "sea of sand", as the *Nilamata* puts it. If the shape of India evokes a woman putting on her sari, as a novelist once asserted, then the Northeast is her extended left arm and Kashmir is her head, poised high in the western Himalayas and mulling warring suitors. The Valley, or Vale of Kashmir, is a 40-km by 140-km floodplain, almost completely surrounded by mountains. [10]Wedged between the subcontinent's deserts and arid plains and a vast expanse of Himalayan glacier, Kashmir is a climactic sweet spot, with all four seasons yet little extreme heat or cold. In winter, snow falls in golf ball-sized hunks and gets waist-high in a matter of hours. In summer, when southerly regions welcome the monsoon, Kashmir too sees torrents of rain. Dal Lake and the Jhelum River occasionally surge into Srinagar's streets, as in 2014 when the city was inundated and hundreds of nearby villages were submerged. In fact, melting Himalayan glaciers — including Kashmir's largest glacier, Kolahoi, which has lost a quarter of its area — are widely thought to have contributed to the devastating summer 2022 floods in Pakistan, which displaced tens of millions. [11]

The Himalaya may not remain "the abode of snow" much longer, but Kashmir remains lush, unlike much of the subcontinent — one reason it has long held a mythic beauty, inspiring visions of the cloud-shrouded Shangri-Las and Shambalas of other remote Himalayan regions.[12] The Valley has been called the Eden of the East, and canal-scored Srinagar the Venice of the East. [13]Like the gods that came before, the Mughals sought to possess Kashmir, filling it with vast parks and palaces. Emperor Jahangir built an elaborate garden along Dal Lake for his wife Nur Jahan, and named it Shalimar, or "abode of love".[14] That phrase might also describe Bollywood's portrayal of the Valley, in swoony romances like 1964's *Kashmir Kil Kali* and the 2012 Shah Rukh Khan vehicle *Jab Tak Hai Jaan*. A million Indians visited Kashmir in 2010, to choose a random year, despite the drumbeat of violence.[15] "If you look at Indian movies, every time they wanted an exotic locale, they would have a dance number in Kashmir. Kashmir was India's fairyland," Bombay-born Kashmiri-British novelist Salman Rushdie told The Paris Review in 2005. "It had that feeling of an enchanted space."[16]

For Kashmiris, the enchantment is gone. Few of the world's people or places can match the Valley for its almost uninterrupted history of persecution. Among the nicknames poet Agha Shahid Ali gave his homeland is "Cauchemar," French for nightmare. This paradise is a living hell, a venomous beauty, and its list of desiccators is endless. Start with Alexander the Great, who after battling King Porus along the Jhelum forced Kashmiri ruler Abisares to send jewels and elephants to signal his submission. In the fifth century AD, the Alchon Huns destroyed countless Buddhist stupas and monasteries, killed or drove into slavery thousands of Buddhists and forced monks out of Kashmir.[17] Rival warrior clans jockeyed for power in the 10th century until the Loharas gained control, ushering in three centuries of corruption and harsh taxation that enfeebled Kashmir.

The Lohara period did, however, lead into Kashmir's golden age, a quarter-millennium of relative amity and stability (Chapter Two) during which a sense of communal harmony, later dubbed *Kashmiriyat*, purportedly reigned.[18] Alas, the good times did not last. Led by Akbar, the Mughals annexed the Valley in 1586, built forts, gardens and palaces and ignored the abject poverty of Kashmiris, who suffered frequent famines.[19]

The Afghans, Sikhs, and Dogras then took their turns. For Kashmiris, each seemed worse than the last. Afghan "rule reduced the Valley to the lowest depths of penury, degradation and slavery," writes Pandit historian Prithivi Nath Kaul Bamzai.[20] British explorer William Moorcroft passed through Kashmir in 1822 with a caravan headed to Kashgar. "The Sikhs seem to look upon the Kashmirians as little better than cattle," he writes. [21]"Their appearance, half-naked and miserably emaciated, presented a ghastly picture of poverty and starvation."

After defeating the Sikh Empire in 1846, Britain sold Kashmir to Dogra leader Maharaja Gulab Singh. Gulab levied exorbitant taxes, banned Kashmiris from owning land and reintroduced the *begar* system, under which the state could put locals to work as needed for little or no pay. In this period Pandits solidified their standing as the local elite while Kashmiri Muslims sunk into debt-saddled peasantry. Very few Pandits died in the 1877-79 famine, for instance, as Muslims bore the brunt of the suffering. "When I first came to Kashmir in 1889, I found the people sullen, desperate and suspicious. They had been taught for many years that they were serfs without any rights," writes British civil servant Walter Lawrence. "The system of administration had degraded the people and taken all heart out of them."[22] Well, not all heart: conscripted to fight for Great Britain in WWI, the Kashmir Imperial Service Corps earned the title of most reliable troops and dozens of decorations.[23] In WWII, the Jammu and Kashmir Rifles regiment fought on Kennedy Peak in Burma. Many did not come home.

This catalog of subjugation finally brings us to the creation of India and the knotty Kashmir problem we know today, which is a legacy of the British Empire's bloodiest failure: the partition of Pakistan and India. The Raj may deserve some credit for helping give shape to modern India — its democratic framework, justice and administrative systems, and robust rail network — yet it surely merits considerable condemnation for the devastation that attended its departure.[24] As many as two million people died as countless Muslims living in India fled to the new state of Pakistan, from whence Hindus and Sikhs surged in the other direction. Partition was an orgiastic spasm of bloodletting disguised as population exchange. At least for those further south it was over in a few months. For the mostly Muslim population of Kashmir, seen as integral territory by both Pakistan and India, Partition continues today, though it took its time getting off the mark.

With Britain's departure in August 1947, Maharaja Hari Singh, great grandson of Gulab, was allowed, like the heads of hundreds of other princely states, to choose to join Pakistan or India. At the time, the population of Jammu and Kashmir was about three-fourths Muslim (77%), one-fifth Hindu (20%) and the rest mostly Sikh. Singh initially favored independence, envisioning himself the ruler of an expanded "Dogristan" that would stretch into Punjab.[25] But after his early August dismissal of the state's pro-independence prime minister, Ram Chandra Kak, many saw the maharaja tilting toward India. This spurred Pakistan to move to lay claim to mainly Muslim Kashmir. Officials close to Mohammad Ali Jinnah's Muslim League rallied a Pashtun militia in Pakistan's Northwest Frontier Province, which joined with rebels in western Kashmir's Poonch district and mounted an invasion. Outgunned, Hari Singh turned to Delhi for help. Indian Prime Minister Jawaharlal Nehru and Lord Mountbatten, Governor General of India, vowed to send troops if Singh signed the instrument of accession. He did just that on October 26, 1947, making Kashmir part of India and triggering the first Indo-Pakistan War.

"The fate of Kashmir is ultimately to be decided by the people," Nehru vowed days later on a visit to Srinagar.[26] A key provision of accession was that, once the state had been cleared of invaders, a plebiscite be held to allow the Kashmiri people to choose India or Pakistan. As the war heated up, India turned to the United Nations. In April 1948, the UN Security Council passed Resolution 47, calling for an immediate ceasefire and for Pakistani forces to withdraw and India to reduce its military presence, in order for a plebiscite to be held. The ceasefire went into effect on the first day of 1949, but the UN Commission failed to persuade the two sides to agree on conditions for a vote. Pakistani officials felt the likeliest outcome in the Muslim-majority region would be to join Pakistan, and pushed for the referendum. India saw itself as in possession of Jammu and Kashmir, since its leader had signed an instrument of accession, and saw no reason for a vote. The status quo held and spurred two more conflicts, in 1965 and 1971, after which Pakistan controlled Azad Kashmir, Gilgit and Baltistan, while India controlled Jammu, Kashmir and the mainly Buddhist plateau of Ladakh. China, meanwhile, held Aksai Chin and part of the Siachen Glacier. As of early 2023, the planned plebiscite remains a distant dream and tensions remain high along the Line of Control, between Indian and Pakistani territories, and the Line of Actual Control, between India and China. None are happy with their lot.

But they've all made out better than Kashmiris. Modern-day politics began in the Valley in the early 1930s, when Sheikh Mohammed Abdullah launched a political party that would become the National Conference and dominate Kashmir's political scene for generations. After a stint in prison for his "Quit Kashmir" campaign against Dogra rule, Abdullah, who today is widely known as "Sher-i-Kashmir" ("The Lion of Kashmir"), became the state's first prime minister in 1948. He was sent to jail again for more than a decade before being named the state's first chief minister in 1975. Upon his death in 1982, his son Farooq succeeded him just as anger and frustrated began to seethe. Buoyed by the success of the *mujahideen* holding off Soviet forces in nearby Afghanistan, the idea of Islam-fired militantism began to take root in the Valley. The pro-independence Jammu and Kashmir Liberation Front (JKLF) and pro-Pakistan Jamaat Islami Jammu Kashmir (JIJK) leveraged growing anti-India sentiment to attract recruits. The 1984 execution of leading Kashmiri separatist and JKLF co-founder Maqbool Bhat sparked widespread outrage, spurring a government crackdown that in turn gave militantism greater appeal. As angry young Kashmiris began to contemplate crossing into Pakistan for military training, communal riots between Muslims and Hindus, as in the mountain village of Anantnag in February 1986, suggested dark days ahead.

For the 1987 state elections, Chief Minister Farooq Abdullah partnered with India's dominant Congress Party.[27] In response, Islamic parties joined forces to create the Muslim United Front (MUF), which called for Kashmiri unity and an embrace of Quranic law in the state assembly. Kashmiris voted in record numbers, with more than 80 percent turn-out. The MUF received nearly a third of the vote (31 percent), yet won just 4 of 43 seats it contested. If the onset of Kashmir's nearly 35-year insurgency could be traced to a single moment, it would be this: Abdullah and the National Conference manipulated the 1987 vote to appease New Delhi. "There was a massive rigging in 1987 elections," Kashmiri Pandit Khem Lata Wukhloo, a former Congress leader, told the BBC in 2002. "The losing candidates were declared winners. It shook the ordinary people's faith in the elections and the democratic process."[28] Not only did Kashmiris never get to choose their fate, as Nehru had promised, their own leader and champion used an election to steal their vote. An insightful observer had foreseen this a dozen years in advance. "The democracy in this city had reached a stage where, one day, it had to take a dangerous turn," Akhtar Mohiuddin wrote of Srinagar in his 1975 book *One's Own Hell*, one of the few novels written in Kashmiri. "The world mistook this turn for an accident, but the charlatans who steered the democracy had deftly negotiated the turn."[29]

Waves of young men soon began to "pick up the gun," as locals say, and head off to Pakistan and Afghanistan for training. In the last weeks of 1989, militants led by JKLF launched an armed insurgency, starting with the killing of dozens of Indian spies and collaborators. Hundreds of thousands of Indian troops flooded in to occupy Kashmir. As of early 2023, some 60,000 people have died in the insurgency, and more than half a million Indian soldiers watch over the Valley, among the world's most heavily militarized regions. Shaped in its early years by the rise of radical Islamism within the Pakistani military, the conflict, for some, became an anti-Western *jihad*. In 1995, Islamist militants kidnapped six tourists — two Americans, two Britons, a German and a Norwegian — from the resort town of Pahalgam. The perpetrators described it as an attack on the enemies of Islam, particularly America. One of the hostages escaped, the headless body of another was found a month later and the rest were never heard from again.

Now you might understand why my Indian friend, back in 1998, urged me to avoid Kashmir. But reality does like to intrude. The morning I arrived in Delhi the heat was overwhelming. It was mid-June, when the humidity ticks up every day, climbing toward the great monsoon release. I was later told it hit 50 degrees Celsius that day (127 F), which seems like overkill. But the Indian capital was unmoved. With his half-closed eyes, the pale, mud-splashed cow in the middle of Paharganj Road seemed perfectly content. Beneath tangles of hanging wires, shopkeepers cheerily beckoned, displaying shawls, flip-flops and various knickknacks. I felt unsteady, having no experience with jet lag or oven-like temperatures. I retreated to my squalid hotel room to lie under the ceiling fan in the hopes of catching a few minutes' sleep. Instead, my body hit on a novel way to get rid of fluids: hyper-salivation. I sat on the edge of the bed, spitting and dribbling into a medium-sized glass until it was full.

I felt chewed up and hollowed out, and knew I had to get out of town. I pushed myself to my feet and made my way to the train station a few blocks away. As I shuffled toward the entrance a young man appeared, grinning warmly and dressed all in white — the cool, calm counter to my frazzled, overheated American. "So hot here, right?" he asked. "Wouldn't you like to be in green mountains, with cool air and beautiful blue waters?" I would like that, I thought to myself, and nodded, as if in a trance. His name was Bilal and he led me to a nearby teahouse and pulled out a stack of photos: snow-capped mountains; vast fields of wildflowers; wooden boats gliding across still waters. Here was that picture-postcard, Bollywood version of the Valley, working its magic. Just looking at Kashmir I felt a cool breeze at my neck. By our second chai I'd booked a flight to Srinagar for the next morning and a week-long stay on a houseboat. I'd needed just five hours in India to do the one thing I'd vowed not to do — and that decision would shape my life.

A few summers later, a group of 19 Muslim men hijacked four commercial US airliners and flew two of them into twin skyscrapers about a mile from where I was working as a receptionist for a boutique magazine. When I heard of the second plane strike, I rushed up to the roof, where a handful of us stood there riveted, blinking, slack-jawed (Chapter Five). Every New Yorker has a 9/11 story — where they were, what they saw and how it changed them. Mine's ongoing. New York, my adopted home, had been crushed and upended.

Yet we soon knew who was behind it, and the seed of an idea began to take shape. I wanted to know why this group of men from thousands of miles away invested the time and resources required to plan and carry out this hugely complex and ingenious plan, devastating the city I'd come to call home. What drove them, and men like them, to dedicate years of their lives to causing such incalculable damage and killing countless innocents they'd never met? Do Muslims hate us, and if so why?

Many were asking these same questions, but I decided to become a journalist and get some answers. I heard Brooklyn College had a strong journalism program, with a Pulitzer Prize winner, a leading columnist and a bestselling author among the faculty, so I enrolled. Strong work in class led to an internship at a New York tabloid, followed by another at a better newspaper and a third at United Nations' headquarters. In early 2006, as graduation loomed, I cast about for a region that checked three boxes: mainly Muslim, news-making, and English-speaking. There was only one, as far as I could tell, and thanks to Delhi's blast-furnace heat, I'd been there. A bit of Googling led me to Srinagar-based daily *Kashmir Observer*, which as luck would have it had hired a Western journalist, a young Briton, for the summer two years prior. I emailed KO editor Sajjad Haider offering my services. He responded with interest and within days I'd been offered a reporting position and confirmed with my British predecessor that KO was on the level. I'd needed more than four years after 9/11, but finally the seed had sprouted and I was headed back to Kashmir.

I can guess what you might be thinking. Why would a reporter driven into journalism by the 9/11 attack — perpetrated by Al Qaeda, a terrorist group led by a Saudi and dominated by Arabs, and followed by American-led wars in Afghanistan and Iraq — go to Kashmir for answers? Is he lazily putting all persecuted Muslims into a box marked "potential terrorists"? Fair question, but the two are closer than they appear. I've already mentioned the 1995 kidnapping of Westerners in Kashmir by anti-American Islamist radicals. That's just the tip of the glacier. In November 2002, Osama bin Laden published a letter to the American people in which he explained why he had attacked the US. He mentioned American support for Israel's fight against the Palestinians, then went on: "You supported the Russian atrocities against us in Chechnya, the Indian oppression against us in Kashmir, and the Jewish aggression against us in Lebanon."[30] This might be dismissed as PR — the leader of the world's top Islamist terror outfit looking to expand his base and ranks by claiming to fight for all major Muslim causes. Yet Osama's were not empty words. "I, myself, drove three Arab fighters into the center of Kashmir," jeep driver Nasir Ali told US journalist Philip Smucker in July 2002, referring to Al Qaeda militants arriving from Afghanistan. "Hundreds have entered Kashmir in the last several months."[31]

The regional chief of Pakistan's Inter-Services Intelligence agency (ISI), Mohammed Muslim, told Smucker there was no Al Qaeda presence in Kashmir and denounced what he saw as an American war against Islam. "The US government destroyed the World Trade Center so that it would have an excuse to destroy Afghanistan," Muslim said.[32] Many in the Muslim world pushed this conspiracy theory in the years after 9/11, and still today it's heard in some circles. Even back then I was confident the US did not attack itself, killing thousands of its own civilians, and did not intend to destroy Afghanistan. But my country was partly to blame for the most successful terrorist attack of all time — and, I have come to learn, for the intensity of the insurgency in Kashmir.

Among the handful of books I brought to Kashmir in 2006 was Steve Coll's *Ghost Wars*, which had won the Pulitzer Prize a few months prior. Coll details how the United States funneled weapons and money, via the ISI, to the Afghan mujahideen to help them battle the Soviet Union. In 1980, the Central Intelligence Agency (CIA) spent $100 million shipping weapons to the jihadis. A few years later that number hit $700 million, marking the US' priciest covert action of the Cold War.[33]

Yet US support of Islamic elements in Pakistan had begun long before. In the early 1950s, the US Information Agency, part of the State Department and abolished in 1999, sent an official to Lahore to ask respected author Saadat Hasan Manto to pen a contribution to its magazine. Over the next few years, Manto, who was of Kashmiri heritage, wrote nine "Letters to Uncle Sam", as he called them. In one he suggested the US fund elements of extremist Islam as a counter to the Soviets. "Our mullahs are the best antidote to Russia's communism," Manto wrote in 1954. "The purpose of military aid, as far as I understand it, is to arm these mullahs...If this sect of mullahs is armed American-style, then the Soviet Union will have to pick up its spittoon from here."[34]

However sardonic, Manto's prediction came to fruition in the 1980s, with the US' funding of Pakistani and Afghan mujahideen to fight off the invading Soviet army. *Ghost Wars* details the subsequent growth of the Taliban and Al Qaeda, flush with US funding and weapons, during the Soviet war in Afghanistan and after the Russians retreated. Robert Gates, deputy CIA director in the 1980s before serving as Obama's Secretary of Defense, later acknowledged the mistake the US made in walking away from the *mujahideen*. US funding helped create the Taliban and led to the first World Trade Center bombing, in 1993, and later to 9/11. "I feel a certain sense of personal responsibility," Gates told Congress in 2007. "If we abandon these countries, once we are in there and engaged, there is a very real possibility that we will pay a higher price in the end."[35]

Through its ISI middlemen, the US similarly helped arm militants in Kashmir. By the summer of 1988, when Kashmiris began turning to militancy, the ISI's main foreign backers included Washington. "ISI enjoyed an ongoing operational partnership with the CIA... with periodic access to the world's most sophisticated technology and intelligence collection systems," Coll writes. "The service had welcomed to Pakistan legions of volunteers from across the Islamic world, fighters who were willing to pursue Pakistan's foreign policy agenda not only in Afghanistan, but, increasingly, across its eastern borders in Kashmir, where jihadists trained in Afghanistan were just starting to bleed Indian troops."[36]

When the insurgency exploded in 1989, Pakistan was ready, thanks in part to the CIA. "Inspired by their success against Soviet forces in Afghanistan, Pakistani intelligence officers announced to [Pakistani Prime Minister Benazir] Bhutto that they were prepared to use the same methods of covert jihad to drive India out of Kashmir," writes Coll:[37]

> ISI organized training camps for Kashmiri guerrillas in Afghanistan's Paktia province...The Kashmiri volunteers trained side by side with Arab jihadists. The Kashmir guerrillas began to surface in India-held territory with Chinese-made Kalashnikov rifles and other weapons siphoned from the Afghan pipeline. The CIA became worried that Pakistani intelligence might also divert to Kashmir high-technology weapons such as the buffalo-gun sniper rifles originally shipped to Pakistan to kill Soviet military officers. The United States passed private warnings to India to protect politicians and government officials traveling in Kashmir from long-range sniper attacks.

Think about that. Not only did the United States finance the training of Kashmiri insurgents — terrorists in the view of its ally in New Delhi — it provided weaponry that was so advanced it felt compelled to warn India.

The US' failures of omission were nearly as bad. Several observers have argued that President George H. W. Bush may have been able to end the insurgency shortly after it began had he been more focused on resolving Kashmir rather than avoiding another India-Pakistan war.[38] Yet no real effort was made, continuing President Harry Truman's policy of non-interference in response to the initial emergence of the Kashmir question. After presidents Eisenhower, Kennedy, and Johnson all tried and failed to resolve Kashmir, war avoidance, rather than dispute resolution, became the default US position. Neither the first President Bush nor his successor, Bill Clinton — who at one point declared Kashmir the most dangerous place on earth — made any real attempt to move Pakistan, India and Kashmir toward resolution. Following the December 2001 attack on Indian parliament and the May 2002 Kaluchak Massacre[39] , the second president Bush stepped in to keep India and Pakistan from going to war. Again the United States had a chance to shape a peaceful future for Kashmir. Instead, Bush stepped back, handing the reins to India and Pakistan with his assertion that the United States could not force nations to agree.[40]

That had never stopped us before. The US helped nurture the insurgency and bore some responsibility for its crushing impact. But rather than working to end it, America let Kashmir burn. "The unwillingness of the US government to take a strong stand on Kashmir not only makes the dispute that much more difficult to resolve," Peter R. Lavoy argued in April 2006, shortly after writing a book on the 1999 Kargil conflict. Lavoy would later serve as an advisor to presidents Obama and Trump on South Asian security. "It also could have the unintended consequences of exacerbating political tensions between New Delhi and Islamabad," he added, "possibly producing greater instability inside Indian-held Kashmir." [41]

Kashmiris merely wanted "azaadi", or freedom — a goal that seemed to align with Bush's repeated calls for global freedom.[42] Wasn't American exceptionalism about encouraging the spread of our ideals? President Abraham Lincoln described the US as "the last best hope of earth". Franklin Roosevelt, during World War II, talked of the US' "divine heritage". Richard Nixon said the US was not meant to have freedom for itself, "but to carry it to the whole world".

As in several of the world's troubled regions, Washington twisted itself up in its own ideals when it came to India and Pakistan. "Bush's counter-terrorism advisers decided that Kashmir-focused jihadi groups posed no direct threat to the U.S.," writes Coll, adding that over the years the Bush administration gave Pakistan nearly $10 billion in counter-terror funding with no oversight.[43] Meanwhile, Delhi talked the US-style talk on terror to garner support for one Kashmir crackdown after another. In June 2002, Indian Prime Minister Atal

Bihari Vajpayee said that for India to stand down Pakistan would have to stop infiltrations and dismantle "the infrastructure of terrorism" — echoing Bush's words about Al Qaeda.[44] For maybe a decade, US leaders saw Kashmiri militants as terrorists when talking to Delhi and as freedom fighters when talking to Islamabad. While encouraging Pakistan and India to resolve Kashmir, the United States did a great deal to ensure failure.

I should have paid more attention when my octogenarian Kashmiri educator friend Agha Ashraf Ali blamed my country for the region's problems. He referred often to Robert Fisk's epic, *The Great War for Civilisation*, which had just been published. "The Iranians used to call the United States 'the centre of world arrogance' and I would laugh at this," the British journalist writes in his 1100-page tome. "But I have begun to understand what it means."[45]

Fisk was nearing 60 and on the far side of several decades of foreign correspondence when he came to this realization. Arriving in Kashmir I was a green reporter in his early thirties holding fast to the conviction that America had a moral edge and couldn't always be bothered with minor details. "The arc of the moral universe is long," American civil rights leader Dr. Martin Luther King Jr liked to say, in a line often repeated by Obama, "but it bends toward justice." This idea owes much to German philosopher G. W. F. Hegel, who argued for the steady march of human progress and development.[46] Each successive generation, to grossly oversimplify his view, distances us further from cavemen, makes us a touch more evolved and civilized, breaking down barriers and increasing our moral clarity. [47]It seemed logical, then, that the United States, founded long after other world powers, would sit at the endpoint of a Hegelian evolution of states. If humanity had evolved to be more united, more thoughtful, just and humane, then the global power founded most recently should logically be an improvement on those that had come before.

Extending this logic would of course make any more recently created state — hello India, born 1947 — more morally advanced than the US. Yet this line of thinking has a long history in America, and probably a bright future. The United States was founded on the highest ideals, and for generations the world's "poor huddled masses" did all they could to reach our shores. In the early 20th century, many Americans' view of history — mostly white Americans, admittedly — placed them at "the speartip of human progress," as Ivy League historian Walter Russell Mead puts it.[48] Among those huddled, starry-eyed masses arriving long ago was one Francesco Capra, the seventh child of a Sicilian fruit farmer. Capra arrived in New York Harbor with his family in 1903. He was just five years old, yet recalls seeing a great lady holding a torch, which his father called "the light of freedom".[49] They settled in Los Angeles; Capra fell into filmmaking and directed three Oscar-winning films in the 1930s. After the attack on Pearl Harbor, in December 1941, he enlisted with the US Army and soon found himself meeting Army Chief of Staff General George C. Marshall, who handed him a massive assignment: make a series of propaganda films explaining to US troops why they're fighting. Capra has acknowledged that the Bible provided the series' foundational idea, that "the truth shall make you free".[50] *Prelude to War*, the first and most popular film in the seven-part *Why We Fight* series, opens by crediting Jesus, in addition to Moses, Confucius, and the Prophet Mohammed, with helping inspire the creation of the free world.[51]

US heroics in that war, and its Cold War victory, did little to disabuse Americans of these delusions of greatness. It seemed clear to me as well, gliding along my entitled flight path, that we had been imbued with a moral superiority, a deeper understanding of freedom and humanity. The world's hopes and millions of immigrants' long journeys had been vindicated, went my thinking — and that of many others at the time. Most importantly, as the world's moral leader, Reagan's "shining city on a hill", the United States would never be like those 19th-century and early 20th-century empires that needed to use force to expand their writ, or make horrifying, continent-shaping errors like Partition.[52] The US needed only the power of its principles to draw people on-side. "American leadership is the one constant in an uncertain world," Obama said in a 2014 speech.[53]

Of course, it's all a steaming pile of manure. A country should aspire to global leadership; the alternative would be to accept inferiority. But to assert that one's leadership is based on a potentially divinely ordained moral superiority while quietly eroding the agency and security of millions of people around the world is hypocrisy of the highest order. The US was never going to live up to its principles all the time. Like its citizenry, it's deeply flawed, prone to mistakes and bouts of wrongheadedness. But should it not, as the world's most powerful country in the post-WWII era and claimant to exceptionalism, strive for a modicum of decency?

US leaders took considerable credit for the spread of democracy in the wake of our Cold War victory. But during that frozen conflict, the United States interfered in foreign elections more than 60 times, according to a 2020 book from Oxford University Press.[54] Ousting leaders like Iran's Mohammed Mossadegh and installing dictators like Chile's Augusto Pinochet turns out to have been more the rule than the exception. Yet somehow enough global belief in US exceptionalism lingered in the early 2000s for it to decline sharply under George W. Bush after his 2003 Iraq invasion.[55] Obama may have quietly done just as much damage to America's reputation. Setting aside the bloody chaos that consumed Libya and Syria under his watch, in his two terms the Nobel Peace Laureate approved ten times more drone strikes than his predecessor, killing as many as 800 civilians.[56] Perhaps to absolve himself, he invoked American exceptionalism nearly a third more often than previous presidents.[57] Biden has carried on the tradition. "America is still a beacon to the world, an ideal to be realized, a promise to be kept," he said in fall 2022. "We're going to make the 21st century another American century because the world needs us to."[58]

It may, or it may not. US leaders have long been wont to express a deep commitment to human rights and justice, yet even before Donald Trump the US was the only country in the world to refuse to ratify international treaties that sought to regulate global arms sales, protect the oceans, enable prosecution of war crimes and genocide, ban cluster bombs and nuclear tests, and ensure the rights of women and children.[59] Then Trump arrived to pull the United States out of the world's most important climate accord, marginalize a significant portion of the world's population by denouncing "shithole countries" and inspire a raving mass of protesters to besiege the US Capitol in an effort to "save" their democracy by toppling it.[60]

Enlightenment-era Italian diplomat and political theorist Niccolò Machiavelli famously endorsed lying and manipulation as invaluable political tools, but deception seems antithetical to exceptionalism. And the word has started getting out. Americans, like much of the rest of the world before them, are losing faith in the myths that long sustained our sense of superiority. From 2012 to 2020, the percentage of Americans who believe in their country's exceptionalism fell nearly a quarter, to 54 percent.[61] A majority of Europeans, in the wake of Trump, no longer trust Americans.[62]

Some argue that Russia's February 2022 invasion of Ukraine — around which the US-led North Atlantic Treaty Organization (NATO) quickly rallied, seeking to defend democracy and so-called Western ideals with funds and weapons — signaled the return of Cold War-style geopolitics and the resurgence of the US-led world order. If that were true, why did leaders of nearly half the global population, including those of several key US allies, view the conflict in such vastly different terms? In the first months of the war, European and NATO-member states such as Hungary, Serbia and Turkey, Gulf powers like Saudi Arabia and the UAE, China and many smaller states across Asia and Africa, either remained on the sidelines, choosing not to back either side, or favored Russia. India, a long-standing US ally, took what might be described as an aggressively anti-Western position, nearly tripling its Russian energy imports as of mid-2022 while welcoming US-sanctioned Russian shipping vessels to its ports.[63] And its citizens largely support that stance, as 56 percent of Indians agreed in summer 2022 that Russia was "justified in wanting to have greater influence over its neighbor Ukraine."[64]

Around the same time, nearly two-thirds (64%) of retirement-age Americans supported US military involvement in the Ukraine war, while just over a third (36%) of younger US citizens held the same view.[65] This suggests, again, that Americans increasingly view their country as less powerful, less able to shape world events — unexceptional, even. Besides, even if the US had again emerged as the global leader in the wake of Russia's invasion, its days in that post are surely numbered. China is set to overtake the US as the world's largest economy in the early 2030's and by mid-century the US and EU will represent a sliver of global population and GDP. Someday in the not-so-distant future, the majority of Americans will accept their country as no better than any other.

The myth of American exceptionalism, like Satisar, is as dry as two-month-old naan. Yet as I arrived in Kashmir, despite widespread disdain for the policies of George W. Bush, his war on terror and invasion of Iraq, most Americans, including this one, still felt deeply wronged when it came to that dark September day. That's not to say I came to the Vale bearing the "white man's burden" — thinking that I could teach locals a thing or two about democracy and freedom. No, I sought to listen and to learn. But when I thought of 9/11, the Muslim perpetrators were "evildoers," as Bush put it, and we the victims. This aligned with my compatriots at the time: polling shortly after 9/11 found that just 15 percent of Americans believed US policies were even partly to blame.[66]

That view has since been leavened with empathy. In 2010, Pakistani-American author Ayad Akhtar's play *Disgraced* — in which a Muslim-American feels a blush of pride as he watches 9/11 unfold — struck a chord, won the Pulitzer Prize and prodded a certain strain of globalized American to begin to reconsider their country's imprint on the Muslim world and beyond. Today there is an emerging literature on Americans waking up to the damage done by their empire, like Akhtar's *Homeland Elegies*, Suzy Hansen's *Notes from a Foreign Country*, Stephen Wertheim's *Tomorrow, the World*, Mohsin Hamid's *The Reluctant Fundamentalist* and Hilde Elias Restad's *American Exceptionalism*. "The world looked to us—and now I speak as an American—to uphold a holy image, or as holy as it gets in this age of enlightenment," Akhtar writes. "We have been the earthly garden, the abundant idyll, the productive Arcadia of the world's pastoral dream. Between our shores has gleamed a realm of refuge and renewal — in short, the only reliable escape from history itself. It's always been a myth, of course, and one destined for rupture sooner or later."[67]

For many around the world, recent years of financial and pandemic peril paired with tarnished US prestige have taken the sheen off of not just the United States, but liberal democracy as a whole. Russian President Vladimir Putin says liberalism has "become obsolete".[68] Who listens to him, right? But in this case he's got a point. In its 2022 report, US-based rights advocate Freedom House found that the global decline in democracy had accelerated: 73 countries representing three-fourths of humanity saw their freedom scores decline. Leading the way was the world's largest democracy, India, which the advocacy group downgraded from Free to Partly Free, which meant that just one out of five earthlings live in countries considered fully free — the lowest total in nearly thirty years.[69]

On this subject, too, we have an emerging literature — *How Democracies Die, The People vs Democracy, The Virtue of Nationalism, How to Lose a Country, The Problem of Democracy, The Twilight of Democracy* and many more. Humanity seems to be moving away from traditional democratic ideals and embracing populism and far-right nationalism. Leaders like Trump, Hungary's Viktor Orban, Turkey's Recep Tayyip Erdogan, Brazil's Jair Bolsonaro and India's Narendra Modi attack democratic institutions, weaponize fear and encourage hate. The decline of American exceptionalism has eroded humanity's faith in a stable liberal democracy that encourages emancipation, equality, dignity and prosperity. Countries around the world have sought to fill this vacuum. Again and again we've seen disenchanted voters embrace strongman types promoting a native form of exceptionalism — the Russian or Ottoman Empire, the Hindu Raj. Modi, in fact, may have been the first to go all in. He swept into the prime ministership in 2014 on a wave of *Hindutva*, or Hindu nationalism, recasting the story of India from a place of Gandhi-inspired diversity to a sacred motherland. But the foundation of his political ascent was laid in 2002, when as Gujarat chief minister he appeared to encourage three days of communal violence that left as many as 2,000 people dead, mostly Muslims (Chapter 10).

Originally from Gujarat, Modi joined the Hindu nationalist Rashtriya Swayamsevak Sangh (RSS) in the late 1950s at eight years old and went on to become an outspoken youth leader for the local chapter.[70] Communalism has some history in Kashmir as well, and India and Pakistan's 1947-48 war over the Valley brought these tensions to the fore. Anti-India and jihadi sentiment spread in the early years of the insurgency, resulting in growing disdain for the Kashmiri Pandit population. These tensions were exacerbated by the 1992 destruction of the Babri Mosque in Ayodhya, Uttar Pradesh, which sparked days of communal rioting that killed nearly 1,000 people, again mostly Muslims. Some 200,000 Pandits fled persecution in Kashmir around this same time (Chapter 10). Hindu fundamentalist outfits like Vishva Hindu Parishad (VHP) and the RSS, both linked to Modi's Bharatiya Janata Party (BJP), denounced Muslims and Pakistan for driving Pandits out of their Kashmiri homeland, while some Pakistani and Kashmiri extremists whipped up Islamist sentiment by denouncing the Hindus' destruction of their centuries-old mosque.

This brings us to the latest chapter in Kashmir's *Book of Job*. Drafted as part of India's constitution, Article 370 granted a measure of autonomy to Jammu and Kashmir — and perhaps a modicum of respect. Under 370, the state had to approve the application of laws issued by India's parliament, apart from those involving defense, foreign affairs and communications. The state could as a result make its own decisions on rights and property, such as barring Indians from outside the state from buying property there. But on August 5, 2019, the Modi government revoked 370, ending this autonomous status and making Jammu & Kashmir and Ladakh separate union territories. Kashmir would no longer have its own constitution and had to abide by Indian laws like any other state. Crucially, the revocation also meant people from outside the Valley could buy property there. The government vowed to bring economic development, but Kashmiris feared the BJP sought to demographically re-engineer the Valley, from Muslim-majority to Hindu-dominated.

Ignoring the reality on the ground, the revocation was essentially a declaration by New Delhi that the insurgency had ended and the time had come to fully integrate Kashmir with the rest of India. To that end, the Indian government deployed tens of thousands more troops and imposed strict security measures. Military bunkers and checkpoints that had been removed years prior returned.[71] "[Kashmir] was heaven on earth and will remain so," Home Minister Amit Shah said in a televised address announcing the revocation. "Give us five years and we will make it the most developed state in the country."[72] In his first speech following the revocation, Modi vowed to bring Bollywood film shoots back to the Valley, and international filmmakers as well.[73] Yet even 18 months later, many shops remained closed and most streets full of soldiers. Visiting Jammu in April 2022, Modi pointed out that, following the 2020 local elections, more than 30,000 representatives had begun overseeing district and village councils. "It's a proud moment that democracy has reached the grassroots level in Jammu and Kashmir," he said.[74]

But it had been years since the region had an elected government, and critics argue that the councils have no power to make or change laws in a territory run by the Center. During his visit, the prime minister announced $5 billion (38,000 cr) in proposed investments in Kashmir.[75] The UAE's Emaar Group, the developer of the $20 billion Downtown Dubai, with its iconic Dubai Mall next to Burj Khalifa, plans to develop a 500,000-sq-ft mall in Srinagar.[76] As of late 2022, none of these proposed projects had begun construction. They may yet come, along with the promised lakhs of new jobs, spurring economic growth. But the government's extended post-revocation internet blockage, which ended when 4G service was restored in February 2021, cost Kashmir an estimated $4.2 billion.[77] A poor start if the goal is economic revival.

Thanks to the Modi government's muzzling of media in the Valley, most Indians are only dimly aware of what's been happening in Kashmir. When the BBC, Al Jazeera, and Reuters reported that 10,000 locals turned out to protest the revocation — and that authorities dispersed the crowds with live rounds — New Delhi dismissed it as "fabricated".[78] Many Kashmiri outlets halted publication after the revocation and Reporters Without Borders described Kashmir as an "information black hole".[79] Reporters took to smuggling news out of the state on hard drives, rather than waiting hours to use one of four computers at the state-run media center. The harassment has been steady, aided by regular arrests and detentions. In November 2021 authorities jailed leading rights activist Khurram Parvez. Weeks later, US-based TIME magazine included him on its 2022 list of the world's 100 most influential figures.[80] Fahad Shah, editor of *The Kashmir Walla*, soon followed Parvez into prison.[81] An array of major organizations and prominent officials, including the International Press Institute,

Human Rights Watch, and UN human rights experts, have called for their release, but as of late 2022 both remained incarcerated — and more than 35 Kashmiri journalists had been detained or questioned since the revocation.[82]

Indian authorities have also zeroed in on news outlets. In June 2020, the J&K administration empowered itself to determine what qualified as fake, unethical or anti-India news and take legal action against the offending news outlet. The likeliest step the state would take would be to stop providing the offending outlet with government advertisements, which for Kashmiri outlets are existential. Since the first days of the insurgency this has been New Delhi's unspoken threat to Kashmiri news outlets: publish any writing that hints at a pro-militant, pro-independence, or pro-Pakistan position and you'll lose our ad funds. Frozen out of government-related news and funding in a bleak economic environment, these outlets would be forced to reduce their coverage, cut staff and perhaps even shut down (Chapter One). In 2021, Delhi cut government advertising for 34 news outlets in Jammu and Kashmir, including 10 in the Valley.[83] To top it off, in recent years many leading Kashmiri newspapers have reported losing parts of their news archives — mainly stories critical of New Delhi — after hacking incidents.[84] This includes *Greater Kashmir, Kashmir Times, Kashmir Reader, Rising Kashmir* and my old employer, *Kashmir Observer*. "Newspaper reports are being disappeared to erase the memory of a particular time," says an official from the Jammu and Kashmir Coalition for Civil Society (JKCCS), which has also lost a sizable portion of its regional news archive.[85] Books like this one may end up helping preserve the historical record of insurgency-era Kashmir.

Media clampdowns have been a regular occurrence since the start of the conflict, but never has one been this harsh and far-reaching. The self-censorship is now at such a level as to all but ensure that negative reporting on India or its security forces never goes public. This has enabled an increase in India's counter-insurgency operations, and a corresponding spike in militancy, to go largely unnoticed. While reporting for KO, I wrote that Kashmiris seemed to have "given up the gun", meaning that they had moved away from militancy. That prediction held true for some time. Starting in 2007, the number of Kashmiri youth who crossed the border for training never returned to the levels of the previous two decades — until the revocation of Article 370. In 2013, just 16 Kashmiris turned to militancy.[86] Seven years later, at least 200 young men, mainly from South Kashmir, turned militant, according to a former chief of India's external intelligence agency.[87]

The number of militants killed in 2020 was the second-highest in a decade, and as of September, 2022 year was on a much higher pace than the previous year.[88] "The withdrawal of Kashmir's special status has triggered a new phase of militancy through the emergence of homegrown militant outfits and local recruitments," Washington-based think tank the Middle East Institute asserted in February 2022.[89] A year later, the government's creation of Hindu-dominated civilian defense units in the Rajouri district, along the Line of Control, underscored the growing threat.[90] The number of foreign fighters has declined amid an increase in local militants, particularly younger Kashmiris, serving as shadow militants who disappear into the population between attacks.[91] At the same time, the Taliban's return to power in Afghanistan may have helped spur a renewed insurgency in Kashmir, as a Pakistan listing toward extremist Islam seeks to again leverage *mujahideen* to irritate India.[92]

In a 1997 poem, Agha Shahid Ali, Kashmir's bard of woe, described Srinagar as "the city from where no news can come".[93] I always thought this line referred to authorities' muzzling of local reporting. But it could just as well refer to the "new" in news — the numbing drumbeat of horrors in Kashmir that makes all news old hat. On one of my first days at *Kashmir Observer* I got upset about a story highlighting Indian security forces violating locals' rights. Sajjad, my editor, stayed calm. "We rarely get upset about news like this because we see these stories again and again," he explained. "This is Kashmir. This has happened before and it will happen again." The Kashmir news cycle has been on repeat for generations. Every handful of years another observer bemoans the Valley's crumbling. "Kashmiri Muslims and the Indian government have conspired to abolish the complexities of Kashmiri civilization," British journalist James Buchan wrote in 1997. "The world it inhabited has vanished: the state government and the political class, the rule of law, almost all the Hindu inhabitants of the valley, alcohol, cinemas, cricket matches, picnics by moonlight in the saffron fields, schools, universities, an independent press, tourists and banks."[94]

Count Pakistan, Great Britain, the United States and the UN among the guilty as well. I'd also include Hindu fundamentalists and non-Kashmiri Muslim extremists, for helping increase communal tensions in the Valley. Finally, the international media, for consistently portraying the Kashmiri struggle as one involving Islamic radicalism, which has always been just a narrow slice of Kashmir society. I include myself in that group, for failing to report with as much depth and insight as I might have, being inadequately critical of Kashmiri, Pakistani and Indian politicians, and lacking the determination and conviction to report more conflict-related stories, despite my editor's opposition (Chapter 1).

After the revocation of Article 370 many feared the Indianization of Kashmir — the return of Pandits and a wave of Hindus snatching up property in an economically revived Valley. But what has happened since looks more like the Kashmirization of India: the perceptions and policies used to stifle and control Kashmiris have gone national. Already the government is using some of the same tools to stifle dissent — police and security forces manning barriers and checkpoints in the streets; strictly controlled internet access; critics, journalists and protesters charged with crimes, detained, and questioned; widespread self-censorship in the media and political class; increased restrictions on what news outlets are able to publish; and most notably, the rampant demonization and persecution of Muslims.[95] Hindu leaders call for genocide against the country's Muslims yet receive no reprimand.[96] Top BJP officials feel comfortable enough to insult the Prophet Mohammed, sparking a diplomatic row. The ultimate goal seems to be a revival of the Partition mentality. "In India today, Muslims are massively under-represented in politics and the professions, discriminated against in the workplace and the marketplace, and taunted and mocked on television and social media. In their suffering and stigmatisation lies our collective shame," award-winning historian Ramachandra Guha wrote on the eve of India's 75th birthday.[97]

I may be thinking too small. Perhaps India is just a harbinger and we'll soon see the Kashmirization of the world, as identity-driven violence lurks just beneath the surface and any region that strives for autonomy or independence, a sliver of dignity and self-esteem, is militarized and muzzled. Look at how an independent Ukraine is treated by its former overlords. There, as in Kashmir, we see that to seek to possess an object of beauty is to view its current owners as an obstacle. Kashmiri-British novelist Mirza Waheed has pointed out that the Bollywood classic *Kashmir Ki Kali*, for all its appreciation for the Valley's natural beauty, has zero Muslim or Kashmiri characters.[98] The muzzling of journalists, the erasing of newspaper archives, the destruction of creativity and education — such steps all have the same end. A week after the revocation of Article 370, Republic TV reporter Sweta Srivastava rode a scooter through an eerily quiet Srinagar. "The situation makes you feel good because the situation is returning to normal," she said without interviewing a single person. "The locals are ready to live their lives normally again."[99]

Frank Capra made *It's a Wonderful Life* immediately after *Why We Fight* — a sequence that puts my family touchstone in a new light. Did the Italian-born filmmaker feel complicit in the American horrors of World War II and seek to return to the moral clarity of family and goodness? Is *It's a Wonderful Life* an isolationist vision? The great ambition of protagonist George Bailey is to leave Bedford Falls and remake the world. "I'm shakin' the dust of this crummy little town off my feet and I'm gonna see the world," he explains early on. "I'm gonna build skyscrapers a hundred stories high. I'm gonna build bridges a mile long." But he never does. Again and again he stays to fulfill family obligations, holding fast to his innocence and emerging as "the richest man in town," as his war-hero brother puts it. "Stay home," Capra seems to be telling Americans. "You'll thank me for it." I might relay to Capra what my brother Bill told my parents years ago: You've created a false paradise that fails to prepare us for a hard, cold world.

But there's no need. Americans largely ignored *It's a Wonderful Life*, which bombed at the box office, and lapped up the assertions of *Prelude to War* — mainly that the US cause is just, even biblically inspired. During World War II and the Cold War that followed, Americans needed to believe in the righteousness of their fight, which in turn enabled them to create happy homes like the one in which I grew up. Without *Why We Fight* we might have stopped believing in places like Bedford Falls. Are these two poles complementary?

Before I left the US for Kashmir in 2006, my mother gave me a necklace of a cross, vowing that it would keep me safe. She also gave me a brightly-colored stuffed animal of a teddy bear clown. "Never forget who you are," she urged. For a while I felt insulted. "A clown? Really??" But I've come to see my playfulness as an advantage, a gift, even.[100] I should probably take myself a bit more seriously, I'm closing in on 50, after all. But much of the time, I'd rather not. Is the world not heavy enough? Playful and mischievous are adjectives rarely associated with journalists, but they're among my strongest character traits, especially when in the field. So too, thankfully, is curiosity.

You may be wondering if I found answers to the questions that drove me to report on the Muslim world all those years ago. I now know that Americans are indeed exceptional — in their limited understanding of the world and their country's pervasive influence upon it. That evil is often a matter of perspective and that some perspectives are less valid than others. And that even in a *desiccated land*, or perhaps especially there, rich and verdant life can emerge. I've learned that the Muslim world is no monolith and that this ever-looming global clash is not between Islam and Christianity, or Muslims and the West, but the powerful and the powerless. Muslims, to take the handiest example, are marginalized and oppressed by Christians in the West, Hindus in India, Jews in Israel, their fellow Muslims across the Middle East, Buddhists in Southeast Asia and non-religionists in China. It's less about religion than the global revival of populist politics that tend toward majoritarian domination.

I've learned that the greatest threat to Western liberal ideals is not Islam or the Muslim world, but Western liberal ideals. Mostly free democratic elections have given us Modi and Trump, Brexit, Erdogan, Orban, Bolsonaro and more. January 6 was frightening, but it was no 9/11; the nadir of illiberal democracy is likely still to come — possibly at the hands of Modi. "We are not bystanders in this ongoing attack on democracy," a major political leader said in late 2022. "It's within our power, it's in our hands, yours and mine, to stop the assault." These words came not from a leading Indian journalist like Rana Ayyub or Barkha Dutt, but from US President Joe Biden, who went on to describe "a battle for the soul of this nation". They could've come from a politician in half of the world's democracies.

I've learned, finally, that we're all wandering the same desert. Progressive-minded Americans and Indians today see the troubling direction of their wildly diverse societies — a moving away from founding ideals; an overzealous embrace of the dominant religion; the marginalization and mistreatment of minorities, and the inclusion of activists, journalists and political opponents within those groups; a spike in deception and misinformation; a tendency toward authoritarian means and weakened institutions. Yet most are satisfied in merely pointing this out. We humble flex our wokeness, but don't endeavor to build better — as if it were an achievement to grasp the rising communalism and condescension or stop believing in the hopeful myths that help build our nations.

As 2023 dawned, leading analysts wondered if this would be the decade, perhaps even the century, of India. New defense and tech deals with the US underscored India's deep ties to the West, in contrast to China, with its fleet of unsettling spy balloons. Delhi's economy ranked fifth globally as it took over the presidency of the Group of 20, with a population set to surpass China as the world's largest. At the Davos World Economic Forum, prominent columnist and TV host Fareed Zakaria described India as perhaps "the most optimistic country in the world right now."[101]

Meanwhile, Kashmir stands out as a black mark. Investments have fallen some 55 percent since the revocation of Article 370, devastating the local economy.[102] Violence has ticked up as neighboring Pakistan has struggled with a surge in terrorism, highlighted by the deadly January bombing of police headquarters in Peshawar.[103] As during my time in the Valley, US weapons again turned up in Kashmir — having been left behind by American troops in Afghanistan, found by the Taliban and routed to militants — even as Washington again said it would play no part in resolving Kashmir.[104] And the late January announcement of a new Jammu and Kashmir Family ID sparked widespread concerns of more invasive government surveillance.[105]

Pointing out and criticising such policies is merely the first step in bringing the visions of Gandhi and the Founding Fathers to fruition, which needs to be done brick by brick, day by day. The next is believing that it is indeed within our power, within our hands.[106] Hailing from the perch of the privileged, perhaps it's not my place to gauge how much leverage people possess, or to dictate what comes next. Some might even argue that, given my background — not Muslim, Kashmiri, or South Asian — I've no place writing on these subjects.[107] But I'm willing to take that risk. And unless more Indians take the risk of responding to the troubles in Kashmir and across their country, India looks set to become to the 21st century what the US was to the 20th — a democracy born with great promise and blessed with great influence that suddenly finds itself submerged in darkness.

Chapter 1

Welcome to the Vale

"Every journalist who is not too stupid or full of himself to notice what is going on knows that what he does is morally indefensible. He is a kind of confidence man, preying on people's vanity, ignorance, or loneliness, gaining their trust and betraying them without remorse."

— Janet Malcolm[108]

I MAY HAVE taken it as a bad omen when nobody showed up to meet me when I landed at Srinagar airport, which at the time was actually an Indian military base, in late July 2006. But later that day I realized that in my most recent email I had told my employers I'd be arriving the following day. So, blame accepted.

After making my way into town I met Farooq Shah, my short, slim, bespectacled new colleague, outside my hotel. We walked to the *Kashmir Observer* offices to meet the rest of the crew, then he took me for tea in the quiet back garden of Tao Cafe, which would become our regular haunt. "We will put no limitations on you and your responsibilities at the *Kashmir Observer*," Farooq vowed. "You can do whatever you want. View this paper as your baby."

I raised my eyebrows in surprise; this seemed too good to be true. But I held my tongue and lit a cigarette as we waited for the check. "Don't you want to live a long life?" he asked me, serious yet grinning. "You should stop smoking because we need good people like you a lot more than we need most other people."

The next day I moved into my new home, a guesthouse on the property of Sajjad's uncle, Iftikhar, in the mainly-Shia Zadibal neighborhood. I was surprised to find I had a servant, Hussein, who slept in an adjacent room and had been working for Iftikhar for years. In India, servants are common, but where I'm from nobody has them. Still, we got along just fine. Around 7:30 every morning Hussain would bring in my newspaper, buttered Kashmiri bread and milk, as I put a pot on the stove to boil water for coffee. "Good morning, sir!" he'd shout as he entered. We quickly fell into a "sir"-ing contest – the winner being the one who could deliver the word with the most voluble and joyous intent. It was a fine way to start the day.

After reading the news I'd squeeze in a bit of exercise before Sajjad would arrive with Abid, his driver. The drive to Lal Chowk — "Red Square," so dubbed in the 1950's when communist sentiment ran high — would be over in a flash, as Abid appeared to have little appreciation for brakes. Today, in 2022, the ride would take considerably longer, due to more military checkpoints and the right-of-way granted to military convoys, which can halt civilian traffic for hours at a time.[109]

I would work at the KO office until 8 or 9 or 10 p.m. before returning home, where Hussain would materialize with my dinner, invariably half a chicken in some sort of spicy sauce, with rice and sometimes a vegetable, and frequently very good. I'd pour myself a whisky and write, go online or relax with a book or magazine. In the days before podcasts and Netflix, I had no television and my radio could find only one English-language station, the BBC World Service, which I came to love deeply and curse when it was elbowed out by the signal of some rival Chinese station creeping over the apparently not-tall-enough Himalayas. Beyond the occasional Sunday night gathering at Agha's place, I stayed in. Srinagar's streets are deserted after 10 p.m.; everything's closed and there is nothing to do but get in trouble. The final screening at the Neelam was at

4 p.m., and the only sound after 9 p.m. was the late night *azaan*. After a dozen years of mostly forgotten parties, I fell easily into this routine.

The vast majority of international reporting from Kashmir focuses on the conflict, on militancy, human rights violations and the push and pull between Pakistan and India. I would focus on the daily lives of Kashmiris after nearly two decades of conflict, and would soon learn, thanks to my editor, that reporting in Kashmir is often less about committing actual journalism and more about simply staying in the game.

☐

Reporting in Kashmir: Gung-slow

(old blog post)

July 25, 2006: Jetlag, the local kite population, and Islamic ritual all made their presence felt early this morning, as I woke up to stay around 3:30 am. My off-kilter body clock was aided and abetted by the noisy raptors that perch just outside my window and scream their lungs out from dawn onwards, apparently hunting Himalayan roosters, as well as the muezzin's morning call to prayer, which occurs pre-dawn. After breakfast and the paper I headed over to the KO offices only to find them shuttered. As I'm leaving, Abid pulled up with Sajjad.

"You're too early for us," my boss said, flashing that Mona Lisa smile.

We went back into the office, which is smaller than my bedroom in Brooklyn yet divided into three smaller spaces and a larger computer room where most of the work gets done.

"You read today's paper?" Sajjad asked once we were seated on facing brown-cushioned benches, glorious view of the Pir Panjal range out the wide-open window to my right.

"Yes, I did." I responded.

"Any thoughts, comments?"

"Well, yes, there are a few things," I said, telling him the stories could use more analysis and perspective. A few of them read like press releases for politicians and power players.

"The problem is that most of our stories come into us in the late afternoon or evening, so we have very little time to do additional reporting," Sajjad explained. "It's difficult enough to get them written up and polished for publication by deadline."

He asked if I had any story ideas.

"Yes, I have a bunch," I told him, and pulled a list out of my bag.

"There is a UN observer group here," I began. "What the heck are they doing? Nothing, it seems, but still they stay in Srinagar, and a new commander has just been put in charge, from Croatia, I believe. I'd like to interview him and see what his plans are, and also see what the locals think of the UN."

Sajjad nodded.

"I've been in contact with a couple of analysts and I'd like to do a piece on the Kashmir conflict in the wake of Mumbai serial bomb blasts," I said, referring to the pressure cooker blasts on a commuter train a few weeks prior, which killed more than 200 people. "How it might affect the situation, that sort of thing."

"Right, sounds good," he nodded again.

"Oh, yeah, and I've been reading about how Indian army soldiers have been committing suicide," I said. "As a result they've been instituting all of these stress-reduction measures, like yoga and therapy."

"Yes, yes, that's a possibility, too," Sajjad said. "But David, these are all very sensitive issues. We have to be careful about offending people here in Kashmir, because there are so many sides to every issue."

What he meant was that if *Kashmir Observer* crossed a certain line it would lose its government-funded advertisements and potentially be forced to shut down. There was also the possibility that the Indian government would banish a meddlesome foreign reporter.

"You, too, might find some difficulty reporting these issues," he added. "Because...well, for one reason because nobody will speak to you on the record."

"Well, that shouldn't stop us from trying," I countered.

"No, it shouldn't. And it won't," he responded. But with his eyes he made clear I should steer clear of conflict-related stories. "For now let's keep you working on other things."

So on one of my first days at work, we established our constant battle of wills: Sajjad looking out for *Kashmir Observer* and angling to keep me away from the conflict, and I keeping an eye out for ways to cover the story that brought me to Kashmir.

◆

A Pleasant Drive with Abid, or Dance of the Dodge

(old blog post)

August 24, 2006 :A few days after I arrived in Kashmir I had just gotten into the car with Sajjad and told him that I would like to get my own transportation.

"But you don't need it – Abid can give you rides," he said.

"Yes, but I'd like to be able to go where and when I need to, to cover a breaking story, for example, or visit a friend."

"Yeah, yeah, I see," he responded, as he often did when trying to think of a good counter. "Well perhaps you should have a bike."

"A bicycle? Well I guess that wouldn't be terrib..."

"No, no, a motorcycle," he corrected. "Something like that," and he pointed out the window to a chap riding a Honda two-wheeler.

"Oh, right, well maybe I could do that. Wonder if I could get a used one."

"Perhaps. But the bigger issue would be learning how to drive on these roads," he said, turning to me and smiling.

"Yeah," I laughed. "There are not many rules."

"Not many?" he looked at me. "There aren't any."

As Abid zoomed the wrong way down Residency Road, a main downtown artery akin to Sixth Avenue in New York, mingling with all variety of pedestrians and honking vehicles around a traffic circle, I could only agree. Imagine, if you are able, the following: Srinagar, a city of one million people and about half that many motorized vehicles, does not have a stoplight. Nowhere in this maze of paved and gravel roads do timed, colored lights regulate the toing and froing.

Actually, that's not completely true. They do have a few of them, on M.A. Road and at Jehangir Chowk, for example. But they stand sheathed and unblinking, commissioned and built but never used, having apparently offended some circulatory sensitivity just prior to their debut. So in reality there are no stoplights. Nor are there curbs or shoulders, barriers, lane markings, speed limits, or traffic signs of any sort. Nor, finally, do policemen keep an eye out for traffic violators; with an insurgency going on, they have bigger concerns. One would guess, then, that the steady stream of pedestrians, animals, motorcycles, bikes, trucks, army convoys, cars, seeking to flow through mainly narrow streets would present endless opportunities for mayhem and disaster, inspiring considerable anxiety in an outsider.

Somehow it has the opposite effect. There is little in my rather hermetic life here in Kashmir that I enjoy as much as the nightly ride home with Abid, weaving through the untold moving and immobile obstacles, buoyant Bollywood songs bouncing from the stereo in rhyme with the scenery whizzing past. Bus in the way? Just lean on the horn and it will slide subtly to the left to give us room to pass. Sheep at 1 o'clock? Whip right and the coast is clear.

Abid is leaning on the horn again as we zip around a corner at 60 kms/hr. There's a dog smack in the middle of the street, which is hemmed in by pedestrians on our left. We neither slow down nor budge from our path and at the last moment the dog lurches a foot or so to the left and we miss him by inches. Further along, on a nearly straight section of boulevard divided by a two-foot wide median, a jawan – Indian security officer – is unloading something from a large white truck on the edge of the road. A black and white cow is standing on the median but leaning his great girth some three feet over the short railing and out into the street. Between the officer and the bovine there is less than a meter, yet we barrel onward, undaunted, as a damsel gleefully hits those high notes, up and away she goes, urging us on, within twenty yards now as Abid leans on the horn again. Without looking at our fast-closing vehicle, the jawan presses his body up against the truck and the cow swings his head, neck, and body back over the median – the two synchronized movements providing the necessary additional three feet and we zoom through unimpeded.

Similar seemingly choreographed moments happen every few seconds, and I would often see my life rushing before my eyes if they weren't so effortlessly perfect, as if all the people, horses, goats, sheep, dogs, chickens and cows had from birth been inscribed with the movements of this dance, knew exactly when a vehicle of a precisely defined width was approaching, and at what speed, and precisely how to adapt without breaking from their conversation or duty at hand. Or as if they all are gifted physical improvisationists, capable of shifting up, down, left, right, contorting and manipulating bodies, vehicles, carts and children in a fraction of a second at the slightest warning while going about their business. I imagine the countless similar instances of near mayhem occurring at the same time at any one moment across the city, the Valley, all of the subcontinent, even, and sense that this inexplicable dance of the dodge is another Indian wonder to behold.

Occasionally someone misses a beat, but accidents just might be more impressive. On my first visit to Kashmir I was on a bus in Jammu that nudged a parked car's bumper as it was coming to a stop at a tea shop. As we passengers unloaded a small crowd of men gathered and began to take the matter in hand. I couldn't understand a word of it, but I got the gist. At first the car owner was upset, his vehicle being visibly damaged, but the subdued tones of the discussion calmed him down. The men who had witnessed the accident began speaking in turn, pointing at the car, the bumper of the bus, and the other available spaces of the mostly empty lot. The bus driver and car owner listened, nodding occasionally. Soon enough a settlement, in which the car owner clearly got his due, had been reached, the bus driver and car owner shook hands, and all went into the café. In the United States it might take a year for a court to decide fault and payment in such a case. In India, not fifteen minutes after the accident occurred, justice and chai had been served.

□

A Trip to the Country… or, Escape From Waterhal

(*Kashmir Observer* report)

November 19, 2006: Any journey into rural Kashmir is bound to be fraught with danger, what with its hidden, unpredictable militants, secretive paramilitaries, anxious soldiers, and conflicted locals caught in the crossfire. Yet last Thursday morning my colleague Farooq Shah and I set off in search of that rare animal: an outdoor primary school, with mud seating for upwards of fifty children, little or no facilities, barely-trained teachers, and nothing but the Valley's bitter late autumn for a roof. A disconcerting image of just such a beast had appeared without warning in our paper the previous week and, being enterprising journalists' game for a good story and an adventure, we packed up our gumption, a Twix bar and some chewing gum, and sallied forth into the relatively uncharted southern reaches of Budgam district.

We hit the road at the crack of 11, my little motorbike as game as could be after 19 Valley winters. Thrumming joyously and adding to the warmth kindled by our huddled torsos and reportorial verve, the old blue lady zoomed around curves and bobbed up and down, in and out of vast water-filled potholes, we two riders twittering like morning sparrows. Neither the previous few days' downpours and bitter cold nor the threat of a run-in with armed men of indeterminate allegiance could dampen our spirits.

Shortly after noon, however, our rural jaunt began to feel more wild goose chase-y. The mud sucked greedily at our bald tires. The road, with its jeep-sized potholes, became a minefield, and our destination, the tiny village of Waterhal, increasingly mythical. Minimal signage, suspicious, tight-lipped villagers, and a bland brown landscape bereft of identifying markers added to the sense of foreboding. Yet we soldiered on, querying a few locals to regain our bearings, and soon enough crossed a little concrete bridge into our dust speck of a destination. Middle-aged men commiserated next to tea shacks. Women carried baskets of spinach-like greens and bulging plastic sacks of rice on their heads. The road grew yet muckier and still on we ventured, finally hearing the high-pitched voices of young children just off to our right as we neared the top of a small rise.

We parked and clambered up a short, slippery slope and found ourselves in the Middle Ages, which is to say the very school from the photo. Children as young as three and four were bundled in sweaters and scarves and pherans, faces unwashed, noses dripping and feet bare and purpling. Shivering yet smiling at their visitors, they sat one behind the other on ruddy jute mats. The two teachers taught while we snapped photos and asked questions. After an hour or so our work was done and we headed towards my bike, and home. But I couldn't get the old girl started. And when Farooq tried he found that the accelerator cable, which should be attached to the right handlebar grip, had been severed. Oops.

"You've got to be more gentle, Dave," Farooq admonished. "You can't just - rgegh, gerhehr, rghea!! - attack everything like a wild animal."

"Yeah, I know, you're right," I admitted.

Then I grabbed my colleague by his puffy coat and shook him.

The sky filled with clouds as the clock ticked past two. My bike had become little more than a useless mass of heavy, rusting metal and worn rubber. I stared at her proud blue gas tank. I considered the wonderful times we had together. I considered pitching her into the stream.

Finally, I considered what Kashmir's most revered foreign observer, Sir Walter Lawrence, would do with such an excellent opportunity. Investigate the local flora and fauna? Query the villagers about their religious practices? Decipher the make-up of their pre-industrial economy? I decided I didn't care; I was cold and wanted to go home. Luckily, my phone had just enough juice to call our editor and apprise him of the situation.

"Hey, Sajjad, we found the school and got a really nice story," I told him.

"Oh, really," he responded, just slightly pleased.

"Yes, but my bike broke down and now we're stuck."

"Oh," he said, not surprised.

"Yeah, the accelerator cable broke and we're trying to figure out how to get back."

"OK," he said. "Let me talk to Farooq."

I handed the phone over and took in a changed scene. Perhaps a couple enterprising villagers had employed the mosque loudspeaker to announce our plight, because Waterhalis had gathered from far and wide. Young and old, big and small, pheran-wrapped and kangri-wielding, staring at my strange mug, fingering my gleaming, muddy machine and foisting up potential solutions. We've got to fix the bike, they told us; it can be very easily done. No, no, others disagreed, you'll never fix it; leave the bike here, hop a Sumo back to Srinagar and come get it later.[110] That's no good, still others interrupted: walk the bike over to Budgam and they can fix it in a jiffy.

Manzoor, the school headmaster, recalled a fellow villager who owned a motorbike, and thought perhaps he could help. He scurried to retrieve him as Farooq and I endeavored to entertain the remaining audience. I made silly faces and pretended to attack the little boys. Learning that the teachers occasionally beat the youngsters, Farooq found a thin switch and made to whip a little boy, to great hilarity.

Manzoor soon returned and after ten minutes of tinkering the man, Ahmed, announced his diagnosis: our accelerator cable was broken and needed to be fixed. Duly noted.

A second plan formed: Farooq and I would walk the bike in a weaving northeasterly direction towards the main road, which would lead us to salvation.

"It's only four, five kilometers," said Yusuf, a 17-year-old who was studying in Budgam to become a doctor and was one of the few villagers who spoke English. "You can definitely make it, and then in Budgam they will fix bike."

The prospect of pushing a motorcycle five kilometers up and down winding valley roads in near-freezing and possibly drizzly conditions did not titillate. I wracked my brain for an alternative.

"Isn't there someone who has a truck around here?" I asked no one in particular. "There's got to be one truck, right? If not in this village, then somewhere near here…"

Excited murmuring in Kashmiri rose. Index fingers pointed northwest among a general nodding of heads and just like that, praise Allah, plan number three solidified: push the bike the kilometer or so to the next village and find the man with the truck.

"Yes, I think it's best idea," said Manzoor, dropping the clincher.

Farooq and I began making our way, pushing the old lady through the muck and up the hill with much of our Waterhal entourage in tow. Thirty meters on we were stopped by an interested passer-by, an eagle-eyed villager with a great red beard. Apprised of our plight he offered up strategy four in the Escape from Waterhal sweepstakes: he would call a nearby mechanic to come and fix the bike straight away! Off he went to retrieve his mobile phone.

Again we sat waiting, the sky darkening as the clock ticked three, children getting restless and finally wearying of staring at the shiny–headed, pale-faced alien. Farooq had a sudden brainstorm and tried to start the bike. Inexplicably, it roared to life. He grabbed the rubber-sheathed accelerator cable near his right thigh and employed it as a sort of jerry-rigged gas controller. He put the bike into gear and chugged wobbily up the hill. Seeing this, the man who had gone off to call his mechanic friend decided we were in no need of mechanical assistance. He stomped off to the fields to resume his work. I went up to Farooq and patted him on the back.

"Hey, nice job," I told him.

"Yeah, yeah, but let me work on it," he said, sputtering off and tinkering with his new system.

Reverting to plan three, I rejoined Yusuf and Manzoor and we continued to stroll towards the neighbouring village, Harden, and the man with the pick-up truck. Minutes later we found Farooq in what passed as the village square, chatting with a young local.

"I fixed it," Farooq said, with obvious pride. "I've figured it out. We don't need the truck at all! Let's just ride to Budgam, we'll be fine."

"Are you sure, Farooq?" I asked.

"Yes, this cable basically works just like the accelerator,' he explained, reaching down near his knee and tweaking a black rubber cord. "You try it."

"Are you sure?" I asked again, not wanting to start something we couldn't finish.

"Yes, I told you," he said, getting impatient with my suspicion. "Try it for yourself."

"No, no, you figured out how to do it," I said. "You can drive."

Yes, loyal reader, plan five: employ Farooq's half-baked accelerator controller to matriculate over hill and vale to Budgam. We climbed on, shook hands with Manzoor and Yusuf and started off down a steep, serpentine decline. Progress was slow, but steady, and we began to feel our little ordeal had ended, that all would be fine. We came to the bottom and just over a muddy concrete bridge the road angled up and away into infinity.

As if in fear or awe, the bike halted at the base of the incline and the engine – eehrerhhr!!!!! – roared loudly, stuck on peak acceleration as the bike stood stock-still. I jumped off in fright and nearly fell down a small cliff. Time froze. The ear-splitting whine echoed across the ravine. Blue smoke shot out the exhaust. Vaguely visible through the haze as he tamed that neighing stallion with steely nerve, Farooq fingered gears and twitched his heels. I thought momentarily that this would be the last I'd see of my charming friend, bravely riding out the death throes of an overheating 1987 blue Yamaha. But it wasn't to be.

The engine fell silent. The smoke and dust settled. Farooq clambered off like a hero, exasperated yet relieved.

"Hey down there!" a disembodied voice called out from overhead.

"Yeah!" the two of us shouted nearly in unison.

"Do you need the pick-up truck?" the voice asked.

"Yes, we do," Farooq shot back.

We looked meaningfully at each other then caught our breath and took in our surroundings. A tiny trash strewn creak dribbled under the nearby bridge and on three and a half sides steep, aspen-pocked hills loomed. We were about half a kilometer from the surface world: no place to be broken down. Thankfully, a revised plan three was back in effect.

"Some friend you are," Farooq said. "You just left me to handle that thing all on my own!"

"You were driving!" I responded. "What could I do?"

"I don't know, but don't leave me to die," he said, making a decent point.

There was a long pause. The creek gurgled. An over-flying kite peered down hungrily.

"I totally thought the bike was gonna blow up," I said, starting to smile. "And you were a goner."

He giggled. "I thought I was going to fly!"

Fly from that ravine we did when the pick-up pulled up some ten minutes later. A pleasant, mostly silent ride to Budgam followed, Farooq and I warming ourselves and thinking of butter chicken and a hot bath. The Budgam pit stop was beyond easy: drop bike at mechanic's, get tea and a snack, retrieve bike ten minutes later and we're on our way to Srinagar. There was just one problem: I left my helmet in the back of the pick-up.

"Look at it this way," said Farooq, wind whipping through his hair, "we owed them."

We arrived in Srinagar in 15 minutes. So our brush with oblivion in a relic of a previous century - a village without electricity, without any sewage system or running water, with roads of foot-deep mud and near-starving children dressed in tattered clothing endeavoring to learn their multiplication tables in the bitter cold - took place only about 25 kilometers from Srinagar, a city of a million inhabitants, a place of Internet cafes and lush golf courses, cozy restaurants and swish hotels.

Walk to Budgam? We could've walked home.

Chapter 2

Limited Learning

Desiccate (verb): 1. To dry up. 2. To preserve by drying. 3. To drain of emotional or intellectual vitality.

— Merriam-Webster[111]

THOUGH BARELY A speck on the map of the world, Kashmir has been a seat of learning for two millennia. The Lotus Sutra, one of the most influential works in Mahayana Buddhism, is thought to have been written in Kashmir in the 1st century AD.[112] Kashmir played a crucial role in the early spread of Buddhist thought, thanks to its links to the Silk Road, the ancient travel and trade route stretching from East Asia to the Mediterranean.[113] In the 2nd century, Kushan ruler Kanishka welcomed some 500 monks to Kashmir for the 4th Buddhism conference.[114] After that event, Kashmir-trained missionaries and scholars like Kumarajiva and Nagarjuna translated the original Sanskrit documents that helped export Buddhism to China, Central Asia and Tibet.[115]

The Alchon Huns crushed Buddhism in the Valley, but this later spurred a wave of Hindu poets and thinkers, such as Vasugupta, who in the late 9th century wrote the Shiva Sutras, the foundation of Kashmir Shaivism. Kalhana, a revered 12th century Hindu scholar, recounted the history of Kashmir in *Rajatarangini*, or River of Kings, an eight-book verse text widely thought to have advanced literature in the subcontinent. During the Kashmir sultanate, a

Persian Sufi, Mir Sayyid Ali Hamdani, a Hindu sage, Lal Ded, and her disciple, Sheikh Nooruddin (also known as Sheikh-ul-Alam, or Nund Rishi), shaped Kashmir's uniquely syncretic blend of Islam.[116] Shaivism and Sufism merged within an ideology that embraced tolerance and equality.[117] In this period Sultan Zain-ul-Abidin, known to Kashmiris as Bud Shah ("Great King"), sent diplomatic gifts as far as Egypt and Mecca, including scholarly manuscripts and musical works.[118]

By the time I arrived in 2006, insightful scholarship and Kashmiris' abiding curiosity had largely vanished. Over the last five centuries Kashmir's intellectual and cultural legacy has been pulverized. Today, to give one example, most school teachers in Kashmir are freelancers working on a contractual basis. As a result, those responsible for shaping the next generation of Kashmiris can often be found at Lal Chowk, protesting for the salary and benefits of a regularized teacher (RT). Perhaps even more troubling, the number of outdoor schools, like the one in Waterhal detailed below, has increased sharply over the past decade as many school buildings have been burnt to the ground.[119] In 2016 alone, arsonists burned down nearly 50 government schools in Kashmir.[120] This is in addition to the nearly 1000 schools destroyed by militants since the start of the insurgency.

□

One Village's Future Left Out In Cold

KO report

November 21, 2006, Waterhal: Like most of his classmates, Mohammad Younis Malik wants to be a doctor when he grows up.

"I want to become a doctor because our village has none of them," said Malik, 8, who foresaw one small problem. "I don't have books to read from."

Considering the state of Malik's school, a shortage of reading materials is no surprise. In terms of distance, the Education Guarantee School (EGS) of Budgam district's tiny Waterhal village is only 25 kilometers from the modern conveniences of Srinagar. Yet it appears to have been dropped there intact from the 17th century.

Bundled in pherans, wool caps, and scarves on a recent near-freezing late November afternoon, sixty-four students huddled together for warmth under a brooding sky. Few had books and most sat barefoot with runny noses on stained and fraying jute mats, exposed feet dirty and cracked. A single green chalkboard and a broken plastic chair were the primary instructional aids.

"It is very difficult to teach the students in these conditions," acknowledged voluntary headmaster Manzoor Ahmad, surveying his school.

With no running water, no electricity, no heater, and just one small table, a nearby tin-roofed, 10-by-12-foot wood shack looked more like an outhouse than an occasional schoolhouse. A few aging posters and several examples of students' work on the walls were the only reminders that this was indeed a place of learning.

"We had to build this shack ourselves," Manzoor explained. "And whenever it rains we have to teach everyone together in this tiny room, all six grades at the same time. It-is pretty suffocating to cram 64 children into a single room. And while we're teaching the other ones are getting confused and not learning or misbehaving."

With a literacy rate of just over 42 percent, Budgam is the least literate district in J&K. Yet education in Kashmir's outlying tehsils is uniformly poor, with Kupwara, Baramulla, and Anantnag districts all under 50 percent. Grave health risk and Exhibit A in the shortcomings of education in rural Kashmir, the Waterhal EGS *guarantees* its students little more than an uncertain future.

"Both sunshine and rain brings suffering to the children due to the school's proximity with the road," said Manzoor, adding that many students stay home in bad weather. Children get sick more often for obvious reasons during the colder months, but because the main road is mere feet from their class space, they are constantly coughing and choking on dust and fumes in the summer.

"Inclement weather conditions of both summer and winter, unsafe drinking water coupled with absence of medical facility," said Tariq Ahmad, another teacher at the school. "The children suffer from ailments of different kinds such as chest infection, abdominal pain and diarrhea."

During a visit last week, many of the children were insufficiently clothed for the bitter cold and drizzle. Many parents cannot afford shoes, and their children come to school barefoot. Regardless, all students are required to take off their shoes during class.

"The wounds in their feet develop pus-filled cavities during winters," said Manzoor, pointing towards the dry, cracked heels of the children.

Until Kashmir's rural schools receive greater support, better care seems unlikely.

"Unless we have adequate staff how can we provide quality education to students in villages?" wondered former education minister Harsh Dev Singh, speaking in Jammu earlier this month. He estimated 12,000 vacant rural leaching posts in the state.

"There is a shortage of staff in rural schools," admitted J&K Education Minister Manjeet Singh, adding that most rural teachers were from urban areas. "The unfortunate part is they are not prepared to work in rural areas."

Upon hearing that the central government had sanctioned a Waterhal school under the Total Literacy Campaign (Sarva Shikhsha Abhiyan, SSA) in 2003, Manzoor Ahmad and Tariq Ahmad, both 10+2 pass-outs, applied as voluntary teachers. Winning applicants must set up the school with their own funding, enroll students via house-to-house survey and teach from 10 a.m. to 4 p.m. - all on a salary of Rs 1000 per month. Today some 2876 Education Guarantee Schools are operational in villages throughout the valley.

"The scheme, funded by the central government, was launched so that education could be delivered to the children right at their doorstep," said A. K. Raina, Joint Director Elementary Education, Kashmir Division.

The government provides books, mats, and funding for a midday meal.

"It was decided that the children owing to their poor background needed to be fed to lure them to schools and hence the midday meal scheme was introduced," said Raina, describing a 2004 dietary conference in Chandigarh in which doctors and dieticians developed the diet plan. "It included a balanced diet comprising carbohydrates, proteins, vitamins and other essential ingredients as per the advice of the dietician."

In Waterhal, that meal consisted of a small bowl of turmeric rice, which was cooked in a neighboring home then carried to the children across muddy backyards in a wok balanced atop Malik's head. Lined up like residents of a refugee camp, the youths stuffed the yellow grains into their mouths greedily before jostling for a second helping.

"They are allotted one rupee per student per day," said Nazir Ahmad Lal, Chief Education Officer, Srinagar, explaining the governmental meal outlay. "Occasionally they can save up for a treat, like pudding, but it's pretty much the same meal everyday."

Raina could not explain the discrepancy.

"I don't know why the scheme could not be implemented in letter and spirit," he said.

Tariq and Manzoor topped the EGS merit list and now, as headmasters of the village's only primary school, find themselves as custodians of Waterhal's future.

"They told us that our services would be treated at par with RT's after the completion of two years," Manzoor said, referring to the label applied to most new teachers, a distinction that includes a salary of Rs 1500. "Yet we haven't heard anything."

Manzoor and Ahmad are not alone. The state government has failed to upgrade 8000 Education Guarantee Schools to primary school level, according to Singh.

"The morale of the staff in these centers has been affected by this," he said.

The teachers' morale is not the only concern. Although Summaya, 8, can spell her name in a matter of seconds, she no longer looked forward to school.

"It is terribly cold in the open," she said, rubbing her hands and blowing on them. Her dark green pheran was pocked with golf ball-sized holes.

Three-year-old Cheelu, with bright blue eyes and an unwashed face, is the school's youngest student. Swinging rhythmically as she answered a visiting reporter's queries, she offered up the contents of her torn blue book bag. One book was entitled "Respiration and Reproduction in Living Things."

"She has got these books from her home," Tariq interjected, acknowledging that the students were still using last year's books.

"The Zonal Education Officer has promised that books to the children would soon be provided," said Manzoor Ahmad, despite the protests of his colleague, who pointed out that last year the books arrived at the end of March.

For eight-year-old Malik, the books can't arrive soon enough.

"There's no one to take care of the sick and the ailing," he said, arms tightly crossed, bare feet purpling in the moist brown mud.

After the above article ran in Kashmir Observer, a reader named Kamila reached out via email. I put her in touch with the state's department of education and she ended up buying shoes for all the students at Waterhal school. I wish I could've seen the faces of Malik, Summaya and the other children upon receiving their gift.

□

Kashmiris Close the Book

(KO report)

November 12, 2006: A two-meter by two-meter slab of pearly white stucco stands alone near the center of a vacant, trash-strewn lot behind a red brick wall across Maulana Azad Road from Regal Chowk.

The faux Spanish tile roofing is cracked and falling off, and on one side a golden inscription in black marble reads: "Sri Pratap Singh Library, Foundation Stone, Laid February 27, 2004."

Zahida Bano, Chief Librarian of the current SPS Library, explained what happened.

"Nothing," she deadpanned, chatting outside her office last week. "There was some controversy between the builders and the government, apparently costs were higher than they expected, and construction stopped before it started."

Nearly three years later the stout monument looms over the vast emptiness like an anti-scarecrow, fending off progress and fostering a return to nature. Instead of thrumming with the quest for knowledge the spot festers, silent testament, if any more were needed, to the Valley's intellectual calcification.

"I've been championing, fighting, writing letters and pleading with all and sundry, but nothing is getting done over there," said Agha Ashraf Ali, former J&K Director of Education and Principal of the College of Education. He had prodded local bureaucrats, politicians, and businessmen not only to restart work on the modern SPS venue but also to add an extension to the children's library in the name of his son, the poet Agha Shahid Ali, all to no avail. "Full of large promises and small excuses, they are not interested in books at all," he said.

In the age of bottomless broadband Internet and 2000-channel satellite television, reading may be on the wane across the globe. But in Kashmir the problem is especially acute, and the stakes particularly high. From Mughals to Dogras to Indians, Kashmiris have for centuries been under one or another oppressive yoke; an unwillingness to read could fate them to remain there.

"Without a library there's no university, there's no thought, there's no progress," Agha added. "Libraries and-universities, these things are on the frontier of thought, where you can move forward and ask inconvenient questions; this is an absolutely dead society, afraid of asking questions."

Indeed, the saddest truth may not be that the library has not yet been built, but that locals don't seem to care. The Deputy Director of Libraries admitted the situation had grown dire.

"Many people are less interested in reading," acknowledged Kuldeep Singh, who was transferred into his new post from the Social Welfare Department last month. He cited electronic media and an increasing lack of time, particularly among wealthier, more sophisticated Kashmiris. "The educated people are reading less, not more, even though it should be the other way around."

Comparing the latest borrowing estimates with historical data revealed a steep decline. The Directorate of Libraries said SPS Library has averaged 1000 visitors and 350-400 borrowers per month this year. Bano, who works at the site every day, estimated that members borrowed around 70-80 books monthly, or one-fifth the directorate's estimate.

According to Dr. Sangita Gupta and Dr. Gurdev Singh, professors of library science at the University of Jammu and authors of the new report "Public Library System in J&K State", SPS Library loaned out 10,185 books from April 1945 to April 1946. Stretched over a year, the directorate's 2006 estimate would come to much less than half that and Bano's on-site numbers would be just under one-tenth. Yet the population of Srinagar has doubled in the last 60 years, which means book borrowing has dropped as much as 95 percent in that span.

Prodded by such data, *Kashmir Observer* undertook an informal survey of passersby on Residency Road and found that about one out of every ten local adults had read an entire book in the last six months. Unemployed engineering graduate Javed Dhar, 27, was representative of those polled.

"I'm online all the time and just not very interested in reading," he said, stopping on the way to meet a friend for lunch. "I'm really busy, too busy...and in terms of books these days. I have no idea which ones would be good."

Detailing a litany of problems in the J&K library system, Gupta and Singh argue that locals should not shoulder all of the blame.

"The collection developed in the public libraries so far is... not relevant to the tastes of the public." they wrote. "[Book] selection is done at a higher level, and the requirement of users of the particular library is not taken into consideration. The librarian is not consulted... this leads to less use of library reading material.

"The condition of these libraries is unsatisfactory and very poor," the authors continued, explaining that professional service is absent, the infrastructure nominal, the locations odd and unpopular, and that all the libraries "are lacking the requisite reading facilities; the reading space is insufficient and the requisite furniture is inadequate."

Finally, Gupta and Singh pointed out that, like current Deputy Director Singh, most library officials are appointed from within the state administrative cadre. "In the history of public libraries, no subject expert has been appointed as Director of the Public Libraries and Research in the state," said their report.

These findings are borne out at SPS Library, which lies tucked away behind the State Museum across from the Jhelum. Although the front reading room is bright, airy, and attractive, in two back rooms thousands of volumes fester in dusty cases surrounded by neglected, brilliantly colored papier-mache walls.

Chief Librarian Bano acknowledged the 1896 building was in need of cleaning and repair, but more than the structure has suffered. A few of the glass-fronted bookcases had been left unlocked, and a recent visitor found that many of the texts inside were fragile and of little use. Upon opening, several pages fell out of a faded, red-bound 1927 hardcover of Dostoyevsky's *Poor Folk*. A bright green 1950's Penguin Edition of Dickens' *Our Mutual Friend* was sticky and unwilling.

"I used to check out Carlisle, Rousseau, the lives of Napoleon and all that from SPS, books for my father," Agha recalled. "Now fifty, sixty years after independence, when money has been coming into Kashmir in cataracts, the library has gone to the dogs. You can't find any books at all, anything that has been released in the last few years is not available here."

Funding materialized for SPS' new Internet Centre, however, which was inaugurated in late April and boasts ten gleaming new computers and a dedicated broadband connection. Yet on a recent afternoon the ten new swivel chairs sat empty. What's more, in the sun-streaked reading room a lone young woman studied her own Shakespeare texts while a half-dozen employees sat and chatted next to the entrance. For nearly 90 minutes there were no visitors, and the workers moved just once, to make way for their boss and a visiting reporter.

One morning last week the offices of the Directorate of Libraries at the SMC compound in Karan Nagar were similarly uninspiring. The entryway overlooked a scrap yard, full of twisted and mangled hunks of cars and trucks and other industrial materials. Inside the air was musty and heavy, as if traffic were irregular. Ripped and dirty maroon-colored carpeting half-covered the floor, light struggled to make its way through broken and papered-over windows, and 6 to 8-inch stacks of bound documents sat waiting on a desk. Chin in fist, an office assistant slept on a scuffed forest green couch.

"I don't know the secret to success, but a sure road to failure is trying to please everybody," chided a poster on the wall. Nearby photographs of then-Chief Minister Mufti Mohammed Sayeed and Directorate staffers at the 2004 SPS foundation stone-laying ceremony commemorated what had become a non-event.

Strolling confidently in the bright sunshine of a brisk November afternoon, Showkat Mohammed, 44 and a businessman, felt comfortable with his reading habits.

"I read one or two newspapers every day and occasionally I look at a magazine," he said. "And yes, I did read a book last year. It was by an American, a thriller-type story, and I enjoyed it!"

That so few Kashmiris are having similarly enjoyable experiences, however, may be for the best. The Valley's population of nearly 5.5 million vies for three lakh publicly available volumes, or about one for every 18 locals, Gupta and Singh found. SPS, the largest library, holds about 60,000 books, with about 35,000 at City Center Library and 25,000 research and reference texts at the Oriental Research Library on the University of Kashmir campus.

In fact, the state of J&K contains only 136 of India's 60,000 public libraries, or less than a quarter of one percent. Compare this to Delhi, where for an urban population of 12 million the public libraries offer over one and a half million volumes (2002 data, most recent available), or one book for every eight residents.

[And then there's the New York City library system, whose 89 buildings offer more than seven million borrowable volumes for a city of just over eight million. And this does not include the 43 million items contained in the network's four research libraries. One should not expect a conflict-torn developing region like Kashmir to compare with the global intellectual and cultural nexus of New York City, but it is interesting to note that the New York Public Library was created in 1895, one year before Sri Pratap Singh.]

"Without a library there's no university, there's no thought, there's no progress," said Agha. "Libraries and universities, these things are on the frontier of thought, where you can move forward and ask inconvenient questions; this is an absolutely dead society, afraid of asking questions."

For readers in Kashmir the difficulties don't end there. Don't even try to find an Urdu or Kashmiri-language bookstore anywhere in the Valley, because there isn't one. And since the Kashmir Bookshop on Residency Road shuttered about three years ago Sheikh Mohammad Usman and Sons has been Srinagar's only legitimate bookstore. The shop opened in 1956 and today offers approximately 25,000 books on all variety of topics, many new hardcopies with a strong focus on Kashmir culture and politics. The shop also operates a small publishing unit, Gulshan Books, which has released over 90 J&K titles in the last eight years.

Usman's efforts are valiant but there is only so much one outlet can do, thus the widespread desire for a convenient, pleasant, and up-to-date learning center. Zahid Ghulam Muhammad, former Deputy Director of Libraries for over three years, mourned the absence of the new SPS library and fingered the state leadership.

"It would have been a very good addition to Srinagar because it was right in the middle of all the educational institutions," he said. "The government has never been interested in promoting intellectual endeavors and promoting this kind of activity. Studying education and raising money to buy books and other matters related to the acquisition of knowledge has always been the most neglected. It is a lost priority, and perhaps the government does not want people to grow intellectually by design."

J&K Education Secretary K.M. Wani defended his department and claimed the new library was still in the works. "There has been a problem with funds which we are working to resolve," he said. "I can't commit to any period of time. We are trying our best to get the funds from the appropriate agency and when we do we will move forward."

But ever since the J&K Construction Company estimated the total cost of the new building at over Rs 17 crore, expense has remained an insurmountable hurdle.

"According to the plan of the city and government, this facility must be the icon of city, with new books and aisles and Internet and computers and all that, and right now that funding is not there," said Director of Libraries Dr. S.M. Fazlullah. "I am hoping...after January it may be possible."

In terms of the reading habits of Kashmiris, Ali Muhammad Dar, Professor of Arabic and Urdu at the Government Women's College, was an exception.

"Oh, yes, I am reading all the time," he said, explaining that in the last month he had read most of three books, including one on Sheikh-ul-Alam, patron saint of Kashmir. Dar owned neither a television or computer, and feared for future generations. "People only watch these days, they read very little. Soon you will see children graduating and doing post-grad who cannot fill out an application."

Agha blamed rampant materialism, especially in the youth-of Kashmir.

"The government is sluggish but it's the people; they get the kind of government they deserve," he said. "The habit of reading and discussing and getting together has gone out. The new rising generation is illiterate; they think by making money they can move mountains, but a library is the greatest thing."

Into the stillness of SPS' bright reading room, a bright blue sign echoed this last sentiment: "Books are keys to wisdom's treasure. Books are gates to lands of pleasure. Books are paths that upward lead. Books are friends, come on, let's read."

Yet the lot along M.A. Road sits empty. Where a grand colonnaded entryway should be welcoming visitors, three broken down jeeps - one bearing the insignia of UNICEF, another the Red Cross, and a third UN blue - seep slowly into the soil.

Where students and intellectuals were slated to pore over meaningful texts at gleaming new desks and tables, wildflowers, shrubs and weeds crowd leaf-strewn stretches of gravel. And where endless aisles of newly bound tomes should be drawing seeks of knowledge, two pairs of rusty white posts mark the cracked and dirt-strewn badminton and volleyball courts upon which scholars from the neighboring College of Education once played.

On a recent sunny afternoon a well-dressed man employed the foundation stone marker as a barrier behind which to relieve himself. He walked off grinning, leaving an observer to wonder if his gesture represented the majority opinion.

BOX: The Fire Still Rages

Sixty years ago this week, famed educator and future President of India Zakir Hussain delivered a fiery speech on the occasion of Jamia Millia University's Silver Anniversary. In attendance were India's soon-to-be first Prime Minister Jawaharlal Nehru and Maulana Azad, among other dignitaries. Although in reference to that era's spreading communal tensions, his words ring no less true in the Kashmir of 2006:

"The fire of hatred is fast spreading, which makes it seem mad to tend to the garden of education. This fire is burning in a noble and humane land. How will the flowers of nobility and sensibility grow in its midst? How will we be able to improve human standards which lie today at a level far lower than that of the beasts? How shall we produce new servants devoted to the cause of education? How can you protect humanity in a world of animals?... An Indian poet has remarked that every child who comes into this world brings along the message that God has not yet lost faith in man. But have our countrymen so completely lost faith in themselves that they wish to crush these innocent buds before they blossom?... The fire is raging. Please extinguish it. For God's sake do not allow the very foundations of civilized life in this country to be destroyed."

□

The Long, Blessed Journey of Fida Hassnain

(KO report)

December 24, 2006: "I had gone to Berlin to speak on the androgyny of man," Fida Hassnain began, wrapped in a red scarf and puffy blue jacket in the study of his Srinagar home on a recent chilly afternoon.

With his wife nearby, the octogenarian scholar recalled how he stumbled into being a healer.

"There's a statue in Indian mythology, half man, half woman," he said, "and I talked of this statue and I opened and closed the lecture with sayings from the Holy Qur'an."

Hassnain paused for a sip of tea, mug brushing against his trimmed white goatee.

"Afterwards these young Germans came and told me they liked my lecture, and said, 'Thank you very much,'" Fida recalled, raising his eyebrows. "They said, 'No, no, you have to come with us.' They worked at a local psychiatric hospital and I went with them...I didn't know what I was going to do there but I remembered some of my learning from Istanbul, where I received my master's, Sufism and whirling dervishes and that stuff, I had learned these things, but what exactly to do?" said Fida, looking slightly embarrassed.

"I said to them, 'please keep your shoes outside,' and I started a little pramayana and then a zikr, and I asked them to 'raise your hands and connect yourself with your God.' 'Professor, Sir, who is God?' they asked, and I said 'Your father and mother — just connect yourself.' And after ten rounds of this they told me, 'You have helped them! This meditation is healing them!'" Fida laughed and went on. "So they sent me to Munich and these other places and that is how I started this Sufi meditation."

A modern-day Prince Myshkin, Fida Muhammad Khan Hassnain lives each day as if it were his first, adapting to his environment, charming everyone in sight and constantly spinning silk from sow's ears. Although his business card dubs him a Sufi Mystic and a Spiritual Healer, he is a great deal more. Author, lecturer, archivist, historian, columnist, lawyer, and archaeologist, this Kashmiri has led a dozen lives, most of which were thrust upon him by family, friends, or happenstance.

He has doctorates in alternative medicine, literature, Sufism, metaphysics and Indology, has traveled to nearly every country in Europe and Asia and lectured, meditated, or studied in most of them. He has been happily married for fifty-six years, has two sons and a daughter, eight grandchildren, and two great-grandchildren. He is 83 years old, has written 32 books — soon to be 33, he says — and may yet have several careers to come.

Originally from Sialkot, Punjab, Hassnain's grandfather Raja Mohammad Ali Khan Khokhar moved the family to Kashmir to become the master jailer for Maharaja Ranbir Singh shortly before the turn of the last century. He served in military campaigns and put Fida's father, Raja Din Mohammad Khan, through the Srinagar EMS School. After returning from battle in the Boer War, the younger Khan married another teacher and the two spent most of their adult lives moving around the Valley opening schools.

"This made an impact on me," said Hassnain, recalling how he returned from Aligarh in 1947 with degrees in political science, history, and law. "I returned to Srinagar and started my teaching career as a lecturer at Amar Singh College."

Regular visits by several of his well-known National Conference friends quickly drew the ire of his superiors. "My friends would come to visit me and the principal told me 'you are indulging in politics,'" he said. "'I don't care to teach' I told them, and I resigned."

Spurned from education, Hassnain turned to law.

"I started a second career as a lawyer," said Hassnain, beginning what would become a trend. "I quickly learned the first trick of the trade - if you speak in Urdu people believe in your legal knowledge. Not English, Urdu. I don't know why, but I became a very successful criminal lawyer."

And that is how he came to represent a suspect client.

"The chief of a pickpocket gang had been arrested," he began in his typically unassuming manner. "And his men came to me, begging, 'Please, please get him released on bail!' So I thought about it and realized I didn't really have a case, but I said to the judge, 'I am representing this poor man trying to maintain his wife, his children, his father, his brother. He is an honest-man, he goes to mosque every day,'" Fida said, cracking a smile.

"And that judge is laughing: 'This is the chief pickpocket man!' 'This man has been wrongly implicated in this case,' I told the judge. 'Sir, in the name of Allah, I request to you, please allow him to go."

Unable to contain himself anymore, Hassnain burst into laughter.

"The judge laughed, but then he said, 'Release this man on bail," Fida recalled. "And then all these thieves and pickpockets came and they raised me in their arms and they cried, 'Zindabad! He's the greatest lawyer!' and they put a big golden ring with a ruby on my finger and they give me a big bag of money."

But that wasn't the end of it.

"When my mother saw me in the evening she asked, 'Where is it that you got this ring and all this money?'" said Hassnain. "I told her what happened and she said, 'You released a criminal, a thief?' I said 'Yes, this is my profession.' 'You're profession is to safeguard these thieves, these criminals, and to take that money, which is haram? You will return this ring and money and don't plead such cases. You just convince your heart that you plead only the cases of the innocent; you must not turn untruth into truth and truth into falsehood.' And I said, 'Yes, yes.' And I changed my attitude," Hassnain recalled.

Honesty, however, is rarely the best policy for a lawyer.

"As a result my law practice diminished," he remembered, thinking of his mother's advice. "Because I was always asking questions, about innocence and what they had done and all that."

Hassnain gravitated back to teaching, and after a few years at SP College he was called by Sheikh Abdullah to work as a state historian. He trained at the National Records in Delhi and in 1954 returned to Kashmir to become the Director-General of Records, beginning another career, as an archivist.

"I got absorbed in this work of reading files and forgot everything else," he said. "Until 1970, when Sadiq Sahab was CM and he selected me to deliver speeches on Buddhist culture to Nagoya University in Japan."

He went and delivered his series of lectures and then his hosts asked about payment.

"I said 'No, no, you brought me to this place and kept me in a nice hotel and provided me with lots of good food. I am a big shoe and I don't touch money,'" said Hassnain, smiling. "This impressed the Vice Chancellor of the University, and he called a big meeting and began to speak and my interpreter told me, 'He is praising you: "For the first time we have this great Buddhist teacher, a Bukhia Sensei, who doesn't touch money!"' And another VC stood up and said, let him please give these lectures at my university!'

"I spent a few months there giving lectures at various universities, and they give me this title of Buddhist master. I was a Buddhist monk and could stay anywhere. They gave me much honor, and I have returned to Japan every year."

The Japanese connection was so great that his second son has settled there, but, for Fida, the incident was not so uncommon that it couldn't be repeated elsewhere. Just about every time Hassnain left Kashmir, it seemed, he wound up with a new vocation.

Stuck in Leh because of heavy snowfall in the early 1980's, Hassnain found some old manuscripts there and became interested in the possibility of Jesus' visit to Kashmir. Ten years later he self-published a book that after further editing was later re-published as "In Search of Historical Jesus".

"It has been quite successful," Hassnain acknowledged. "It has been published in various languages, German, French, Italian, this year it was translated into Russian. People became interested and I got lots of letters asking questions and I became a well-known scholar on Jesus in Kashmir.'"

Perhaps you can guess what came next.

"I went to England and Scotland and gave lectures on this," said Hassnain. "I wanted to show that in the West they have monopolized Jesus, although he belonged to the East."

Hassnain was asked how he came to be a successful lawyer, a published author many times over, and, particularly, an international lecturer on the history and practices of three different religions.

"In my life certain things happened for which I had no control," he explained. "How could I go to Japan and start teaching this Buddhism?

I had no connection with Buddhism. And how could I go to Germany and these other countries to practice Sufi meditation? Lecturing about Jesus in England?! I was destined to do these things.

"There is some purpose in the creation of every human being," he added. "Nobody is created without some purpose; God is not a madman, that he would create anyone without some purpose.

"But my going towards occult sciences and these other things has a long history in Kashmir, where Islam came through Sufism, through fakirs and through saints...It is a different kind of Islam that came through the sword in other places. You may say that Islam never came through sword, but it has, and in those countries it will go back. Why did you go to Spain and conquer it? You had no business conquering it. You can spread Islam through your good deeds, and your example. What was the result? You were thrown out of Spain after seven hundred years. Wherever Islam has gone through sword, it has to come back."

The discussion of Islam and war brought the historian back to Kashmir.

"We are in a transitory period here, and God has willed it," he said. "We have suffered, suffered, suffered, and due to circumstances, these vestiges of our history are being lost. But all will not be lost; you can't lose the tradition and heritage of thousands of years in a decade or so."

"As for the departure of the Pandits, that is a great loss, surely, but they will come [back]," Hassnain said. "This has happened earlier, during Sikander's time they ran away, but during Bud Shah's time they came back. So this happened before, this coming and going. Naturally when there is peace, they'll come back — when everything is OK, when there is no India, no Pakistan here.

"Lal Ded says 'there's no difference between Hindus and Muslims,'" Hassnain continued. "So it's a fact that it's a different kind of Islam here. Yes, yes, during the last few years there were all these changes, some people won't allow you to hold sessions, to do this or that, but that was Wahhabi brand of Islam, Orthodox, terribly Orthodox. It is not a permanent thing here in Kashmir.

"Pakistan used the energies of these people but you can't have it now, because you can't go back, the world is progressing," he said. "On one side you have this system that wants to make you pure Muslim, on the other side is this modern globalization. Now two trends are going on. Can they fight this globalization? You try to keep women in the house, not to go to school, but it won't work. You are fighting against time. The world has to progress and we have to go by it. How can they stop this wave? Tomorrow they will say this computer is un-Islamic, but it won't work."

Hitting his stride after some more tea, Hassnain roamed on.

"It was the honorable Prophet (PBUH) who said, 'The sun will rise from the West.' Progress from the West will bring Islam to the world. Not the East; the East has lost its chance. Their time, their period has finished. It is the Muslims of America, Europe and England, not these people here. All the wisdom of the world is in London, and in New York. That's the New World. Those Muslims will tell you what Islam is, not this man with a beard and a big turban, no. The new Islam will be explained by someone from New York or London, wearing a very nice suit and a fine hat."

☐

BOX: Kashmir's Scholarly Traditions

"I have studied the history of Kashmir," says Fida Hassnain. "It is an ancient land with its own civilization, and it will become the focus of Asiatic civilization one day. It will become a miniature England within Asia."

"We have this tradition of great historians here," Hassnain added, naming nearly a dozen, including Kalhana and Soka. "I am keeping that very tradition alive."

He listed four books he was working on, including a memoir of his travels, an analysis of Islam in Kashmir, and another Jesus study. Friends had asked him why he had yet to write about recent Kashmiri history.

"This is a transitory period," he explained. "And you can't write well about a war until it is over, when you can explain how it happened and what it means and all that."

Hassnain disparaged the majority of writing in the Valley.

"You can't write on Kashmir by sitting in Srinagar," he said. "You have to go out of this state, where you can think independently and write independently. At this point there is no independence here: if you write in favor of Pakistan, the government of India will stop you; if you write in favor of India, people will say it is manipulated."

Returning to his educational roots, Hassnain saw reason for hope.

"If you go to the rural villages, right across the street from militant hideouts and orthodox mosques you will find these English-Medium Schools," he pointed out. "English is international, when you learn it your mental vision changes. This is the language of progress...So you may think these are only educational institutions but they are changing the destiny of Kashmir. If you look deeply at these schools, they are bringing a revolution here, the salvation of Kashmir."

Chapter 3

My Lion of Kashmir

Without a lamp I look for him in houses buried, empty —
He may be alive, opening doors of smoke,
breathing in the dark his ash-refrain:
"Everything is finished, nothing remains."

— **Agha Shahid Ali**[121]

And when I am forgotten, as I shall be, and asleep in dull cold marble, where no mention of me must be heard of, say, I taught thee.

— **William Shakespeare**[122]

READING THIS PROFILE of Agha Ashraf Ali fifteen years later, I remember that he had been more of a friend than a subject, despite our half-century age gap. I recall long evenings of conversation and whisky at his Rajbagh home, where visitors might include an ex-terrorist or an acquaintance of Nehru, a Pandit of Kashmiri origin, and how he affectionately called me "Professor of Honolulu" because it sounded ridiculous and rolled off the tongue. In particular I recall his halting, almost reverential memories of his son Agha Shahid, who in the first decade of the insurgency emerged as Kashmir's bard of woe, penning weighty verses about his troubled homeland from thousands of miles away.

Born in Delhi and educated in Kashmir, Agha Shahid Ali left for the United States in 1976, but returned to Kashmir nearly every summer. In 1987 he published his breakthrough, *The Half-Inch Himalayas*. A decade later came the work that would make him a Kashmiri icon, *The Country Without a Post Office*. "For many of us growing up amid this horror, it was Shahid who shone a light on the darkness," Kashmiri novelist Mirza Waheed wrote in 2016. "I remember I had a near visceral reaction when I first read *Country*... It was akin to listening to someone making sense of my world to me for the first time."[123]

The title refers to the extended halt on mail delivery in Kashmir during the height of the insurgency, and was sparked by the discovery of an undelivered letter meant for Agha Ashraf.[124] The poems, centered on nostalgia for lost landscapes, conflict and exile, struck a chord beyond Kashmir. "Extraordinary formal precision and virtuosity," prominent intellectual Edward Said said of *Country Without a Post Office*. "This is poetry whose appeal is universal, its voice unerringly eloquent. A marvelous achievement."[125]A naturalized American citizen, Shahid taught for years at the University of Massachusetts-Amherst, served as a guest lecturer at Princeton University and won a Guggenheim Fellowship before he succumbed to brain cancer in late 2001.

Centuries of persecution topped off by a bloody, three-decade insurgency have left Kashmir with very few Agha Ashrafs, and even fewer Agha Shahids. The educational and cultural infrastructure that might encourage such ambition, creativity and bold thinking, and envision various routes to success, is no more. It is a sad ode to Agha Ashraf and his son that in the wake of India's 2019 revocation of Article 370, mail delivery was suspended until further notice — again rendering Kashmir a place without a post office.[126]

□

The Life and Times of Agha Ashraf Ali

(KO report)

October 17, 2006: I first met Agha, as he is widely known, on a July visit to his cozy Rajbagh home. Arguing politics over drinks with several close friends, the octogenarian educator was in high spirits and rare form: accusing me, the imperialist American, of most if not all of the world's problems; brushing aside challengers for talking "rot;" and jovially lording over his kingdom like a knighted duke. As the months passed, tales of his family's notable Kashmiri heritage, the literary achievements of his revered poet son, and the mark he left on Kashmiri education and politics filtered down and we at *Kashmir Observer* decided that his 84th birthday – Wednesday, October 18 – presented the perfect opportunity to take a closer look at this long and well-lived life. So with pen, notebook, and recording device at the ready I returned to his house last week and, after exchanging pleasantries, asked him about his family's rise to prominence in Kashmir.

"The family of my grandfather's grandfather has fallen on hard times, 1872, and Hari's Singh's son, Pratap Singh's father Maharaja Ranbeer Singh is going in a big boat, 24 rowers, on the way to Mansbal Lake down the Jhelum, and he gets, luckily for us, a wind colic and he is in terrible pain," he began with a typical single burst of breath sentence-story, bobbing grey moustache keeping time and dark-rimmed spectacles lending gravitas.

"So they stopped the boat and they ran into that area of woebegone humanity, Sixth Bridge, 'Is there any doctor here?' And out steps my great great grandfather, Aga Hakim Baqir. He gives him black salt and the Maharaja starts farting away. Farting away! And he totally recovered and he appointed Aga Baqir as his royal physician. True story. And over a century later my son the poet said to Amitav Ghosh: 'The fortunes of the Agha family we're hanging by a fart.'"

From this tale sprung forth not only a wealthy, cultured assemblage of kin but also a long, meandering stream of words, a seven-hour marathon of memory that regularly doubled back on itself and spanned three afternoons, the four score years of his life, five continents, and the modern story of Kashmir and the communal divide. One man's psychological and professional journey, a trip intertwined with the story of India and full of the spice and contradiction that define the subcontinent.

With the fighting spirit of Turkoman Qizilbash commanders in his blood, Agha remains a bear of a man, with thick features, an able body and a vigorous, agile mind prone to three-minute digressions that conclude with a shake of his square, silver-topped head and a thin, subject-changing "anyway."

Wearing a wool sweater over a plaid dress shirt with pressed khakis, he leaned back in his favorite, floral-patterned chair, rested his navy blue-socked feet on a round wooden coffee table and recalled his childhood.

"I was an adopted child," he said, explaining that his mother had wanted a daughter and so delivered Agha into the hands of her father, his grandfather, to raise him. "In a way I was a compromise the day I was born, and thereby hangs the story of an unhappy childhood."

It was not for lack of money. Noticing that Agha's grandfather, Aga Syed Hussain, was a bright student, Aga Hakim Ali Maki, the farting curer's son and royal physician to Maharaja Pratap Singh, helped him win a post as a junior government officer shortly before the turn of the century.

"Sir Walter Lawrence and other English officers made calls and they went on hunting and fishing trips and so he kept rising up," Agha related. "At his peak my grandfather was making 2500 rupees a month, this at a time when you could get in Kashmir 64 large breads for a single rupee, which also happened to be the average teacher's salary at the time."

Along with his cousin he built a grand feudal estate in Shaheed Ganj, where he lived with his three children. Nearby were Agha's mother and father and two brothers. Empty now, the manor house still stands, having narrowly escaped a watery grave.

"There were floods in Kashmir in 1928 and King Hari Singh offered us one of his grand guesthouses, but my grandfather said 'no, we're not leaving.' I remember as a child, the water is about this much" — Agha brings his hand to his waist — "in the house and my adopted mother and others are walking through it to the road where the car is. The water's coming into the house and our books are in the yard and about a mile away, floating. His elder son, he goes in a shikara collecting them.

"And my grandfather's cousin Sher Ali, retired, he would read huge books like 'Mysteries of the Courts of London' – stories of sex and lords running about, that sort of thing – with a magnifying glass. But there was one story, about when a particular village was supposed to be flooded there was a wall in which there was a hole, so he told him to put his finger in that and the village was saved. He had read this. Now water is coming through at least two feet in his house, and he's yelling to the servant: 'In the back door, the pine door, there's a knot, put your finger in it!' And he does, but of course the water just keeps pouring in."

Agha doubled over in giggles before returning to his parentage.

"My stepmother, 22 years younger than her husband, doted on me in the hopes that I, the youngest, would get some of the property… So she was giving me everything, showing to her husband, 'Look how much I love him,' but she made too much of me, got me the best things, and occasionally for no rhyme or reason other than being frustrated she would beat me," he added. "She was insecure and transmitted a bit of that insecurity to me."

[That insecurity may partially explain why so few of Agha's millions of words have been preserved on paper; in 84 years he has written only one lengthy prose piece, his doctoral thesis. Asked why he had not written more Agha responded with a question: "Did Socrates write?" He had Plato, I countered. "Yes, well there are many great men who did not write, for various reasons. I don't have the patience for it. The craft of writing takes real patience, a virtue I do not possess."]

"My grandfather loved me as he loved all his children, but he loved me more because he'd brought me up in his old age," Agha pointed out.

"Treated me like his own son…and he gave me more of his property, not equal to his sons but more, handing me his daughter's share. So I became an apple at the scarlet age of twelve.

"Then came my mother — she created a tremendous debate based on the following: since I have given half of my property to him, he is my son," Agha went on. "So I was taken back at twelve; it was a trauma in chief. There I was the third child and unwanted and not taken care of as well. It was a very educational atmosphere, etc., etc., but I could see that I was not loved as much as I was by my grandfather and grandmother."

His adolescent years were strung between the grand, Westernized life of his grandfather in his younger days and the stolid, more traditional ways of his mother's home. And as Agha spoke of his formative years a glittering gallery of writers, philosophers, politicians, and academics made regular and unscheduled appearances, shooting from his memory like kernels of popping corn, fully in character and offering up personal anecdotes or paragraph-long quotations sprinkled with buttery sentimentality or salty wisdom, or both. He employed them to further an argument, to emphasize the dramatic moment, and to delve into his own psychology. Dr. Zakir Hussain, then-future president of India, materialized first.

"1941, I'm a senior, fourth year in college. I'm merely going to be twenty," he started again, excitedly approaching an early milestone. "I've seen good teachers but nothing first rate, and because of my bewildered and bewildering childhood, I'm lost.

"And I in my state of total liquidity, I am like wax, and Zakir Hussain comes and – whap! (slaps his hands together) – he spoke and I was totally won over. It was my first unsophisticated love. I fell in love with Dr. Zakir Hussain, governor of Bihar, future president of India, studied in Berlin, a brilliant man. I hear this speech and I'm bowled clean. Bowled clean!"

He scooted to the edge of his chair and sat up tall before unleashing, without pause, the bulk of Hussain's October 2nd 1941 speech for the All Jammu and Kashmir Student's Conference.

"'Young friends,' he began, as if in my melting wax the needle is making the grooves. Can you imagine?! I'm just bewitched, totally bewitched! 'It's very kind of you to ask me to preside over your deliberations. But if in asking me to do so you want me to make a long speech or a good one, I shall have to disappoint you. I must abstain on medical advice from making a long speech and my personal limitations will see to it that I will not make a good one. Fortunately I can turn this necessity into a virtue. I shall refrain from flattering you. I will not tell you that the future of your country, nay, the future of the world was safe in your hands: you are the promise, you are the hope. Because I know, alas, there have been others young before you. They also were a hope and a promise. Their story, alas, is a sad tale of hope unfulfilled and promise unrealized. No one can predict the story of the generation that's now growing. But if it has to be different, our young men will have to start by realizing now,'" Agha continued, index finger pounding out key words. "'Life, young friends, is real. Life is hard. Life is earnest. Life is striving forever higher. Life is service. Life is a vision. Life is virtue.' He goes on and on then he brings up the end, a devastating sentence. 'Young friends, youth is not an attainment, it is an opportunity, do not let that opportunity go by.'"

Agha grinned and rubbed his hands together with glee.

"I was bewitched!"

The young student quickly embraced the open-minded, liberal idealism of Zakir Hussain and his Jamia Millia colleagues, but the shift was short-lived.

"The Partition of India...knocked out the basis of Jamia Millia's ideology and philosophy, which was Hindu-Muslim culture, which was unity. So the whole philosophy of Zakir Hussain and the Jamia Millia crumbling led to: what is the future of the Muslims in India? So, by 1940, when Jinnah spoke about the partition of India, Muslims would come and say to us, 'You are not in the Muslim League? You are not a Muslim?!' Dr. Zakir Hussain would talk to them patiently and say, 'Look, you are welcome to have Pakistan, but you will weep tears of blood one day. Remember.'

"So the whole idea that we were bargaining with the Hindus for official equality, that several hundred years of Muslim culture had also done some good, was knocked out. We'd just become fourth class citizens of India. So I thought Marxism was the only way, that communism was the only way, which is that the poor of Hindus and Muslims would get together to fight for freedom," he said, looking back. "That was innocence incarnate."

PART II

In the living room of Agha Ashraf Ali's Rajbagh home, multi-colored Kashmiri rugs cover smooth brown carpeting. Thick books and ruffled newspapers, odd objects of sculpture, and photographs of family and friends lay about the bright, airy space while misty portraits of Gandhi, Jesus, and Maulana Azad hang near a maroon couch. The scent of black tea and old wood mingle with the occasional creaking of walls and furniture, the only sounds of a still mid-afternoon.

Until Agha speaks, that is.

"My first clash with Farooq Abdullah and I cut him to size," he resumed, recounting with a broad grin an early incident as J&K Inspector of Schools. "Eighteen-year-old cheeky lad, 1953. He came into the office, says, 'There's an understanding between the PM and this office that my cousin will not be transferred. He's a teacher and you have transferred him.' I said to my secretary, 'Please find where is the order of the Prime Minister that his nephew should not be transferred.' And he said, "Sir, there is no such order." And I said to Farooq, 'Mr. Farooq, I will talk to Sheikh Sahab myself. Goodbye!'"

Concerns about the state of education in Kashmir, however, could not be similarly dismissed. The Indian Constitution had recently been made law, stipulating that within ten years all of India should have free, compulsory, and universal primary education up to the age of 14.

"Within ten years?!" he recalled, referring to Kashmir. "They don't have it today! They wished it, but they didn't realize what would be the problem."

Trotting a couple centuries back in time to strengthen his argument, Agha turned to 18th century England and the rural to urban migration of the Industrial Revolution. Several decades later it had led to mass education.

"They were able to do it, but we in fifty years have not been able to do it because we are not ideologically and philosophically wedded to the idea that the masses have to be educated," he explained. "Here we thought without any industrial revolution, we'll have mass education! It's just not possible, you see. You have to generate the resources to establish infrastructure and all that. When I go to that damned country called the United States…underground there are tunnels, under the roads. And hundreds of pipes through which everything flows and if anything goes wrong you go in and you put it right. But here there is nothing underground except my bottom!"

Towards tea time the chirping of chickadees rose, muezzins wailed from down the street and across the Jhelum, and puttering, chatting servants produced a muted clamor in the connecting kitchen.

[By turns fierce and gentle, berating then caressing, Agha embraces his domestic help as he does life. From his living room throne he will shout across the dining room and into the kitchen with specific instructions. When later some small oversight is committed he will erupt, scolding a man a mere foot away, then quickly subside. Yet he dines and takes tea with them, remembers the names of their children and children's children, and knows what they do when they are elsewhere – one's a computer programmer, another studying to be an engineer, and his kindly, white-bearded gardener once worked for one of the wealthiest men in Kashmir.]

Sipping black tea and crunching marmaladed toast with his gardener, Agha waxed philosophical.

"It was in England that I came upon the great Jewish philosopher Martin Buber. He gave me my motto, my creed, my Bible, which destroys both Jinnah and Gandhi in one sweep. Listen, this is just fantastic, devastating: 'In an age which is losing form, the highly praised persons who serve its fictitious forms and in their name learn to dominate the age count no more than those who are diligent to corrupt those forms… The ones who count are those who though they may be of little renown respond to and are responsible for the continuance of the living spirit each in the active stillness of his sphere of work.'"

Many Kashmiris believed Sheikh Abdullah to be the embodiment of that living spirit, and as the Lion of Kashmir pressed India for greater autonomy in the early 1950's the Central Government pushed back.

"Because he was behaving like that, fighting India for Article 370, which was being eroded since the day it was created, Sheikh Abdullah was being disobedient like a naughty boy, creating a problem for India," Agha said. "The day Sheikh was arrested they came and took away my vehicle. The whole of Kashmir was risen; there was civil commotion. They took machine guns to kill people in Anantnag. Shops closed. It was a tremendous uprising. In that atmosphere suddenly my rule in Kashmir was finished, as was Sheik Abdullah's."

After a two-month stint as the acting principal of the College of Education and a year as the head of the National Education Training Center, Agha was appointed the full-time principal of the College of Education in 1955.

"That is when I began my work," Agha recalled, his face brightening. "Becoming a teacher of teachers; and I was able to devote myself to academic work!"

But that work was cut short in 1956, when Soviet Premier Nikita Khrushchev provoked a deep philosophical crisis.

"I had returned from England a rabid Marxist, but Khrushchev's secret speech changed everything. I picked it up from my local bookshop, came home and read it through. I was shocked. I've been envisioning Russia as a utopia and I've been criticizing everybody. I was so embarrassed," he admitted, again growing quiet. "I was on the verge of suicide…I was feeling so bad…Oh god, it was terrible."

Reading cleared his mind of suddenly troubling Marxism and put the wind back into his sails.

"That period, that crisis period, is fantastic!" he recalled, perking up again as he toured his personal journey of philosophy. "After Zakir Hussain and Erich Fromm, and moving away from that, through Marxism after the Partition of India, and then coming to Dr. Zhivago and Azad and back to the innermost self via Krishnamurthi....aahhhhh," he finished, sighing.

"I live by ideas," he explained, "whatever that means to you."

I asked if he noticed any agitation towards independence during this period.

"Of course, it's all the time here," he explained. "A few people are dying every few months instead of every day. They throw stones at the army and things like that; Sheikh Abdullah is continuing this agitation. It's building…the middle class Muslim is coming to the fore. Youth are going to high schools and colleges…and they see the government of India promoting only Hindus, in all the banks, in all the government offices: discrimination, that's what Partition did to this country. Greatest tragedy.

"Here, because of the Partition and the communal divide and the two-nation theory, the Kashmiri Pandit professors would go to the Indian government and complain about how a Muslim man twice their age and half their ability had been promoted. Seniority and experience and ability didn't matter…Pandits saw that they were being superseded, and they offset it by employing only Hindus in their own domain.

"The quality of education dropped because on the whole the Pundits, who were the better teachers, stopped teaching well. If Muslims were going to be promoted why would they teach? I'm talking about the 50's, 60's, 70's. And slowly as Muslims started coming up, the Hindu was being squeezed out of this."

In an effort to place these developments in greater relief, Agha scooted to the edge of his seat and huddled his shoulders close to transform himself into Maulana Azad circa 1945.

"I'm taking you back again, but this is detonating. Three Pandits come to visit him on a houseboat in Dal. He's sleeping but calls them in anyway. Only a five-minute interview, but Azad could pierce to the heart of the matter; he had a luminous mind."

Agha leaned forward conspiratorially, crouched further and spoke meekly, like a wise man aware of the power of his words.

"'Brothers, this movement of Shiekh Abdullah, the masses coming up, does it make you feel a little afraid?' 'Oh, no, no,' they said. 'Oh, it can be frightening, it can be, you don't have to deny. But my advice to you is' one single sentence, like a doctor's prescription for Cipro 500! 'devote all your creative energies to the uplift of the masses and therefore remain at the head of it.'"

And like flipping the channel, Agha suddenly inhabited two very different characters from an earlier era.

"Lord Rutherford, British physicist, split the atom you should know, was at some fancy gathering and an American professor of physics, cigar in his mouth, comes up to him and says," and here Agha employed brash, flat American tones, "'Ha! Hey! Lord Rutherford! How do you manage to remain at the head of the wave? You are always at the head of the wave!' And Rutherford, with his British understatement, 'I'm sorry. I made the wave.'"

On Agha roamed, shouting now in his excitement.

"What Azad meant was in this vast movement, if you help Kashmiri Muslims to learn math and science and use your creative energies to bring them up you will remain at the head!" Agha said, leaving the UK behind and returning to Kashmir. "This is what they didn't do and this is why they were thrown out. Not only from the college but out of Kashmir. They didn't want the masses to come up…but the masses have got to come up!"

Most, unfortunately, were unable to come up as far they had hoped.

"The products are the unemployed, the unemployables, and that leads to the movement, Yasin Malik and company," he said, speaking with less force, as if wearying of the familiar tale. "And they went across and brought the gun and in the last fifteen years the whole thing has been destroyed, and Kashmir become a luckless, lawless society."

PART III

In an attempt to simplify his eight-decades-plus bildungsroman, Agha Ashraf Ali, like China's ruling party, breaks his life into negotiable chunks.

"If you split my life into ten or eleven five-year plans you'll never go wrong," he told me. "Then you can divide, move them around and connect with this or that, etc."

So we rejoin our tale in 1971, in plan number seven or eight, or ten, depending on who's counting, and Agha has become the Director of Education for all of Jammu and Kashmir as more urgent concerns begin to haunt the Valley.

"Now the communal question is coming into its own," he said. "You can see the brazen stupidity of the minority Hindu community of Kashmir."

Even though Kashmir was 90 percent Muslim, he explained, the College of Education had 19 Pandit professors and only one Muslim. "The Hindus were the more educated community; Muslims were 'get us some wood, draw us some water.' Because I had powers of a government secretary, I transferred eight of them out of the college and transferred in eight of the Muslim professors that I had earlier produced."

I asked him why.

"The Hindus had raised an agitation: 'We won't educate these Muslims. We've seen through your game! You want us to educate these Muslims, because then they will usurp our places. If the Muslims come up, we'll be eased out!' They were right, from their own short point of view…They didn't have the farsightedness to realize that the able Muslims must also be accommodated…I was not communal, they knew that. I had helped them…had gone out of my way to help them," he said. "But good Muslims had been produced and they had to be accommodated…So I threw them out! And brought in the Muslims. It was a radical transformation, it was revolutionary, throwing eight people out, never done by anybody but I did it…It caused a hubbub, yes, but I had gathered in twenty years of work the moral prestige.

"If the majority people cannot be in a revolutionary manner brought forward, you can do nothing," he said, continuing his defense. "In a backwards society you have to take revolutionary steps…This was on a communal basis, the same basis Sheikh Abdullah wanted. But they were not intellectually refined, Sheikh Abdullah and the leadership, to realize that we must promote the Hindu and encourage him to teach Muslims and convey trust without disheartening them."

Agha's transfer of the eight Pandit professors led to charges of corruption, but he patiently filled out a police-brought questionnaire and the charges were dismissed. The witch hunt, however, raged on. Years later Agha stumbled upon an expected ally.

"Mufti Sayeed is against me, sends for me," he began. "The Mufti is a dejected man, sitting in his room, smoking his hubble bubble, he says, 'What are your relations with Sheikh Abdullah like?' 'Same as with you,' I told him, not being totally honest. 'But you don't know me?' Syed asked, 'You don't know?' he asked again, as if I should recall…'A long time ago when you were Inspector of Schools we came to you during winter break, nine students from Beijbihara, we were nine students who needed additional teaching and we couldn't afford it,' he told me. 'Next morning at 10 a.m. you arrived in your big truck and you worked with us throughout the break.'

"So I had helped them, these nine students who later sat for the exam," he said. "Seven failed and two passed. Mufti was one of the latter; my misfortune."

Mufti remembered the debt, and when he became Chief Minister in 2002 offered Agha a position in the upper house of the state Senate.

"But I declined," Agha said. "At the age of 80, what would I do with those robes and that money and all that? And oh, the humiliation they suffered," he added, grinning.

Alternative histories suggest Agha had accepted the position but that JKLF leader Yasin Malik, his friend, dissuaded him at the last minute. Either way, Malik has played a key role in bringing Agha into 21st century Kashmiri politics. The latter explained how the two became close.

"In October 1994 professors had been killed in the university, and I was scheduled to make a speech. Many of my colleagues told me, 'No! Don't go! You'll be killed!' But I went, and after I made my speech, Malik heard about it and loved it and came over to my house at 8 p.m. in the evening and told me I must be part of his book release. And so at Ahdoo's Hotel a few days later they release his book, Our Greatest Enemy, and I spoke, said, 'There are no goons in Islam, no killing people' and all that, 'It's not allowed,'" he recalled.

But his comments fell on deaf ears, and the violence has brought the cause low.

"All separatists, in fact, 9/11 has killed them," he said, diving back into contemporary Kashmiri politics. "The Hurriyat leadership couldn't unite. For years I told them, 'Unite or perish.' And they have perished. And they met Advani! After Gujarat! And shook hands with him! What will the Kashmiri people think of them after that?...After 1975 Sheikh Abdullah was nothing because he was corrupted, and now his family, too. They have their money and their houses and they do nothing.

"Yasin is the only one who's remained uncorrupt, living in his little hut. Presidents and ambassadors have visited him in his tiny home where you can barely go up the stairs. But he is not embarrassed at all," he said like a proud father. "Malik has stood on the shoulders of Sheikh Abdullah."

I asked about the legacy of Sheikh Abdullah.

"There is no doubt in my mind," he responded immediately. "Land to the tiller! The land reform was a revolutionary act: today there is no poverty in Jammu and Kashmir, no poor villagers – they used to come and beg in Srinagar, but today there is no movement from the village to the city!"

Do you see any new, similarly all-embracing leadership emerging in Kashmir?

"I don't have much hope," he said. "This is the period of the rise of the middle class in India…They're uppity, nouveau riche; they are rude, they are crude."

And as is his wont, Agha cited not one but two well-known social theorists to further his point.

"Tagore wrote of such people, 'This rudely elbowing age of relentless rapacity,' just brilliant. And Karl Marx in the New York Herald Tribune, wrote of the 'the profound hypocrisy and inherent barbarism of bourgeois civilization …did they not in India…resort to outrageous extortion when simple corruption could not keep up with their rapacity?'" he recited again from memory.

"That is what this middle class is, in Kashmir and elsewhere," he said. "I still believe that until Kashmiris have the character and the consistency and the integrity to act and behave in a responsible manner, their freedom will not amount to much."

This collapse of the Valley's character and the turmoil of conflict in his paternal homeland inspired Agha's poet son Agha Shahid Ali to become, by the early 90's, one of the great chroniclers of the troubles in Kashmir. He studied under revered American poet James Merrill and pioneered the lengthy and complicated gazal form in English to great acclaim. From Shahid's Guggenheim Award-winning *Country Without a Post Office*, Agha recited his son's most well-known verse.

We shall meet again in Srinagar,

By the gates of the villa of Peace,

Our hands blossoming into fists,

Till the soldiers return the keys and disappear.

After a nearly two-year battle with brain cancer, Shahid died in late 2001. His father was present when the illness first struck.

"He was visiting professor at New York University, and I was visiting him in his beautiful home on Washington Square, 2000, February or March," Agha recalled, averting his gaze and slowing his words. "He had a fall and I heard a shriek….An. Unearthly. Shriek. I went there and saw him flat on his back, in his bathroom. Rang up, an ambulance came and we took him to hospital…for a year and a half after he wrote poems, he delivered lectures, and he made people laugh…then he quietly passed."

Thoughts of his son led Agha to reminisce about his family, how all four of his children had earned their doctorates and taught at American universities, just like he and his wife of nearly 50 years, Sufia, who died in 1996. He also reflected on his 84 years.

"I feel good. I feel good. I feel alive, despite a few minor failures of health here and there," he said. "I look back on my life with my wife and my children and my friends, the greatest things in my life have been laughter and friendship and the vision of beauty both in nature and in art,…I regret the fact that I was often too domineering. I lacked that genuine humility which would have made me have a greater impact on the lives of the young. That's why as I have ripened in the last 10-15 years I have focused on simplicity and humility."

This last word reminded Agha of one of his favorite quotes, and again he scooted to the edge of his chair and moistened his lips, rubbed his hands together and sat up straight as an eager schoolchild.

"Joseph Needham, brilliant historian, author of the greatest work of the 20th century, *Science of Civilization in China*, 10 volumes, he wrote, 'Humility is a concealed form of love,'" and Agha paused, a broad smile creasing his face as the words sunk in, then bursting with explication. "Love in the sense that another religion can be equally good given the benefit of doubt, another civilization can be equally good! Study with humility, don't say my way is the best; this is what he's saying, and this is what I love."

We've come such a long way, dear reader; I am as weary as you. Pray forgive me for invoking the voice of another in farewell.

"Age does not make us childish," Johann Wolfgang von Goethe wrote in *Faust*. "It only finds us true children still."

■

Chapter 4

The So-Called War on Terror

"I do not know of any people who could be as frank with and about themselves as Americans are. That, of course, is a healthy thing and the sign of a well-founded self-confidence, and gives one reason to hope that no matter how grave mistakes America may make, she will always have a chance of recognizing and undoing them before it is too late."

— Bulent Ecevit[127]

"We need to feel shame. Our policies must begin from a place of shame."

— Rory Stewart[128]

THE DEVASTATION OF post-Saddam Iraq marked the low point of George W. Bush's war on terror. More than 700,000 people died in that nine-year conflict, which tore the fabric of Iraqi society and helped lay the foundation for the emergence of the Islamic State. Starting in 2003, the steady drumbeat of war crimes, gross incompetence and bumbled nation-building drove much of Europe and the Muslim world to turn against the United States. This helps explain why in 2009 the Swedish committee handed recently inaugurated US president Barack Obama the Nobel Peace Prize for "creating a new climate of international politics" and giving "people hope for a better future".[129] The next year Obama authorized 128 drone strikes on Pakistan, killing at least 89 civilians.[130] A few years later Obama's first strike on Yemen killed 55 people, including 21 children and 12 women, five of them pregnant. Drone strikes by the US-led NATO alliance in Afghanistan also increased. "The Americans are benefitting from the nature of this war," Karim Popal, an Afghan-German lawyer who represents the victims of a 2009 NATO airstrike that killed dozens of Afghan civilians, said in 2020. "They believe they are above the law."[131] In recent years I have been surprised to find, in a number of personal conversations, that many in the Muslim world preferred George W. Bush to Obama, because at least the former tried to help rid them of dictators.

President Donald Trump came to power in 2017 vowing to end America's endless wars, and did go on to reduce the American footprint in Syria, Iraq and Afghanistan. Yet he also significantly eroded the US' international reputation, with his limited interest in facts, constant public attacks on critics and instigation of an 11th-hour insurrection. Two weeks later, in January 2021, Joe Biden took office with an understanding of how the United States had lost considerable standing around the world. He vowed to get to work "renewing our role in international institutions and reclaiming our credibility and moral authority," aiming to "earn back our leadership position".[132] Among his earliest policy shifts was ending Trump's so-called Muslim ban and dramatically increasing the number of refugees the US would welcome, from 15,000 in 2020 to 150,000 in 2021.[133] Yet a handful of months later, Biden implemented a policy that curbed Muslim freedom and opportunity — pulling American forces out of Afghanistan and allowing the Taliban to take Kabul and reinstitute Islamic law.

☐

The Bully and the Bruised, the Slingshot and the Stone

(KO report)

September 10, 2006: On a gorgeous Tuesday morning five years ago I stood with several co-workers on the roof of an office building in downtown Manhattan and watched in stunned silence as the south tower of the World Trade Center collapsed, sending great khaki-colored plumes of smoke, dust, and debris shooting across the southern tip of the island.

In a daze I drifted to the stairs and out of the building, stepping into a Gothic scene. Dust-covered zombies shuffled northward from Ground Zero, stopping to catch their breath and stare into the middle distance, eyes wide and mouths half-opened. Buzzing crowds gathered around storefront televisions and radios on Broadway, yearning for the whos and hows and whys while others embraced and conferred in desperate tones. Attacked on its own turf unawares, New York, and America, had been shocked and deeply wounded, and the world would never be the same.

You might recall the outpouring of sympathy from across the globe (or you may not). Parisian headlines carried condolences and in Germany 200,000 gathered at Berlin's Brandenburg Gate to express their sorrow. Palestinians held not one but two candle-lit vigils and in Tehran's largest stadium 60,000 soccer fans and players observed an unprecedented minute's silence in sympathy with the victims. French political analyst Nicole Bacharen summed up the solidarity that swept the world: "At moments like this, we are all Americans."

"International notes of sympathy and empathy are fine," Rand analyst James Mulvenon responded prophetically at the time. "But what will separate those who are with us from those who are against us is military action."

And so it has passed that the bellicose rhetoric and mostly unjustified, Islam-trained aggression of American foreign policy that followed has erased that great goodwill and exacerbated already-extant tensions with the Muslim world. Numerous major terror attacks and the combative belligerence and often ignoble proclamations on the part of Muslim leaders have also fanned these fires, and, as a result, the intervening five years have left that 21st century sword of Damocles, the long-feared clash of civilizations, hanging by a thread.

When the US sought to retaliate that October with the toppling of Afghanistan's Taliban, most developed nations were behind the move. Syria, North Korea, and Iran predictably sounded the first discordant notes, and as the US' widespread and seemingly indiscriminate bombing raids led to vast civilian deaths condemnations poured in from the United Nations, Oxfam, and Doctors Without Borders, prodding Donald Rumsfeld to trot out that infamous term of obfuscation, "collateral damage," and signaling the great tides of diversionary rhetoric soon to flow from the Bush administration.

But if Afghanistan was a grenade to global American approbation, the invasion of Iraq was an atomic blast. The Bush team linked then-Iraqi leader Saddam Hussein to Al Qaeda and claimed he had great stockpiles of weapons capable of mass destruction, both of which represented imminent threats to the United States and both of which history has since Swiss-cheesed. In a reversal of post-9/11 solidarity, protest marches from New York to Chicago, London to Paris, Damascus to Sydney, Tokyo to Milan and beyond, tens of millions of demonstrators expressed vehement opposition to the US' planned preemptive war. France and Germany, which had so eloquently shared New York's sorrow, stood out as America's most vocal detractors. Yet shock and awe was unleashed on Iraq in March 2003, a point in time future historians may mark as the beginning of the end for American hegemony.

Recent developments in five key stories traceable to 9/11 provide an excellent overview of the current global situation.

1. Rising sectarian violence has reached a new post-invasion peak in Iraq, with a fifty-one percent rise in casualties among Iraqis in the past three months alone and more than 3,000 killed each month, according to a US Defense Department report released last week. "This is reality catching up with Rumsfeld and the Pentagon," said Brookings Institution military analyst Michael O'Hanlon. Where there was once no Al Qaeda, the cells are now legion, prodding Bin Laden to dub the struggle in Iraq the "third world war…a war of destiny between infidelity and Islam. The whole world is watching this war and it will end in victory and glory or misery and humiliation." Far from the stable democracy Bush, Rumsfeld, Cheney and the

neo-conservatives envisioned, Iraq is embroiled in a civil war with global ramifications.

2. Afghanistan's 2006 poppy crop, estimated last week by the UN Office on Drugs and Crime at a record 6100 metric tons of opium, or ninety-two percent of world supply, is certain to please heroin addicts, poppy farmers, and the warlords expecting a piece of the action. This is an increase of nearly sixty percent from 2005 for a trade that accounts for over one third of Afghanistan's economy and continues to bankroll insurgent elements. Five years after the toppling of the Taliban, three years into the Hamid Karzai regime, and months after NATO took over security responsibilities from coalition forces, the Taliban is resurgent and much of Afghanistan is a warlord-ruled, chaos-rife narco-state. Oft-lauded US anti-terror ally Pakistan essentially ceded parts of its Afghan-bordering North Waziristan province to the Taliban and Al Qaeda in a just-inked truce, giving Osama bin Laden and his cohorts their own private mountain redoubt. "This country could be taken down by this whole drugs problem," the US top narcotics official admitted. "We have seen what can come from Afghanistan, if you go back to 9/11. Obviously the US does not want to see that again."

3. For most of the Muslim world, this summer's Israeli-Lebanon war was a shorter, more satisfying sequel to the Afghanistan-USSR conflict that ended the Cold War. Islamic radicals fought and essentially defeated a great global power, even if by proxy, and a charismatic, militant, devoutly Muslim leader (bin Laden then, Hezbollah's Hassan Nasrallah today) stood up to a regional and international bully, sending his status through the roof. The fallout included an Israeli investigation into military failures, a Saudi Arabia that had urged other Arab states to be careful of Hezbollah when the Israel-Lebanon crisis was brimming suddenly dissatisfied with the US, and the exact opposite of stated intentions – a more vigorous Hezbollah and Iran. The over one thousand Lebanese casualties brought accusations of war crimes from the UN and increased international opprobrium.

4. Opinion within the US reveals increasing disapproval of the Bush administration and its war on terror, as over half of Americans support neither the Iraq War, their president, nor the linkage between Saddam and Al Qaeda. In an online interview this week, Pulitzer Prize-winning New Yorker journalist Seymour Hersh said, "By going to war, instead of criminalizing what Osama bin Laden and his minions did—there's no question that, in terms of military operations, this is the worst government in the history of America." As if on cue, the *World Citizens Guide*, a pamphlet recently published by a Texas-based nonprofit in the hope of ameliorating anti-Americanism, blithely underscores the faults of US' post-9/11 leadership. The document offers Americans traveling abroad diplomatic insights the American president could take to heart: dialogue instead of monologue; be proud, not arrogant; check the atlas; talk about something besides politics; and keep your word.

5. Polling data published recently by Harris and the Pew Global Attitudes Project reveals considerable drops in US esteem across Europe and the Middle East. Out of the five most powerful European nations, according to the Harris Poll, only Italians believe the US is not the greatest threat to global stability. And overall polling data found that nearly twenty-five percent more of those surveyed believed the US more dangerous than Iran. Since 9/11, outbreaks of Muslim violence, deadly terror attacks, and/or major arrests have occurred in the UK, the Netherlands, Spain, France, and Germany, and just this past week authorities arrested accused plotters in Denmark. Europeans may well blame these new problems on recent US foreign policy. Less than one quarter of Spain's population holds a favorable opinion of the US, according to Pew, and Turkish regard has dropped from over half to a mere twelve percent.

Often cited as the very type of democratic, secular, and Muslim nation the US would like to import to the Middle East, Turkey has long served as vibrant evidence of the Western argument that Muslim nations could willingly and successfully embrace democratic institutions. But this bridge between the West and the Muslim world is crumbling, mainly because of American foreign policy, making Turkey the new poster boy for the world's post-9/11 attitudinal adjustment.

Since the American-led and UK-supported invasion of Iraq, the Turks have turned away not only from the US but from long-sought EU-membership. Instability in its mainly Kurdish southeast, which borders the predominantly Kurdish northernmost province of Iraq, has ignited separatist sentiments among Turkey's 15 million Kurds. Turkish leaders fear chaos in Iraq could lead to renewed calls for an independent Kurdistan, with the blame placed squarely on American shoulders.

The latest Transatlantic Trends survey, released last week, confirms this development. Favorable US opinion has dropped twenty-five percent in the past two years while views of Iran have received an equal bounce in the same span. Perhaps even more telling is the data regarding Iran's tough stance on the nuclear issue: approximately forty percent of Americans and Europeans approve of the use of force to keep Tehran from getting nuclear weapons, compared to only ten percent of Turks polled, more than half of whom approved of an Iran with nuclear weapons. These figures become more chilling considering that in his landmark work, *The Clash of Civilizations and the Coming World Order*, Samuel Huntington cited Turkey as a potential barometer of West-Islam relations. "At some point, Turkey could be ready to give up its frustrating and humiliating role as a beggar pleading for membership in the West and to resume its much more impressive and elevated historical role as the principal Islamic interlocutor and antagonist of the West." That time may be nigh.

How have we arrived at such a tangle of crisscrossing anguish? One reason is America's military aggressiveness, to be sure, but its tin ear, which invariably results in uninformed rhetorical bombast, does not help. In a speech in Washington last week Bush reiterated his latest theme: "Bin Laden and his terrorist allies have made their intentions as clear as Lenin and Hitler before them. The question is: Will we listen? Will we pay attention to what these evil men say? America and our coalition partners have made our choice. We're taking the words of the enemy seriously. We're on the offensive. We will not rest. We will not retreat. And we will not withdraw from the fight until this threat to civilization has been removed."

This is a slightly different iteration of Bush's post-9/11 "for us or against us" paradigm, which reduces the world to black and white, good and evil, painting people as either secular, democratic and Western-leaning or wrong-headed, fascist and terror-plotting, whereas in reality over half the world's population fall somewhere in between. The fascist analogy has been torn to shreds elsewhere, and the reference to communism not only brings to mind precisely the kind of global conflict the US should seek to avoid but also links today's terrorists with an ideologically powerful popular revolt that controlled a large chunk of the world for some 70 years. One of the primary goals of any terrorist group is getting their opponents to overestimate their importance, and here once again is Bush falling into that trap. What's more, a US on the offensive is precisely what Islamic terrorists want, Americans playing the bully, the big kid on the block who knocks around his smaller neighbors; the belligerence and the resulting death count are excellent recruitment tools.

"For decades," Bush continued, "American policy sought to achieve peace in the Middle East by pursuing stability at the expense of liberty. The lack of freedom in that region helped create conditions where anger and resentment grew and radicalism thrived and terrorists found willing recruits." Yet America's universalist pretensions, its continued reliance on military means, and a surfeit of dead Muslims are creating those same conditions today.

Indeed, the Bush team and its allies have since 9/11 sought to drive their enemies into submission by hitting them atop the head with a stone. The blunt objects of traditional warfare – technologically advanced as Bradley fighting vehicles, killer drones, and laser-guided cluster bombs may be, they are but bombs, planes, and tanks – have not only wrought immeasurable physical damage on the infrastructure, humanity, and psyche of Afghanistan, Iraq, and Lebanon, but have also provided great grist for the terrorist mill. At least 100,000 dead civilians in Iraq and increasing local animus with inadequate NATO forces in Afghanistan do nothing to bolster the image of America in the Muslim world. And the pictures of slaughtered Lebanese civilians that shot around the globe in July and August were a public relations bonanza for Hezbollah that contributed significantly to leader Hassan Nasrallah's burgeoning esteem.

Al Qaeda, meanwhile, has consistently endeavored to build the better slingshot. Call it cowardly if you must, but hijacking planes and using them as giant missiles was a brilliant tactical innovation. And the recently uncovered UK terror plot in which operatives had planned to combine several innocuous fluids to build bombs while in flight revealed a terrorist network constantly looking for new and unpredictable means of destruction.

Much of the reasoning behind stodgy American policy can be found in the White House's newly-updated National Strategy for Combating Terror (available in full at www.whitehouse.gov), which argues "the long-term solution for winning the War on Terror is the advancement of freedom and human dignity through effective democracy... Effective democracies honor and uphold basic human rights, including freedom of religion, conscience, speech, assembly, association, and press... are responsive to their citizens, submitting to the will of the people. Effective democracies exercise effective sovereignty and maintain order within their own borders, address causes of conflict peacefully, protect independent and impartial systems of justice, punish crime, embrace the rule of law, and resist corruption...They are the long-term antidote to the ideology of terrorism today. This is the battle of ideas."

More than a decade ago Huntington warned of precisely such efforts, writing that these same ideals "make Western civilization unique, and Western civilization is valuable not because it is universal but because it is unique. The principal responsibility of Western leaders, consequently, is not to attempt to reshape other civilizations in the image of the West, which is beyond their declining power, but to preserve, protect, and renew the unique qualities of Western civilization."

President Bush has done just the opposite since taking office – spending lavishly on foreign wars, slashing taxes, and overextending his armed forces in supporting a new and more aggressive form of American exceptionalism. Like a Rip van Winkle who dozed off at the dawn of the Clausewitzian era, the Bush team has blindly maintained its reliance on military might to impose their will even as Europeans and Americans have begun to apprehend vast cultural differences. The Transatlantic Trends survey shows only one-third of Americans and a mere quarter of Europeans support the use of military force in promoting democracy abroad. What's more, fifty-six percent of Americans and Europeans believe their form of democracy is not compatible with Islam.

This weakened US, then, is in for a long slog, not only because Islamic societies are inherently different from the West, but more importantly because they intend to stay that way. Regardless of its sectarian form, the reaffirmation of Islam exploding across the earth's mid-section is also a repudiation of Western influence upon local politics, society, and morals.

As this Islamic resurgence is not entirely open-minded and benevolent, the blame for the current loggerheads cannot be placed solely at the feet of the US. Iranian President Mahmoud Ahmedinejad and Hezbollah's Nasrallah, who in the past year have risen to pre-eminence in the Muslim world, the former for his defiance of the West in regards to nuclear armament and the latter for beating back an Israeli army long viewed as an unstoppable regional juggernaut, have played key roles in bringing the world closer to the brink.

Although the recent Israeli bombardment of south Lebanon may well have been disproportionate, pronouncements such as the following make it difficult for a sober-minded 21st century adult to join Hezbollah's fight: "We will win because the Jews love life," said Nasrallah in early August, "and we love death." Similar words had been uttered previously by bin Laden and his terror-minded ilk, but these were so patently unnecessary and obviously inaccurate as to make one question Nasrallah's sincerity, if not sanity. If you love death, why did you not embrace it when Israelis offered it to you on a platter?

August news reports from New York to Mumbai highlighted how the Arab street and the Muslim tide had swelled behind Hezbollah and its increasingly powerful and popular leader. Why? Because Hezbollah had been so staunch and stealthy in the face of Israeli aggression, because they had fought well and survived, embracing life. Nasrallah later clarified his remark: "Regardless of how the world has changed after 11 September, death to America will remain our reverberating and powerful slogan, 'Death to America.'" This specifies the very sort of death Hezbollah loves, but it is not a statement from which harmony and understanding might flower.

Similarly, Ahmadinejad delivered this message to the American people in July: "If you would like to have good relations with the Iranian nation in the future, bow down before the greatness of the Iranian nation and surrender. If you don't accept to do this, the Iranian nation will force you to surrender and bow down." And now the Iranian president is bent on an ideological cleansing, purging his nation's colleges and universities of all liberal and secular professors.

That Nasrallah and Ahmadinejad are in cahoots is not surprising, but one would hope the Islamic resurgence could hang its hat on more cogent, sober and inspiring words of wisdom. Where is the Mustafa Kemal Ataturk for this century?

Neither is it a surprise that these two can make such dull and blandly ignorant statements as those above and still be as revered as they are in the Muslim world, by both extremists and moderates. Because they stood up to Israel, and particularly the US, the country that attacked and decimated Iraq unjustifiably, in violation of the UN and against the wishes of millions. Further, bruised by the end of the Caliphate five hundred years ago and subsequent centuries of imperialism, subjugation, and West-backed autocracies, a deeply rooted animus towards the US and Britain is burned into Muslim hearts. In the last five years the US, UK, and Israel have merely fanned the embers.

Osama bin Laden has for his part stepped back from the spotlight in recent years, increasingly ceding MC duties on Al Qaeda's regular video releases to his second in command, Ayman Al Zawahiri. The leading terror organization even tapped a former infidel, converted American Jew Adam Gadahn, to deliver its most recent message in early September. In the video, Gadahn urged Americans to "surrender to the truth," convert to Islam, and "join the winning side." One is reminded of the rhetoric of the leader of Gadahn's homeland.

The lone voice of eloquent near-reason has been British Prime Minister Tony Blair, but riding shotgun with Bush and American foreign policy has compromised his position and erased what understanding he may have engendered in the Muslim world. The UK has thus emerged as Europe's top terror target and almost three-quarters of recently polled British believed the nation's foreign policy is to blame, prodding Blair to announce last week that he will resign in late spring 2007.

In this war, then, no promising leader has emerged from any quarter. Instead of reason, restraint, and understanding, we have insults, threats, and ignorance. Two goons brawling in a back alley, a bar fight between drunken belligerents, one angry, dimunitive and occasionally crafty, the other a lumbering, thick-skulled ox attempting a lobotomy with a crowbar. Is it to this we have evolved? Is this how the world ends?

In increasingly dark times, a look to two historical anniversaries may help light the way.

One hundred years ago to the day – September 11, 1906 – an Indian lawyer working in South Africa kick-started a movement that would change the world. At a political meeting in Johannesburg, Mohandas K. Gandhi took from his countrymen the first oaths of what would become satyagraha, literally a firmness in truth but more accurately a categorical commitment to nonviolent resistance. I'm not so idealistic as to expect international relations to become a forum for Gandhian nonviolence, but leaders of Islam and the West would be wise to consider the Mahatma's philosophy: "the nonviolence of my conception is more active and more real fighting than retaliation, whose very nature is to increase wickedness." India's sober response to the

July bomb blasts in Mumbai, which could certainly inform both Western and Islamic policymakers, bear out this belief.

And fifty years ago a Canadian diplomat serving at the UN helped defuse Western-Islam animus when he brokered an agreement between the US, Europe, Israel, and Egypt to end the crisis over the Suez Canal. Lester Pearson, who later served two terms as Canadian Prime Minister, won a Nobel Peace Prize for his efforts, with the Nobel panel claiming he had "saved the world." One could be sure that realizations such as the following, uttered years previous, played a part. "It would be absurd to imagine that these new political societies coming to birth in the East will be replicas of those with which we in the West are familiar; the revival of these ancient civilizations will take new forms." It is precisely such new forms that the West must be willing to accept, for our divergences are integral to our civilizations.

The cultures of Islam and the West diverge at numerous points, making each glorious in its own way; the democratic institutions of the US, France, and the UK on the one hand and those of Afghanistan, Lebanon, Mali, and Turkey on the other bear this out. An understanding and an acceptance of these separations between Islam and the West is necessary, but so too is an appreciation of shared values. The importance of family, friendship, and community, the need for education, adequate food and decent healthcare are common across humanity. The US should commit to reconstruction in war-torn areas and increase its partnerships with Muslim and non-Muslim NGOs and humanitarian organizations to foster development and human rights in less-developed parts of the Muslim world. And after gruesome beheadings and deadly terror attacks in Amman, Istanbul, Egypt, and Saudi Arabia, the Muslim majority is maintaining a significant distance from terror organizations. Pew's Global Attitudes Project reveals decreasing support for suicide bombing in Jordan, Pakistan, and Indonesia – offering another opening for Western leaders to communicate with Islam, about the threat of terrorism. Such a dialogue needs to be sincere from both sides of the divide. Ahmadinejad has offered to debate President Bush during his visit to the UN General Assembly this month. There is little reason to expect Bush to take the offer seriously, but why not take him up on it? Little harm could be done, and much could be gained from a friendly parley.

In fighting terror, the US must alter its methods of foreign policy in order to avoid sparking further, deeper, deadlier conflagrations. By relying less on the hawkish, blinders-wearing Defense Department and leaning more on the crime-solving abilities of the Central Intelligence Agency and the diplomatic solutions of State, the American stance could be softened without compromising security. Instead of military means, a renewed reliance on inventive intelligence gathering and advanced surveillance technologies should be the chief means of counter-terrorism. Instead of crusading condemnation, a softer tone would likely result in less animosity, and a touch of empathy might ultimately lead to a better understanding of the root causes of terror, for only he who knows his enemy can defeat him.

As an American and a New Yorker, the events of 9/11 were painful, but the ensuing five years of awesome failures and disheartening fallout from the US leadership's international actions have been even more so. Last week's ho-hum global response to Bush's confirmation of the use of secret prisons to detain terror suspects is an expression of precisely how much things have changed since 9/11. The world no longer expects greatness or high moral standards of America. Today such ethical breaches from the US instead garner a "what else is new?" global shrug. The fingerprints of Thomas Jefferson, Benjamin Franklin, James Madison, and Abraham Lincoln, on America's social and political institutions are fading fast.

Yet the opportunity to alter American foreign policy, salve Muslim wounds, and vastly improve the global outlook is still before us. Allowing each other to embrace and protect our cultural, political, and religious differences while engaging in constructive dialogue on shared concerns will help ease the looming threat of a cultural clash, and make 9/12 seem not so very far away.

□

[PRESENT-DAY WRITING] FEW have had a fuller life than Rory Stewart, who graduated from Eton and Oxford, tutored British princes William and Harry, walked 6,000 miles across South Asia and toiled as a public servant in occupied Iraq and a social entrepreneur in Afghanistan before returning home to England to serve in parliament. After a stint as International Development Secretary under Prime Minister Theresa May and Foreign Minister Boris Johnson, Stewart campaigned to succeed May in mid-2019. Johnson won, became prime minister and expelled Stewart and 20 others from the party for disagreeing on Brexit. Stewart later stepped down from parliament to run for mayor of London, but ended that campaign after COVID-19 postponed the vote. In late 2020 he excoriated Johnson in a widely shared book review, calling him "the most accomplished liar in public life" and warning of darker days ahead should Britain fail to return to virtue.[134] Weeks later, Johnson invited India's Narenda Modi to be a guest of honor at the June 2021 G-7 gathering in Cornwall, England, to help lay the groundwork for a G-10 that would challenge authoritarianism.[135]

Like many progressive-minded figures, Stewart initially supported the Iraq War. Yet three years later, as detailed below, his position had changed. He later co-wrote a book about interventionism. Stewart may still be mulling some of the key issues addressed in our interview; in August 2022 he expressed his desire to improve the impact of international development work.[136]

☐

Bridging the Great Divide: An interview with Rory Stewart

(KO report)

October 15, 2006: Scottish writer and former diplomat Rory Stewart has in his thirty-three years covered a lot of ground—figuratively and literally. Born in Hong Kong and raised in Malaysia, Stewart studied at Oxford before traversing Iran, Afghanistan, Pakistan, India, and Nepal on foot for nearly two years and then popping over to Baghdad to help rebuild Iraq. Somehow he found time for diplomatic stints in Eastern Europe and Southeast Asia.

His first book, 2003's *The Places in Between*, which won several major awards including the Royal Society's Ondaatje Prize, details the difficulties and dangers of the Herat to Kabul leg of his epic stroll and paints a picture of a desolate post-Taliban Afghanistan torn between war and peace. Released last year, *The Prince of the Marshes* recounts his eleven months as the deputy governor of two impoverished southern Iraqi provinces, offering rare on-the-ground insights and revealing the hazards, frustrations, and foibles of trying to establish a stable and functioning democracy.

Stewart recently spoke with *Kashmir Observer* correspondent David Lepeska from his office in Kabul, where he manages Turquoise Mountain, an organization that seeks to restore Afghan culture via investment in traditional crafts and historic buildings.

DL: You've spent much of your adult life toiling and "vacationing" in danger and combat zones: as a British diplomat in Indonesia and Yugoslavia, walking across Asia for some twenty-one months, a year as a deputy-governor in Iraq; and after a stint at Harvard's Kennedy School of Government you've now returned to Kabul. Are you a glutton for punishment?

RS: I am very bad at talking about my motivations…I met a man in Istanbul who had driven a camel caravan from China to Turkey who assured me that I would know why I was doing the walk before the walk ended. But apart from a glimpse of something almost religious on the last day's walk into Kabul, true explanation never came and these activities seem so obviously fulfilling to me, that I cannot quite understand why everyone else doesn't do them. I felt more alive crossing the desert East of Herat or walking around the Baghdad souk than I ever felt in Scotland or behind a Foreign Office desk. Here in Kabul, every piece of the organisation - seeing a completed building, providing employment, contributing the design and crafts, improving living conditions for people in Murad Khani, dealing with the comic entrapments of bureaucracy – is absorbing and fulfilling.

DL: I've read that Afghan President Hamid Karzai is connected to your organization, Turquoise Mountain. How intimately is he involved?

RS: Well, he had the idea for the project, so I've been very much following through on a vision he dreamed up. He's very conservative and traditional, and wanted to maintain Afghan culture, being from a very traditional Afghani village.

DL: Like Afghans, Kashmiris have great pride in their culture, their craftsmanship and artistry, yet because of the lengthy insurgency much of that tradition is being lost. How can this cultural devastation be slowed or halted? Can the work of Turquoise Mountain be translated or franchised to other countries?

RS: Well, what we are trying to do is implement a different culture, the basic thrust of which is implanting an abstract aesthetic that has real meaning to people, for their identity, and has a real impact on people's livelihoods and their quality of life. I'm not interested in simply repairing cultural devastation but in helping the people that live around it.

And yes, I think it's something we'd be very interested in doing in other countries. One of the things we believe here is in the need to remain relatively flexible because heritage tends to be a very pressured environment, with connections to politics, economics, and society, and in our relationships with the community and the government we almost spend as much time as in preparing the actual technical work. So what we'd try to do if we went into another country would be to keep that sense of political realism, of realpolitik, as an underpinning for achieving things.

DL: You spoke of giving people identity and meaning. One recent development here in Kashmir is the damage done to the emotional and mental state of Kashmiris – mental illness, depression, suicide, and PTSD are increasingly common, much more so today than even at the height of the insurgency in the mid-90's. Have you any experience with this sort of psychological fallout? Is there any remedy?

RS: That is something that is very difficult to pin down. Some Afghans certainly…have a hard time, but those that are trying to correct the situation seem to be coping in a very impressive way. I mean I'm astonished by how they've done: half of our staff has lost close relatives or themselves participated in combat, and yet they remain astonishingly pragmatic, idealistic, and vigorous in their projects and their work.

DL: You dedicated The Places in Between to the approximately 500 villagers of various tribes you met en route. Why?

RS: The journey was possible only because of them; they are the reason I made it across the country. I mean I only made it because they offered their homes and their care. The most memorable part of the journey was about my interaction with them. So for me the interest of the journey and therefore most of the credit should go to those people.

DL: You are a non-Muslim, I presume, and…

RS: Yes, I am definitely a non-Muslim, yeah.

DL: Does this come into play in your work in Kabul? Is it a factor in any way?

RS: A great deal, yeah. It comes into play certainly because we have to be very careful painting Islamic art and Islamic culture not to offend people or denigrate Islamic heritage or history. We have to be very careful that we use the officially approved representations. We have a security problem as well; there are people who disprove of our presence, particularly non-Muslims and non-Afghans, but fortunately that seems to be a minority.

But yes, fundamentally a lot of the support and the energy behind the project is Islamic energy and that's something that we have to be very careful to negotiate, as non-Muslims.

DL: Many people in the Islamic world – and some in the Western world – believe the West could use some ambassadors to bridge the yawning gap between these two cultures. Any chance you might return to diplomatic, ambassadorial, or reconstruction work?

RS: I certainly want to complete this project first before I think about anything else, so at least not for a couple years.

DL: One place where such leadership is still needed is Iraq. You wrote in *Prince of the Marshes* that by the early 2005 national election Iraq felt like a police state; many Kashmiris hold a similar opinion of their valley home. Can security be implemented by outsiders without making the civilian population feel overwhelmed, or "occupied?" What did you find was the best way to avoid or alleviate animosity between security forces and civilians of a different religion and culture?

RS: Military occupation is intrinsically unwelcome. Armies, however well-trained or well-intentioned, offend. Trained for battle, defined by discipline, fiercely proud of their own corps almost to the point of despising civilians, armies are unlikely to be sympathetic to the disorderliness of governance or the compromises of political action. Add to this nationalism, xenophobia, cultural pride, honour codes or radical Islam among the subject population and there is a high probability that military occupation will spawn insurgency.

Many of those who recognise the perils of relying exclusively on military force make the equal error of assuming all can be solved through development economics. They suggest that people attack the military largely because of poverty and thus if jobs, incomes and infrastructure were delivered the insurgency would cease. Yet, [Western nations] hardly have a track record of delivering sustainable economic growth anywhere in the world and it has never been achieved in the short-time frame required to meet the timeline of an insurgency. The kinds of prosperity which people demand are not the kinds of things development agencies like to deliver. And even if we delivered such prosperity on time it would be unlikely to stop resistance.

The reason why a strong section of the population in Southern Afghanistan wish to fight the coalition is not primarily for economic reasons. They have real political, nationalist, religious – in short ideological – problems with the presence of foreign troops in a quasi-occupation. These grievances are now intensified by aerial bombardment and vendettas arising from the death of family members. People are perfectly happy to work on coalition road projects during the day and blow up the coalition at night.

DL: The Iraqi insurgency grew during your deputy-governancy, was there any way to contain it, and did you have any specific concept of what the insurgents wanted, and thus, how to combat or deflect it?

RS: The key to addressing the needs of an insurgency – though easier said than done – is to have local leaders prepared to engage in the tortuous politics of encompassing and marginalising the insurgency leaders. Foreigners are almost by their very nature disempowered. And guns and money on their own are insufficient – politics is the key.

DL: Yet the politics was left to founder. You've written that no foreigners – journalists, CPA officials, generals, diplomats, yourself included –knew what was going on in Iraq. How then could they presume to shape the political future of the country?

RS: This is not a specific criticism of the individuals in the ground. Even Iraqis struggled to understand a situation with 54 new political parties and 14 tribes, each with three rival chiefs, emerging in a single province in the aftermath of the Baath. Most middle class Iraqis argued that the Sadrist party was led by a discredited man and supported only by a few bribed unemployed illiterates. When the elections came the Sadrists took three times as many votes as the next nearest party in the province of Maysan. But ignorance is of course relative. Any Iraqi was likely to know far more about the local politics, history and personalities of the province than any foreigner, however earnest in their desire to learn.

DL: Yet you've spoken of an "instinctive apathy" on the part of Iraqis. Some recent studies suggest that Kashmir's endless conflict has led to widespread lethargy here. Does your reference to apathetic Iraqis refer to cooperating with coalition forces, efforts toward progress in general – apathy to what in particular?

RS: It manifested itself as a reluctance to take responsibility – most noticeably in the political sphere but also in security and economic development. This may have been in part due to Saddam's deliberate hollowing out of local society and aggressive centralisation. But instinctive apathy also reflected instinctive antipathy towards coalition troops and officials.

DL: Is that why you left Iraq?

RS: I left Iraq because we transferred sovereignty to an Iraqi governor and my job, therefore, no longer existed.

DL: British Defence Minister Des Browne recently supervised the gradual handover of security forces in several southern Iraqi provinces. Will the handover make a difference?

RS: In effect most of those provinces have been running themselves; coalition troops have had only a minimal impact on the practicalities of governance and daily politics for months now. The withdrawal should, therefore, make more a symbolic than actual difference. That symbolic change may, however, take some of the urgency and anger out of the insurgency.

DL: Speaking of that insurgency, you supported the war initially but changed your mind because three years later Iraq was still an unstable, chaotic, and very dangerous state with few functioning governmental institutions. Do you blame yourself and the CPA in anyway? Or is it more a case of, after having worked in Iraq, you realized that because of the situation on the ground the mission was doomed to fail from the start?

RS: My instinct is that the mission was doomed from the start. Of course we made a number of errors – de-Baathification, abolition of the army, looting, etc. – but these were ultimately minor. Even had we avoided those errors, the invasion would still have failed. The reasons lay deep in the limitations of contemporary Western government institutions, which in turn reflect the limitations of our own politics and society on the one side and on the other the fractures within Iraqi society.

DL: The "limitations" of contemporary Western institutions, politics, and society – could you expand on that a bit?

RS: Sure. The associates in a position to affect these changes – people in the coalition government, which is made up of three basic institutions: the military, the foreign service, and developmental institutions – are not comfortable with the basic job of administering this kind of occupation in an effective way. They are basically concerned with fighting wars, drafting treaties, and developmental work geared towards alleviating poverty. Yet the job on the ground in these kinds of engagements is much closer to that of a Chicago ward politician of the 1920's. So institutionally the people who are recruited and apprenticed are not compatible with the type of administration required. Secondly the public and the politicians back home are so often constrained and confused about why we are engaged in these kinds of bureaucratic projects, and still the reality usually proves something different. For example, you shoot for a specific future but it's very difficult to accomplish in the face of a changing reality on the ground.

Some of the critics of these kinds of interventions say the problem is we're not being Machiavellian enough or aggressive enough. But the reality is that our societies don't produce Machiavellian princes, but even if they did produce Machiavellian princes the public and those officials would not be comfortable with such treatment. And even if they were it is unlikely it would be successful for the final reason, which is of course the destruction of Iraqi society itself, which has been significantly hollowed out: the political administration has for the last twenty or thirty years lacked any autonomy, financial responsibility, or independence; people are very reluctant to take political office or exercise political power; most of the traditional forces such as the Sheikh were largely obliterated over fifty years of land reform and change; and Iraqi society essentially is struggling to reconcile itself to the reality of a foreign occupation. Nationalism is extremely strong, insurgency and sectarianism is extremely strong. In different ways all of these things meant that the Iraqi society is extremely unlikely either to consent to the occupation or to provide people who are prepared to take on the sort of administration involved in this sort of occupation.

DL: So in light of the troubles in Iraq and the deteriorating situation in Afghanistan, are the tools of Western foreign policy and reconstruction incapable of building and securing democracies in foreign countries?

RS: I think the creation of democratic institutions is something that needs to be led from people within a country. It's not something that can be imposed from outside. There are minor roles that these institutions can play – providing information, providing basic security – but it's extremely unlikely they would be capable of building the required institutions of government.

DL: There have been a great many well-documented human rights violations – rapes, disappearances, murders without cause – here in Kashmir, most on the part of the military and paramilitary forces. What is your experience in dealing with such abuses on the part of the occupying force? How are they best handled? How can cooler heads prevail?

RS: I think this goes to the heart of the question. What do we believe in our hearts about the kind of society we possess? And I believe there is considerable friction there, between our [Western] representatives abroad. For instance in the United States some talk a very aggressive and hawkish line, and there's an entire neo-conservative counterculture with its own extremist rhetoric, and I think what can be seen again and again in everything from Guantanamo to Abu Ghraib, is this oscillation between taking an extremely aggressive stance against this threat of terror and a debate about the use of military force. This debate between military and security is a very nasty, unresolvable debate. But I'm convinced that the liberals are right, that there's no conscience at all. That you can keep security perfectly well maintained without making any compromises, equal and clearly.

My sympathies are obviously going to be on the side of the liberals, on the side of human rights, and that we should take steps to better enforce security. But I also think we should be honest about our intentions.

Chapter 5

Islam and Politics

"The image which the 'established', the powerful ruling sections of a society, have of themselves and communicate to others tends to be modelled on the 'minority of the best'. The image of 'outsiders', groups who in relation to the 'established' sections have relatively little power, tends to be modelled on the 'minority of the worst'."

— **Norbert Elias and John Scotson**[137]

"Repel evil with what is better; then you will see that one who was once your enemy has become your dearest friend."

— **Quran**[138]

DURING THE KASHMIRI Sultanate, Islam spread across the Valley and eventually emerged as the dominant religion. Apart from Sikandar, who reportedly taxed non-Muslims and forced them to convert or flee, the sultans tended to be accepting of other religions. Sikander's son Zain-ul-Abidin, or Bud Shah, ruled for more than fifty years and welcomed back the Kashmiri Pandits who had been chased out by his father. This period saw the emergence of the communal harmony and religious syncretism later known as *Kashmiriyat* — a swirl of Shaivism and Sufism linked to Valley pride, and a term that has become deeply politicized in recent decades. Whatever label one might use, Persian Sufi Mir Sayyid Ali Hamdani, Hindu sage Lal Ded, and her disciple Nund Rishi played key roles in shaping a uniquely tolerant strain of Islam in the

Valley. For centuries, Hindus and Muslims intermarried and even celebrated holidays together. The uniquely Kashmiri hereditary clerical title of *mirwaiz* also traces its origins to Mir Hamdani and this more pluralist era.

Over the past century, Islam in Kashmir has turn toward the conservative. One reason for the emergence of Sheikh Abdullah in the 1930s-40s (see Introduction) was his ability to weave Quranic recitations into his speeches. Later, he placed his followers in charge of the main mosques and shrines. In the 1970s he was asked how he had sidelined traditional Islamic voices, including the mirwaiz. "By becoming a mullah myself," he joked.[139] When rural Kashmiris first began sneaking across the Line of Control for training in the 1980's, Pakistani ISI officers encouraged them to join the Islamist group Hezb-ul-*Mujahideen*, and later the Salafist Lashkar-e-Taiba. Slowly a more radical, extremist Islam crept into Kashmir. Asiya Andrabi, the wife of a co-founder of Hezb-ul *Mujahideen* and head of an all-female extremist group, is among those who encouraged this shift. She was widely thought to be in close contact with ISI chief Hamid Gul before his death in 2015.[140] As recently as 2018, her extremist group, possibly funded by Pakistan, continued to distribute monthly pensions to dozens of Kashmiri families that had had a member killed by Indian security forces.[141]

Yet even 15 or 20 years into the insurgency, maybe five percent of the Valley's residents subscribed to extremist interpretations of Islam — which explains some local journalists' response to my reporting on Asiya Andrabi. I leveraged the interview into a short profile of her in *The Economist*. The day after that article appeared (reproduced in full below), Farooq and our journalist friend Shabir Hussian asked me to join them for lunch. They explained how my article would be perceived in the West: as a sign that the Valley would soon be overrun by anti-American jihadis. I pushed back, pointing out that the article mentioned Kashmir's tolerant strain of Islam. That didn't matter, they said — look at the headline, the photo, the lead. "You have highlighted somebody nobody here cares or thinks about," said Shabir. "Asiya Andrabi? This is not us."

I began to see their point. In focusing on a troubling, yet largely ignored, corner of Kashmiri Islam, I had depicted the Valley as a future Islamic state. I had come to Kashmir seeking to learn more about the Muslim perspective. Instead I had selfishly used a marginal Muslim voice for career advancement — and in so doing likely fueled Western misconceptions about Muslims, Islam and Kashmir, falling into the very trap I had left the United States in an effort to avoid.

Several times during my stay in Kashmir, Shabir half-jokingly accused me of working for the CIA. I'd wave it away with a laugh, but this incident made me see how close he'd been to the truth. If my stories are read by policymakers in London and Washington, I'm providing intelligence that may help shape policy. How many dispatches from Kashmir, I wondered, appear in *The Economist* every year? And of those, how many are focused on religion? In 2007, my article was likely one of just a handful of stories about Kashmiri Muslims to appear in a mainstream Western news outlet. Consider that in 2018, after interviewing Andrabi, *Kashmir Observer* contributor Auqib Javeed was summoned to Delhi for three days of questioning, and you begin to understand how India views Andrabi and those who engage her.[142]

Spies and journalists cultivate sources because both are in the business of intelligence — a reality that highlights the foreign correspondent's dilemma. A spy is by definition partial, working for her homeland. A journalist is supposed to be impartial, weighing the evidence to find a reasonable middle ground. Andrabi's comments, particularly her threat to kill the American president, were of course newsworthy. But this is presumably why she said them — to draw attention to her outfit and fan the flames of conflict between Islam and the West. I fell into her trap and amplified her message. This is not to say that foreign correspondents should refrain from reporting on marginal but potentially influential sub-sections of society. But that they should do so only with clarity and balance.

My story was accurate — it highlighted words and incidents that did actually happen. But it did Kashmiris a disservice. In writing this story for *The Economist*, one of the world's most influential publications, I raised the specter of an extremist Kashmir. I was Joe McCarthy frightening Americans about the Red Scare. As one reader responded to the article online: "Interviews such as this prove to the world that Islam spawns psychopaths—a nation of psychopaths and sociopathic killers. What kind of a god demands blood and rewards those who slaughter their brothers with celestial decadence?"[143]

□

Lock up your daughters

Kashmir's Islamic puritans

Economist — April 12th, 2007[144]: "IF MY son would kill Mr Bush," says the burqa-wearing head of an all-female Islamist organisation, "it would be a great honour for Asiya Andrabi." Those who threaten the leader of the free world and refer to themselves in the third person tend to be crackpots or dictators. Asiya Andrabi may be a bit of both. But Dukhtaran-e-Millat (Daughters of the Faith), which she founded in Indian-administered Kashmir in 1981, is no joke. Older than al-Qaeda and the Taliban, Dukhtaran supports terrorists, and was banned by the Indian government from 1990 until 2004.

One consequence of the 17-year-old insurgency against Indian rule that still simmers in Kashmir is that the region's centuries-long tradition of a moderate, tolerant Islam with its roots in Sufi mysticism, has been under threat. Many liberal Kashmiris blame Pakistani-financed militant outfits for blurring Islam and nationalism, and trying to turn the conflict into a *jihad.* Throughout the 1990s militants tried to enforce moral rectitude, bullying local women, for example, into wearing burqas. They had limited success. But now the puritans are on the march. Last month, for instance, a furious mob beat up customers and smashed furniture in a hotel in Srinagar, accusing the owners of operating a sex ring. A week later conservatives forced the black-out of "vulgar" English-language cable-television channels.

The turning-point was an earlier sex scandal, which shocked Srinagar last year. Civil servants and policemen were linked to a prostitution ring in which teenage girls had been drugged and abducted to a brothel. The scandal prompted days of mass protests, and the torching of the home of the accused brothel-keeper.

Leading the campaign against licentiousness, Dukhtaran helped found a Forum Against Social Evils. Its burqa-wearing members wrecked beauty parlours and liquor shops, ransacked dimly-lit restaurants for encouraging smooching and celebrated Valentine's Day by burning cards. Their cause has been bolstered by the uncovering of two more "sex rings". In one, young women were lured by a fake charity. In another, policewomen were allegedly coerced by male superiors.

Yet Kashmir's liberal traditions are proving stubborn. Kashmiri women continue to pursue further studies, hold professional jobs and move about alone, some without headscarves. Shutting cinema halls has led to a boom in satellite dishes and video-rental shops. Progressive locals winkingly refer to Ms Andrabi as the "Angel of Death" and on the streets of Srinagar burqas and long beards are still rare.

"Islam came to Kashmir not by the sword but through teaching, preaching, Sufis and saints," points out Umar Farooq, a separatist politician and mirwaiz, a hereditary spiritual leader. "You can't threaten people with Islam," he argues. "You have to educate them." Dukhtaran, however, is trying to do just that. It runs 75 part-time *madrassas* in Kashmir.

□

ABOUT ONE YEAR after my interview with Asiya Andrabi, Indian authorities outlawed Dukhtaran-e-Millat and arrested its leader. In the years that followed she was released and detained a number of times. In 2018, still awaiting trial, she was moved to Delhi's notorious Tihar Prison. The next year the National

Investigation Agency included Andrabi in a charge sheet for terror funding that included JKLF leader Yasin Malik.[145]

In July 2020 her children expressed concern about the health of their 57-year-old mother, who has hypertension and asthma.[146] In early 2021, Pakistan's Human Rights Minister Sireen Mazari and Andrabi's son Ahmad urged the UN to help secure her release.[147] Days later the Pakistani Senate unanimously passed a bill denouncing India's treatment of Andrabi and Malik.[148] As of late 2022, Andrabi was continuing to appeal a Delhi court's decision allowing authorities to seize her Srinagar home.

□

We are working to create an Islamic State: Asiya Andrabi

(KO report)

March 19, 2007: Born in 1963 in Srinagar's Khanyar locality, Asiya Andrabi was more interested in science than spirituality in her youth. Today, however, she leads Dukhtaran-e-Millat (Daughters of the Community), an all-female Islamic fundamentalist group that is older than both the Taliban and Al Qaeda and which the Indian government has branded a "soft terror" group. Dressed in her habitual dark hijab and black leather gloves, an engaging and fervent Andrabi welcomed me into her home on a recent Friday morning. Over tea and biscuits we discussed the conflict between Islam and the West, the progress of Kashmir's independence movement, and the assassination of the President of the United States.

DL: I've read that as a teenager you wanted to be a scientist but were diverted and became interested in Islam. Tell me about that.

AA: After my graduation I was planning to go to India for my studies because biochemistry was not offered in this KU in those days. My brother, who is a doctor, didn't allow me to go to India for further studies as he was aware of what was happening in India to Kashmiris, especially to Muslim girls. So after a few days I went into my father's library and found this book *The Inner Feelings of a Woman*, compiled by Indian author Mya Faribad. One of the lead stories was of Miriam Jamilah and how she converted to Islam from Christianity. She had a conversation with Maulana Maudoodi and they spoke and wrote letters and she was converted. When I read this whole it was the turning point of my life. And I made up my mind that Insha'allah I too would spend my whole life devoted to Islam.

Before that I did not even know the ABC's of Islam, and that too from such a family that was known for their prominence in Islam (Andrabi is part of the Sayyid clan, originally from Afghanistan). And then I decided that a Muslim is incomplete unless he or she knows Arabic, because most of the books and key Islamic works are in Arabic. So I started reading Arabic. My father too was an Arabic scholar, and he guided me very properly, and I graduated in Arabic from Kashmir University.

DL: And soon after that you started Dukhtaran-e-Millat?

AA: In 1981 I started a school, a madrassa in Srinagar, and the response was very warm from the women folk. And then I started my organizational work. I went door to door and I went to the mosque and delivered speeches from the loudspeakers. I talked to women just to tell them the status of women in Islam, and how we were exploited by West as well as East – everybody exploits us. So let us see what Islam has given us.

DL: Wasn't it unusual for a woman to speak in the mosque?

AA: Yes, it was unusual in those days. There were confrontations and hurdles from our priests, from the ulema. But I showed them how Allah and Mohammed (SAW) never denied a woman from speaking about Islam. Finally they decided you are the best among all the human beings because you preach the real Islam, you go for the right and you are telling the people to follow the right path and take them away from all the evils.

DL: And how big is the organization today – how many schools and members?

AA: We operate 75 schools across Jammu and Kashmir. These are part-time *madrassas* for only girls where we teach the Koran and Arabic. I cannot give you an exact member total but we are in all districts and areas of the state.

DL: And what is DeT's goal, its mission?

AA: Our goal and aim is that this whole universe belongs to Allah the almighty and so should be governed by the laws of the Almighty. It's not only Kashmir; my strong belief is that all human beings should accept Islam, and Islam is not only for the Muslims it is for the whole of humanity. As I'm talking to you my brother I don't know whether you are Christian or what you are, Jewish or atheist, but this is my inner feelings in my heart is that I want to tell you please go and study Islam.

But don't study the Muslims of this era! Because there is a lot of difference between Muslims and Islam. If you are to study a Muslim you would say Islam is nothing, no different than any other religion. But if you would study Islam, the teachings of the Koran and Prophet Mohammed (Salassam) then you'll come to know what Islam is.

This is what I tell everyone. Even when I met the Indian agencies when I was arrested, RAW and IBS, CBI – they talked to me. I told them you please go and study Islam.

DL: And how did they respond?

AA (giggles under her veil): I gave them my humble request, and they said 'OK, Insh'allah Rahman, we will, Insh'allah, go and study Islam'."

But we are not going for the Dawa work only. Our job is not confined to Dawa only because first and foremost we should liberate Kashmir from Indian clutches, that too for the cause of Islam.

DL: So you seek the re-establishment of the Caliphate, under Sharia law?

AA: Yes, we want an Islamic state, why not? Islam should be in power. They should be powerful, the Islam. And that should be governed by the laws of Allah the almighty. Koran is rules and regulations of all parliaments and assemblies – there is nothing that has not been revealed in the Koran.

DL: Does that mean you believe in hudood punishments such as that a thief should have his hands cut off, adulterers stoned and apostates killed?

AA: Yes, of course. These are the punishments from Allah the Almighty. If you cut the hand off one thief, the whole society – none of them would dream of the theft.

How do you say that this is not justice? So when you punish a man in this way, there will be a totally pure society. One man will be killed and whole humanity would be saved.

DL: Even if your son had committed the crime?

AA: Yes, why not. I myself would kill him. In the time of Omar the second Caliph, his son committed a crime and he said: "My son should be punished first then any other."

DL: Does that mean there is no room for compromise in Islam? That there is no room for moderates in Islam?

AA: There will be no change in Holy Koran; it will be around until doomsday. Nobody can have even a single change, even Asiya Andrabi or any clergyman. Now it is the West who is dictating and wants to see the whole world like the West. In certain areas of the West they are not allowing the women to wear the purdah, because they don't like it. Some people ask them: 'What's the problem, why can't women wear this hijab?' But in the West Muslim women do not wear the purdah and should be exploited and sold like commodities and be made commodities like those in the market.

DL: Following that line of thinking, does this mean that the West and Islam cannot coexist?

AA: We don't have any grudge or anything against the West. One thing we want: If West will try their best to understand what Islam is. What happens is that there are some attacks on Western countries. This is a reaction to what the West is doing! They are trying their best to dictate that the whole universe should be governed by laws of Western countries or laws of America – nobody is ready for that.

So what is happening to Iraq, what has happened to Afghanistan: Muslims have a full right to react now. Now that reaction is not always fully according to the laws of Islam, but when somebody is reacting he cannot react in any other way. If there were dialogues between the West and Islam, that could be positive. And there is a place for dialogues in our religion. Just last year when there were cartoons they were trying their best to show our Prophet Mohammed (Salassam) was a terrorist and everyone knows our Prophet Mohammed (Sullahu Alaihi Wasalam) was the most humble man on this planet. So they are inflaming our emotions and all that – how do you expect there will be civility between the West and Islam?

DL: OK, but these attacks in Saudi Arabia, Jordan, Turkey, Indonesia, Afghanistan and Iraq – many are Muslims killing Muslims, which is un-Islamic, as you say. Are these not bad for the ummah?

AA: That is the conspiracy against Islam. There are some hired persons everywhere. As you can see what's happening in Pakistan, there are blasts in mosques even. Nobody can justify that! Nobody can say that's Islam, that's *jihad*. They are hired persons – hired from the West, hired from India. So what they are doing, this is not Islam.

DL: You mentioned the need for dialogues. The US-Islamic World Forum took place last month in Doha, an event organized by an American political organization to give the US an opportunity to hear reaction and advice from a wide variety of leaders from the Muslim world. Mehbooba Mufti spoke at the gathering, what do you hope she said?

AA: This is a very sad thing that they called Mehbooba Mufti. She is a Muslim woman but she doesn't know what Islam is. She can't represent Islam anywhere.

DL: Why do you say that?

AA: Because she is not a practicing Muslim woman. She has nothing to do with Islam. She is a secular woman who believes in secularism and all that. So as far as the Islamic representative is concerned you must be aware of Islamic rules and principles and you must know what Islam is. It was just a government-sponsored program but she has no authority because she doesn't represent Islam.

DL: What would you have said? What do you think needs to be said at such a gathering?

AA: Until and unless they change their policies, there will be hatred against the US. And whenever and wherever you go, you ask anyone, not Muslims only, whosoever is part of the weaker section of the world, you ask them who do you most hate and they will say George Bush. Because George Bush is against the weaker sections, George Bush is trying his best to have an upper hand on the whole of humanity.

So this is my message for the US: You have your whole United States, you have your own set of rules in the United States and you have no right to involve yourself in other people's lives in other countries. So let us govern ourselves. Let us live our lives how we want. Who are they to dictate to us? Who are they to dictate to Iraq? Who are they to dictate to Iranians how they use their nuclear energy and all that? Why are they interfering? Wherever they see that Muslims have some power they interfere to destroy that power! Why not the Israelis?!

DL: So then what was your reaction to 9/11?

AA: As far as my perception, 9/11, this was done by the CIA. I don't think there was the hand of Al Qaeda in that. But when it occurred Al Qaeda said we have done it. But I think it was the handiwork of the CIA because they were trying their best to destroy Afghanistan, so for that this was all fabricated.

DL: But there is clear proof of these 19 Al Qaeda men on the planes.

AA: No, no. It is very easy, you hire someone else and you tell him to please tell other people: "I am Al Qaeda man," and all that. It's not necessary that whatsoever they spoke was true. Because this was the basis to destroy Afghanistan, because they had no reason, and immediately after 9/11 they destroyed Afghanistan, bombed everything and the Taliban system was destroyed. There are hundreds of documents proving that this was the handiwork of the Pentagon. And I don't think Muslims have as much ability to do such a big job. I don't think militarily they are mature enough yet.

DL: Speaking of maturity, has DeT made progress towards its goals?

AA (smiling eyes): Very nice progress here, yes. We are progressing very nicely. There are some laws from the government – we are not allowed to preach or go anywhere freely – but still progress for us has been very nice lately.

DL: How do you get around these laws?

AA: We used to get arrested and booked regularly under the Public Safety Act even though we are trying our best to make this Kashmir society pure from all obscenity and all the evils. So whenever we used to go anywhere we used to have confrontations with police. But (alhamdulillah) we are trying our best to carry on.

DL: Last month Duktharan helped destroy hundreds of posters and cards and broke up meetings between young couples in public restaurants. Please tell me, what's wrong with Valentine's Day?

AA: In Kashmir we have a purely religious society. We had – nowadays it's not. We were a very pure society based on Islamic rules. And Valentine's Day vulgarity is not permitted in Islam. We can share our love with our husband only.

DL: OK, but what about two young people showing their appreciation for each other by giving each other cards? This does not seem a terrible thing.

AA: This all leads to vulgarity.

DL: But that's not...

AA: Who is St. Valentine to you?

DL: If I remember correctly, the holiday as celebrated in the West really has nothing to do with the historical St. Valentine. It was the English poet Chaucer who romanticized the event and the holiday has passed down from...

AA: In Kashmir we know this Valentine was a man who promoted this vulgarity and who promoted that young girls and young boys should go for courtship and all these vulgar activities. And then he was hanged. Here in Kashmir they want to celebrate this...and as far as our Islamic culture is concerned we are not allowed to celebrate such affairs. I can show my love to my husband, and it is not just one day, it is 365 days a year and 24 hours a day.

DL: Maybe not all Kashmiris want to be more devout Muslims.

AA: On Valentine's Day we saw them and told these youths, young Muslims girls and boys, we told them the ethics of Islam, the principles of Islam. And we asked them "What is wrong with you that you are indulging in these activities?" And with the help of Allah the Almighty they understood what we were telling them and some of them they wept, "What is wrong with us we are not following the rules of Islam?" They told me: "Baji, give us your number" — they called me baji – "give us your phone number, please, we want to contact you, please teach what Islam is."

DL: But isn't tolerance a basic principle of Islam? Doesn't the Koran preach tolerance – for other individuals, for other traditions, i.e. "No compulsion in religion"?

AA: We are tolerating everything but we are also preaching.

DL: But tolerating and preaching seem contradictory. "To every people have we appointed rites and ceremonies." (Al-Hajj 21:76-69). Doesn't that suggest that people should be able to practice such traditions the way they want?

AA: No, that's not what Islam says. Islam says all the human beings should accept Islam and practice Islam, this is what Islam says. That this holy Koran has been given to the whole humanity by Allah the Almighty and whosoever accepts he will be in the life hereafter he will enter the paradise, and whosoever doesn't accept it, he will enter the hell. So now it is up to human beings. It's your will and wish. If you won't accept Islam, it will harm you. This is the holy Koran, if they will accept it it's good for them, if they won't accept it they have to face the tyranny in life hereafter.

DL: If they won't accept it, should they be forced to accept it?

AA: No. They won't be forced. It's just we preach Islam, let them know what it is. If they won't accept it, OK, let them do what they want to do.

DL: But the Taliban – not to mention Al Qaeda – they seem to force others to accept their beliefs and practices. Do you support their methods?

AA: Al Qaeda is something different: nobody knows where Al Qaeda is or who Al Qaeda are. But as far as Taliban is concerned, they were practicing Islam under Islamic government, with rules and principles according to Islam, but on the whole that was an Islamic government.

DL: So you support their ideal?

AA: We are not in power. There is a difference between Muslims and non-Muslims. If we were in power and there would be a government of Muslims, we could have some rules for the Islamic government that whosoever doesn't accept this, he will be punished. But as far as non-Muslims are concerned, you can't force a non-Muslim. For instance, in an Islamic government all the Muslim women would have to accept the purdah, but this order would not be for the non-Muslims. Non-Muslims have their own way of life; they can act as they want. But as far as Muslims are concerned, they have to accept Islam and they have to practice Islam.

DL: And part of the practice is accepting the veil.

AA: Islam has given us respect, has given us honor and to protect this honor this purdah is very necessary for us and we feel that it is security for a Muslim woman.

DL: But is it not sometimes difficult to wear in the modern world, both physically and psychologically?

AA: I think it's easier, to wear it and go everywhere, as compared to living without the purdah. This whole society is totally vulgar now. With the purdah wherever you go nobody knows who you are and no remark is passed on you. As you compare the girls wearing the jeans and semi-nude girls – I think that's very difficult.

DL: You have been quoted as saying, "Women are supposed to look after the kitchen and men are supposed to work." But you seem to contradict this statement – you are out of the house, working quite publicly. Further, you yourself wanted to study and become a scientist – why shouldn't other women be able to follow their dream?

AA: We are not telling them not to study. They can go for the studies wherever they want to. They can go for the study but according to the rules of Islam. Most of our girls are MBBS doctors, PhD doctors – nobody is telling them not to study. But even their mentors haven't seen their face, even when they visit their guides they are with full purdah.

Let them go for studies. But one thing is there in Islam: duty of earning is not the women's duty, in Islam. This duty has been given to man, that he has to earn and he has to feed a woman. There is this unemployment problem in Kashmir and as a result both men and women are working. If there were no unemployment problem I'm sure there would be no women working. Go for studies, whatever you want, but as far as the duty of earning the money, that is the duty of the man.

DL: So the studies of a Muslim woman should not be part of building towards a career, towards earning a living.

AA: Right. We are not studying to earn money. I don't think you need to study to earn money. We are studying just to learn.

DL: Some experts have argued that because men are busy doing the fighting and also the dying, women are the surviving victims of the conflict – half-widows, etc. They are taking the brunt of the Kashmir conflict's suffering and sorrow. Do you agree?

AA: I too am a woman and since I married I have spent just two years with my husband. He has spent his whole life in jail and he is still languishing with life imprisonment. Many other Muslim women also have lost their brothers, their husbands, their sons, to go to *jihad.* So there are some problems, nobody can deny. I am a woman, without a man, and I am facing hundreds of problems. But (alhamdulillah), I am ready for that.

I have sacrificed my life, I have sacrificed my love even. I was very closely attached to my husband and I don't think there will be any husband and wife who love each other like we two. I have sacrificed this for Allah and I believe we will be together in paradise and nobody can separate us – Insh'allah Rahman — over there. So this is for the cause of Allah the Almighty, for the cause of Islam, for the cause of this freedom struggle. So it is for these other women also, we know there is a lot of psychological depression and they are facing threats from different corners. We cannot deny that men too are facing the same. We all are facing these problems at the hands of India.

DL: As a means of combating these problems you've said all young Kashmiri men should become militants. Do you still support the insurgency?

AA: My husband was a *mujahideen.* When we started the struggle in 1988 we called all of the Muslim men to *jihad.* Until and unless India will leave this Kashmir, until and unless all the Indian forces will leave Kashmir, jihad will continue (Insh'allah Rahman) and there is no option that mujihadeen will lay down their guns.

DL: What about your sons?

AA: Yes, I believe in that, and not only in Kashmir. I believe jihad is the most sacred job in Islam, and we believe we will be rewarded in the life hereafter. So if Kashmir will be liberated from Indian clutches and there will be jihad somewhere else in Muslim world it's my dream that my sons will go there and fight.

DL: Even if one became a suicide bomber?

AA: Yes, why not.

DL: Wouldn't you, as a mother, miss your son?

AA: I would miss them but I'll see them in heaven (Insh'allah Rahman). I would sacrifice anything to please Allah the Almighty.

DL: But they would be killing people.

AA: They won't kill people. No. They would kill the enemies of Islam.

DL: And who are the enemies of Islam?

AA: Here in Kashmir the enemies of Islam are the Indian army. To kill Indian army is my dream. So are the Indian politicians — they are the enemies of Islam and they are the enemies of our freedom struggle. Not the common man. If you are from America, I don't have any grudge with you. But if I see George Bush anywhere, and my son would kill Mr. Bush, it would be a great honor for Asiya Andrabi.

DL: I see. And who are these Indian politicians you mention?

AA: Ghulam Nabi Azad, Mufti Saeed – politicians like this.

DL: What about *Mirwaiz* and Yasin Malik?

AA: They are not Indian politicians. But they have changed their ways and I think now they are in the hands of some agencies (smiling eyes). Though they were the freedom fighters, but as far as the present situation is concerned there is something fishy in their character now.

DL: What do you mean by that?

AA: You know we don't believe in Mirwiaz Omar Farooq now. We believe he is ready for compromise but we don't believe in compromising politicians. We started this movement with this aim: Kashmir should be liberated from India, this one thing. And whosoever goes with compromise less then liberation from India we call him a traitor, and *Mirwaiz* is leaning that way.

Yasin Malik is also I think somewhere engaged.

DL: Speaking of the current situation, what are your thoughts on these discoveries of encounter killings?

AA: It is just for the elections now, and they are playing a card now. It is nothing more than that. A CBM for Kashmiris, and it is not a good sign. It's not the first time that they've come to know about such encounters. If it were the first time we could say that they are doing it for the cause of Kashmiris, but it is a political card. They are not charging the Indian army for that, the CPRF or BSF – they are charging just the Kashmiri task force with that. And they want to give the signal that the Indian army is very loyal and Indian army security forces are for your security, but as for your own Kashmiri security they are no good.

DL: And what about the independence movement – how do you think it's progressing?

AA: I am hopeful because (alhamdulillah) a movement that is now backed by one lakh martyrs cannot be stopped. But there are ups and downs in the movement and this is a time that I think there is a lot of confusion in our movement because of *Mirwaiz*. India was ready to have another Sheikh Abdullah but nobody was ready to play the part. But now they have hired *Mirwaiz* for that. So there is confusion among the common masses but I'm sure they are with the movement. As you may have seen Geelani Sahab was going for kidney transplant and hundreds and thousands of youths were ready to donate their kidneys. Because people are with the ideology of Geelani Sahab, and Geelani sticks to his word that Kashmir should be liberated from India – nothing less than that. I am sure with the passage of time the movement shall gain the momentum. If not today then in several years, Kashmir will be liberated – Insh'allah Rahman.

□

TOWARDS THE END of my conversation with *Mirwaiz* Omar Farooq he talks of back-channel communications and a looming announcement. This is a reference to the secret diplomacy between top Indian and Pakistani officials that had been going on for more than a year and had by the time of our chat made significant progress. "By early 2007, the back-channel talks on Kashmir had become 'so advanced that we'd come to semicolons'," Pakistani Foreign Minister Khurshid Kasuri said of this period.[149] The countries' leaders planned to announce a Kashmir agreement, but Musharraf's political stability evaporated and the deal fell apart.

As of late 2022, Omar Farooq remained the leader of Hurriyat and claimed that authorities had barred him from leaving his home since the revocation of Article 370.[150]

□

'You can't threaten people with Islam': *Mirwaiz* Omar Farooq

(KO report)

April 8, 2007: THRUST into the spotlight by the 1990 assassination of his father *Mirwaiz* Muhammad Farooq when he was just a teen, Omar Farooq shifted gears and committed himself to earning the hereditary and unique-to-Kashmir mantle of religious and social leadership. Today he has become a well-regarded *Mirwaiz* and risen to prominence as head of the moderate faction of the All Parties Hurriyat Conference, which he helped found.

Days after PDP patron Mufti Muhammad Saeed returned to Srinagar touting the Centre's miserly handouts on demilitarization and black laws repeal, *Mirwaiz* spoke to *Kashmir Observer* correspondent David Lepeska in his heavily fortified Rajbagh office. Before the chat was cut short the two discussed the prevalence of political gimmicks in the Valley, the making of a *Mirwaiz*, and a pragmatic approach to the resolution in Kashmir.

DL: Let's start with current events. What are your thoughts on the latest developments regarding demilitarization?

MO: First of all we believe that demilitarization should not be seen in isolation. It's not just one step the government of India has to take; it's a step that is very much linked to other steps they need to take on the ground. India and Pakistan must agree to complete withdrawal of forces from the state of Jammu & Kashmir on both sides of the ceasefire online. Also, demilitarization should not be confused with relocation or redeployment of forces: we have seen in the past that what has happened that they take one contingent away and they bring another, so we believe that it should be a genuine attempt on the government of India to cut down the number of troops.

The situation is improving day-by-day in terms of violence. The government of India can no longer continue with the excuse that militancy is active or is the main reason for not demilitarizing. So we believe there is an attempt by certain vested interests to confuse the situation - especially the PDP, which is trying to take political mileage out of it. India and Pakistan are very much involved and they are thinking along these lines and they are close to an agreement as far as demilitarization is concerned. So I think the fact that the PDP is trying to sabotage the whole thing for their own political gain is confusing the whole situation.

Secondly, I think the establishment of committees and these things has complicated the issue. It's very simple, now we are in a situation where even the government could have taken decisions on the lifting of bunkers or on the issue of Special Powers acts. But now they have given the authority to the committee - the state government has essentially no role.

DL: But isn't it reasonable to assess the security situation in Kashmir before they take decisions?

MO: Yes, of course. But if you look at it, it is a prerequisite for the Indian government, for the parliament to review the situation every six months wherever they can apply the Armed Forces Special Powers Act. So it's nothing new that this committee is going to do.

Secondly, as far as the security scenario is concerned, the very fact that the army chief is making a statement that infiltration has completely stopped. It's a very good indication - the army is saying it!

DL: Right. And two days before that Defence Minister AK Antony is saying there will be no demilitarization until infiltration stops; there seems to be some disconnect in the Centre.

MO: The problem from Delhi is that they don't have a consistent policy on Kashmir. They don't have a plan. Their only plan is: "how do we talk in terms of the current situation." They don't foresee that if you're talking about a solution, of a settlement - demilitarization or other initiatives - you need to take the entire scenario into account.

DL: Some have suggested that Mufti and the PDP are taking the political middle ground that separatists such as Hurriyat have occupied for some time.

MO: Hurriyat's efforts are not based on the politics of power. We are not looking at the forthcoming elections, not looking at vote bank politics - we are looking at the settlement of Kashmir. The PDP thinks it's alright to accept the current reality. But if things have not gone well, let them come forward in sincerity. You can't have your cake and eat it, too. You say the government is not doing enough. Well, you're in the government - come out; show your resentment to the Centre.

DL: But some say the best way to make change is from within.

MO: OK, but the fact is that they have been in power for the last few years and they didn't initiate such things when they were in power. Fine, the situation was not as conducive as it is today, but I believe whatever the PDP is saying it is with an eye on the coming election, trying to give a good impression to the common man... Hurriyat is not at all disturbed that they are son of taking our agenda or anything of this. We feel vindicated when the PDP or the National Conference, who are in the mainstream of Indian politics, when they talk about resolution and demilitarization - it proves we are on the right track.

DL: You say Hurriyat doesn't play power politics, yet there are rumors that you and Hurriyat may run in the 2008 elections.

MO: Elections are not a taboo for Hurriyat. But elections come after settlement. We believe that the bigger issue is that India, Pakistan and Kashmir have to reach a consensus as far as the culmination in the peace process is concerned. Yes. if the peace process culminates in elections on both sides of Jammu and Kashmir -elections not only for administrative purposes, elections for a settlement, for a resolution, for looking at different options - Hurriyat would join in.

But we can't jump to a settlement now because we don't have that amount of commitment or trust between the two countries that we can talk of a final settlement at this juncture. Hurriyat is very much looking at the fact that yes, if India and Pakistan and Kashmir agree that this is going to be an interim arrangement and elections are going to follow. But not elections to strengthen India's game over Kashmir, as these parties are doing. When you go in these elections you are saying you believe in Kashmir's accession to India - you give away the very basic right of your struggle.

If you are trying to look at the 2008 elections as something that will change the face of the government, and the PDP are replaced by the separatists - I don't think that's going to help unless and until you genuinely talk about change in the political structure of J&K on both sides of ceasefire line.

DL: Towards that end, many believe that India and Pakistan have reached a back channel agreement.

All we know is that India and Pakistan are working quite hard at the formal level and informal level about the possibility of an interim arrangement. Our stand is that we're not averse to it but the fact is that whatever happens the common Kashmiri should feel the change. It should not be old wine in a new bottle; it should genuinely be something people have struggled for. It's very important that Kashmiris feel the change.

DL: I'd like to go from the political to the personal for a minute, and I apologize for taking you back to what must have been a traumatic time. Could you tell me where you were when your father was killed, and how you reacted?

MO: I was very much at home and we heard the shots. That day there was a strike and every one was home and we rushed to the spot and he was injured and we took him to the hospital and unfortunately, you know, he was pronounced dead there. It was a very difficult period for us, for the family, and the times were very volatile - militancy was at the peak. And of course the incidents that followed where his funeral procession was taken out and the Indian army fired at the procession, and 67 people were killed – it's still one of the bloodiest days of the history of Kashmir.

DL: You were very young at the time.

MO: I was 16, and had just finished my high school. I was looking into going to college. I was interested in studying computers - that was my objective. At no point in my life did I visualize that I was going to enter politics. But you know, you plan one thing and you are destined to do something else. That's how destiny works. But it took me some time to understand how things were.

Apart from the political, my family had been predominantly involved in preaching Islam, and in terms of the faith and the reverence we have as a family, that is where the bonding came in. But I was a kid of 16 and I didn't know much about Islam. I had just read the Koran as a normal kid would do. But there was so much support and love and affection from the people and from my family, that gradually I started picking up the preaching aspect. You need to know Arabic; you need to know Kashmiri to communicate well with the people. There's a special, traditional approach in Kashmir in terms of preaching, it's quite different from mosques in the rest of the world. Here it's more interactive, the audience as well as the speaker are very much involved, because of the Sufi traditions of Islam here. That was something that I had to learn and I had just finished my high school and was looking forward to college. That all had to change.

DL: You must have learned quickly because Hurriyat's first meeting was only a couple years later: 15 years ago this coming December, actually.

MO: Yeah, exactly. I was 20 years old when the Hurriyat was formed. It was difficult, especially Hurriyat's existence in the sense that I initiated it. I invited all the political players of that time to sit and to talk but I had no intention that I would be able to lead them or something.

DL: But that's how it happened.

MO: Yeah, that's how it happened, and things started changing, and Hurriyat has had its ups and downs. But politically as well as religiously, I've kept moving forward. I completed my master's in Islamic studies at Kashmir University. I'm now studying to get my PhD.

DL: The position of *Mirwaiz* requires both religious and political leadership. How do you balance these demands?

MO: I consider myself first a religious leader, and religion can never be separated from society. So it's very natural that politics becomes a part of society. In this way it's very easy to balance. Whatever I believe as a human being, as a member of society, whether I belong to this religion or that religion is immaterial when I talk of the people's interests.

For example I give the sermon at the Friday mosque. I talk about the religious aspect of the situation, and analyze it accordingly. You can't go to the mosque and talk about religion and not talk about what happened in the past week. So it does give me a soil of edge in the sense that I'm in a position to talk of religion as well as politics.

And also the position of *Mirwaiz* - the institution of *Mirwaiz* - is now 300 years old, so there is a long tradition of education and social awareness behind me.

DL: Speaking of social awareness, since last year's sex scandal there seems to be greater visibility for the more conservative, more aggressive elements of Islam in Kashmir. The Valentine's Day protests of Dukhtaran and the Forum Against Social Evils and the recent attack on the De Meridien Hotel, for example. Is fundamentalism rising in Kashmir?

MO: The tradition of Islamic teachings in Kashmir is very strong on harmony. The fact that Islam came to Kashmir not by the sword - it was through teaching, preaching, Sufis, saints - that's a very strong weapon in Kashmiri society. And. I think that by and large people realize this. A while ago the militants started to threaten people: wear burqas, do this, do that. But it didn't really work. You can't threaten people with Islam, you have to educate them. We completely disapprove of these raids conducted by Dukhtaran and others. You reach people through seminars, discussion and debates, this type of teaching - that's how you move forward.

DL: Back to the Hurriyat. It's been divided, so that now it doesn't represent all parties as the name claims. Also, the party no longer seeks freedom, per se. Has the APHC failed?

MO: No, no, it has not failed. I think that there has been a change in strategy in terms of how to approach our objective. I don't think our objective has changed, but we are now talking about a phased, step-by-step approach.

I believe when it's all said and done today, whatever is happening I believe that is because of the efforts of Hurriyat - trying to convince Delhi and Islamabad to make them realize that we have to find a common program. I believe we're on the right track. Yes, there are issues, but the attitudes have changed. Pakistan has shown flexibility, and for the first time the spectrum is wide open: we are talking about possibilities, talking about new ideas, new suggestions, because to be honest it had suited India.

If Pakistan was not willing to budge from resolutions that were not going to be implemented it supported India's case. Now Pakistan is saying if A is not possible let's go for B or C or D. That has opened the whole spectrum and given us a lot to work with. I'm very optimistic that this is the line to take. Some people who are also part of the movement are taking a very traditionalistic approach. Let them do theirs, but we believe that if an issue like Kashmir is to be resolved a traditional approach is not going to work, and it is the people who suffer.

DL: What do you mean by a traditional approach?

MO: I mean those people who are saying, 'If position A is not achieved, nothing doing, we are going to stick with that.' This strengthens India's hand in Kashmir, slowly and gradually they are consolidating their position on the ground. We need to counter it, because India will not come on its own. They will never say: 'OK, I'm coming and let's solve the problem.' You have to take the initiative. You have to create circumstances for India to realize that it has to come to negotiations.

DL: What would Musharraf's four-point proposal mean for the lives of Kashmiris?

MO: I think the four-point proposal would give Kashmiris something to work with. For example, we are talking about sixty years - this is the sixtieth year - gone by since the passing of UN resolutions. But if we continue to say UN resolutions or nothing else 60 years will again bypass us. The UN is not going to help us. No outside power is going to intermediate. India will not liberate Kashmir. These things aren't going to happen.

So Kashmir needs to be realistic and say let us prioritize, what is step A. Step A is an end to violence, from both sides. Let the Indian army start moving out of Kashmir. Now we're seeing it as Pakistan sort of played its role - militancy is down, infiltration is down, attacks are down. Now let's move to the political level. Let's try and talk about demilitarization, withdrawal of troops, abolishment of acts. Demilitarization first means moving back to the garrisons, then moving out. India's strength in Kashmir is India's army, so if we are in a position to get the army out of Kashmir, withdraw the acts, people will feel the change, they'll feel there's no more harassment, no more crackdowns, no more killings. Number two is self-governance.

Self-governance is not something India or Pakistan is giving Kashmir as a compromise. Self-governance is the right of the people to govern themselves, to feel the freedom to take decisions on their own. Self-governance means, as we look at it, that maximum authority is given to the people, to the regions, whether it's four regions or five regions or seven regions, that is to be determined. On the issue of joint management, maybe the foreign affairs is something that India and Pakistan can keep, but let the rest be given to the regions: in terms of trade, people-to-people contact, movement across the LoC. That is what the people want - they want some genuine change on the ground.

The basic problem has been that India and Pakistan have always indulged in Kashmir. Their policy has always been that there have been weak governments here, whose dictates have come from Delhi and Islamabad. People of Kashmir should be able to govern themselves.

DL: As in the case of Northern Ireland's Good Friday Agreement.

Exactly. For example, the PDP and NC are talking strictly in terms of Delhi and Srinagar relationship. We are talking about Delhi and Srinagar, but also Srinagar and Islamabad, Srinagar and Muzaffarabad. We are bringing new dimensions into the picture.

DL: But doesn't that further complicate the issue?

MO: I don't think so. That's where the solution lies. Kashmir is not just Jammu, Ladakh, and this Valley. Kashmir is Azad Kashmir. Kashmir is Northern Areas. So I think what we're looking for is India and Pakistan building a consensus on Kashmir in terms of managing certain things on their own but also giving Kashmiris on both sides of LoC a say in their future, building a better and brighter tomorrow. And that will go hand in hand with India and Pak's interests.

If you look at it historically Kashmir has much less in common with South Asia. We are historically not a part of South Asia, we are historically a part of Central Asia. Whether it's Iran or Uzbekistan, Tajikistan, the cultural, the traditions, the Sufi, it's all Central Asia. We could renew our links to Central Asia. We could have access to Central Asia, and India and Pakistan would benefit politically, culturally, diplomatically, economically.

We have to move from confrontation to cooperation because our futures are linked. Kashmir's future is linked to India, is linked to Pakistan. Even if we wanted to remove that link it's not possible. So we are saying that let us try to strengthen the linkage but at the same time give Kashmiris something to work with. After ten years, when we've seen the benefits of this process, then we can visualize, do we have to stay here or can we move forward? I think this is something that is possible.

DL: In a recent interview with a Pakistani magazine you said the next few months will be "very crucial." Why did you say that, and what did you mean by it?

MO: India and Pak seem to realize today that we have to get our acts together. The status quo is not going to work. And the peace process is good, but it's now been in place for the last two years.

DL: And it seems to be working...

MO: Yeah, yes! It's good. But the fact is that Kashmiris are still getting killed. So how do we answer that? The step-by-step approach is something we support, and we are hopeful in the next few months something will be announced.

DL: Have you heard something? Is there something you're not telling?

MO: In the back channels I know a lot of effort is being made on how we can build a consensus in Kashmir. Both the countries realize that this is going to be in the interest of South Asia.

Chapter 6

Vanishing Culture

My friend, this youth is loss.

I lost all day on the way.

Why were we born?

Why did we not die?

Why such beautiful names?

We must wait for the Judgment Day

And I lost all day on the way.

The way of the world is a meaningless storm

I invited a difficult fate

And I lost all day on the way.

— Habba Khatoon[151]

THE MOST REVERED poet and singer in Kashmiri history emerged at precisely the right time — in the late 16th century, just as the two-and-a-half-century Kashmiri sultanate withered and collapsed. No one born and raised in greater Kashmir has since held full power in the homeland, underscoring the Valley's abiding melancholia.

The story goes that a young Yosuf Chak, soon to rule Kashmir, was out hunting on horseback and heard the young Habba Khatoon singing as she toiled in the field. He was drawn to her voice and beauty. The two fell in love and were together until Mughal leader

Akbar imprisoned the Kashmiri sultan in Delhi, after which Habba became a nomad, wandering the Valley singing songs of mourning. Khatoon's story echoes that of Kashmir — from peasant to queen to outcast; paradise found and quickly lost — which helps explain why her works remain popular today, when cultural creativity and joy have largely evaporated.

Even simple pleasures like the cinema. Decades ago, Kashmiris flocked to the movies. At massive cinema halls like the Broadway and the Neelum, the Shiraz and the Palladium, every major release sold out, forcing many moviegoers to buy their tickets illegally, via a local black market.[152] Tea stalls outside the theaters saw strong business after the credits rolled, as the predominantly male audience would discuss and debate the film late into the night. Until the fall 2022 opening of a new cineplex, younger Kashmiris had never been able to watch a commercial release in a local theatre.[153]

In June 2015, years after Kashmir's last cinema had been shuttered, Bollywood star Salman Khan urged Indian authorities to re-open the theaters. In response, Asiya Andrabi criticized Khan as an Indian agent aiding its cultural aggressions.[154] In September 2022, the Valley enjoyed its first commercial cinema screenings in more than 15 years with the opening of a three-screen multiplex in Srinagar, backed by Kashmiri Pandit businessman Vijay Dahr.[155] But will it last? Most of the gorgeous old cinemas are used by Indian security forces as camps and detention centers. In the 1990s many jailed Kashmiris were interrogated and even tortured in the converted movie houses. The message from the state was clear: "These places, where in the past you could escape, now bring only nightmares."

□

The Last Picture Show

(KO report)

July 27, 2006: Beyond coils of shiny razor-wire and an eight-foot-high fence of tin sheeting along Neelam Chowk, two policemen peer over rotting nose-high sandbags and into the street. Some twenty yards behind them, an aging, windowless stone building appears empty and derelict, its curvilinear chlorine blue façade faded by sunlight.

What sort of space-age, tumbledown edifice could require such protection – government offices? Top secret scientific labs, or the headquarters of a hard-line separatist party, perhaps? Not quite. A prominent, unlit neon sign and a trickle of young men passing through a swinging tin door as 1 p.m. looms provide subtle clues.

"I couldn't live without watching movies in theatres," said an entrant named Rakesh, a perfume seller from Uttar Pradesh who braves the security for the respite of a breezy viewing experience about once a week.

This is the Neelam, Srinagar's last working cinema, and exhibit A in Kashmir's culture wars. Apart from its long-sought autonomy, little in Kashmir is as fiercely protected and oft-embattled as culture, particularly entertainment and leisure activities.

The predominantly Muslim population of the Kashmir valley may not have the domineering clerics of neighboring Pakistan or Afghanistan to keep them in line. But they maintain an upright Muslim sensibility of their own – witness the dearth of alcohol and music – and with extremist elements ready to crack the whip and a pervasive anxiety on the streets, urban amusements are almost nil.

After a decade and a half of protests and occupation, bombings and burnings, cinema is poised to become the next casualty of this almost 60-year conflict.

Prior to the renewed insurgency in 1989, Kashmir had many well-attended movie houses. The Palladium, centrally located and then one of Srinagar's most popular theatres, was in 1991 destroyed by arson, widely believed to be the work of Muslim extremists.

Seen through the prism of the proceeding decade's flared religious passions, increasingly risqué Bollywood fare suddenly seemed overtly vulgar. Many theatres were closed while several others – including the Firdaus, Shiraz, and Naaz – were taken over by the Central Reserve Police Force (CRPF). Indeed the Neelam itself was shuttered for over a decade until the state government helped reopen it in 2002. The Regal Cinema was opened to much fanfare that same year, but on the first day of screenings a bomb blast killed one audience member and injured several others, and the theatre has been shuttered ever since. The Broadway, the Neelam's last competitor, succumbed to the pressures last year, shutting down and selling its lot to a mobile phone company.

All of which explains the machine-gun wielding policemen at Neelam, as well as the thorough bag searches and full-body pat downs. In a region where traditionalist passions can lead to explosive violence, a bastion of modern pop culture requires great security.

Kashmir University's Director of Kashmir Studies, M.H. Zaffar, for one, will not be shedding any tears. "It doesn't matter whether one or more movie theatres are functional in Kashmir," he said. "With new state-of-the art TVs, DVDs, and cable television, people in Kashmir have managed to stay entertained, knowing that going to the movie theatres involves a fair amount of risk."

A few locals were willing to take that risk.

"I usually come once a week with my friends, at times alone as well," said Pattan resident Zaeeshan Haider, moments after the Neelam security check turned up a small box of matches, which were confiscated. "We don't have cable TV in our village and watching movies is the only means of entertainment to us, despite the fact that it could be dangerous."

Indeed, the theatre was near empty on Wednesday despite scorching heat. Although the picture was slightly out of focus, the overall theatre experience at the Neelam was quite pleasant at Rs 40: a ceiling fan kept the auditorium cool, the sound was good, seating comfortable, and refreshments cold. And most of the score of attendees enjoyed *Shaadi se Pehle* ("Before Marriage"), a two-year-old sex comedy.

"It's not the best form of entertainment in town, but it's still good," said Narbul resident Taureef, 24, who comes about once a month and is very excited about an upcoming film starring Sharukh Khan.

"I'd rather play cricket or football, but there are no facilities," continued Tuareef, a recent college graduate looking for a teaching position. "There were barren fields where we could play, but those were taken over because of the insurgency."

That insurgency is the very reason many locals had little interest in going out to watch movies.

"I have a big-screen television, DVD player, and a great sound system," said Srinagar resident, Javed. "I have total control over the viewing environment. Why should I leave the house and take the risk?"

Yet there were several for whom the gathering clouds were a reason to mourn, including the Neelam's house manager, who was initially reluctant to talk but opened up on condition of anonymity. Along with other local cinema managers, several times in the last decade he approached the government to request alternative sources of income, and even filed a writ in court – to no avail.

"Some associated with the cinema have installed shops or run auto-rickshaws," he said. "Others have died."

Today the exposed and cracked concrete walls of the Palladium's open-faced avocado-colored shell offer eloquent testimony to those lost lives. Sycamore trees rise from where the seating area had been and sunflowers sway in a net-covered courtyard next to a heavily-manned red brick guardhouse. Nearby, a CRPF poster reads, "We are the guardians of the wishes of Kashmiri people."

Apparently the Kashmiri people wished the Palladium to become an arboretum.

"With the priority attached to life and property given the current circumstances, entertainment in Kashmir has taken a back seat," said Zaffar, placing the demise of Kashmiri cinema within the broader context of living in the conflict-ridden Valley. "It is the society that determines whether a facility should be in place or not. If people at some stage rejected cinemas, there should be no qualms with it. If the society thinks it needs them, they will automatically return."

The Neelam's manager reluctantly agreed with Zaffar about the uncertain future of movie houses, yet felt cinema could exist in the Valley, partially because of the popularity of films about the ongoing clash, such as *Fanaa*.

"We had almost a full-house every day," he said of that film's run last month, "and we ran the movie for four weeks."

Arshad Mushtaq, director of the first ever Kashmiri-made feature film, *Akh Daleel Loulech* ("A Tale of Love"), which premiered earlier this month, believed the real problem was a lack of a local film industry.

"Indian cinema has been pretty biased as far as portraying Kashmir and making films that have distorted its cultural ethos," he said, urging the involvement of Kashmiris in film production. "The need is not a great number of cinema theatres but to establish film institutions where we could train local people to make movies that give a correct interpretation of the facts."

One local resident had more personal concerns.

"We live in a constant state of fear but we brave all odds for the livelihood and the sustenance of life," the manager of the Kashmir Valley's sole movie house said proudly. "Cinema is the only means to earn a living for my family and I can't think of doing anything else."

□

THE ARTS INSTITUTE did indeed become a fully-fledged department of Kashmir University, but the move has done little to change its fortunes. Students remain largely unable to create works that take any position on Kashmir other than pro-India.

□

Kashmiri Creativity Under Siege from Indifference

(KO report)

September 21, 2006: One would think arts student Bilal Ahmad would be in a good mood. He earned his graduate degree in August and his jarring, brightly colored paintings have won numerous national competitions. Yet his recollection of a violent 1993 confrontation in his native Bijbehara reveals a seething soul.

"A big crowd had gathered in the market and they reached a peak, protesting against the security forces," said Ahmed, 23, who was a young boy watching with his parents at the time.

"Suddenly the security forces opened fire," he said, staring out the window with saucer-wide eyes and quivering lips. "So many people were killed, there was blood everywhere…I was shocked. Shocked. To see all those people shot? I was so shocked and frightened."

He paused and blinked once, twice, before turning to face his questioner.

"That was when I started to think."

Rarely seen, occasionally mourned, and on the brink of extinction, the Kashmiri artist is not unlike the mythic snow leopard that supposedly still prowls the Valley's sheltering mountains. More than twenty years of governmental and societal ignorance, educational disinterest, and a cultural shift away from creativity have endangered all variety of fine arts in Kashmir.

The conflict too has played a part, as pervasive fear and an erosion of freedom have placed creative endeavors - often considered subversive - in the crosshairs of the authorities. As artists and musicians look elsewhere to start or further their careers, the Institute of Music and Fine Arts has become one of the Valley's last bastions of creativity. Drawing on their anguish as a tool for expressing and understanding a brutal, frustrating, and often inexplicable world, its students hope to promote a deeper understanding of their past as a means to improve a cloudy future.

Created in 1965 under the auspices of the J&K Academy of Arts and Culture, the Institute peaked at approximately 150 students before the insurgency began in the late 1980's. Today the student body is about half that.

Despite spartan rooms, minimal financial support and inadequate materials, the modern Rajbagh building crackled with life on a mid-September afternoon. Sunshine poured through large, wood-framed windows, filling studios with light. Sculptural works, paintings, and exhibition photos filled the narrow cement hallways. Instructors sipped tea and chatted amiably in a cozy break room. Several painters stroked canvases with care and consideration; three music students strummed sitars for a vocal accompanist; and a sculptor chipped steel-gray granite into apple shapes with a hammer and chisel.

"When I was a kid I used to go to all these great historical places but now they're turning into ruins," said a diminutive, bright-eyed Snober Hassan, 21, as she flipped through computer images of her graphic design project on Kashmir's underappreciated monuments in a small interior office. "My main goal is to get people interested. Parents and teachers never advise their children to visit these places; the only people that see them are tourists."

She dug up a two-inch stack of photos and pointed out her favorite sites: Nishat, which "Akbar built when he fell in love with Kashmir;" the ruins of Avantipora; and King Lalitaditya's Sun Temple among them.

"This is our legacy; why can we not protect it?" she wondered. "When we teach our kids history, why not this?...Violence is not our only history."

Showkat Kathjoo, who graduated in 2000 and recently returned to teach, had a theory.

"Because of the conflict, the Centre has been propagating culture in its own way," he said, citing *Kashmiriyat*, Dal Lake and 'paradise on earth' as talking points. Crafts and tourist-related artisan industries have survived and even flourished as a result, while fine arts and music have withered.

"To create decent culture, arts, and literature you have to look back at your history, yet this is probably the only state whose own history has never been taught in its schools," Showkat added. "Nobody knows the history of Kashmir, so the result has been a cultural genocide."

The decline of arts education can be traced to an early 1980's National Council of Education Research and Training law that eliminated required art classes from public schools. Thus downgraded, art fell precipitously in the eyes of the public and the government.

"At this point, we can't say there's any state of art in Kashmir," said Sajad Hamdani, another 2000 grad who returned to the Institute this month after teaching for two years in Thailand. He pointed out that Srinagar has no art galleries, no concert halls, no periodical publications, no debates, nor any meeting place for discussing arts and literature.

Professor Masood Hussain, whose work has been exhibited internationally and who has taught at the Institute for a decade, fingered both locals and politicians.

"People aren't really aware of this particular field. They don't see any future in art," he said. "The government is also responsible because of ignorance; they don't understand the artist community."

Examples of this lack of understanding were common among the Institute's student body.

"I exhibited my work earlier this year, but people saw the paintings and left without asking what they were about, what they meant," said Ahmad, the Bijbehara painter. "They are not interested; how can they understand?"

The result has been an artistic brain drain, as students are forced to seek graduate education and careers outside Kashmir, where they are held in greater regard.

"Most students go outside the state and find success because they cannot find it here," Hussain acknowledged.

Several have accepted prestigious fellowships and faculty members have been featured in magazine profiles and, most recently, presented works as part of an Indian Art Exhibition in Damascus, Syria this past July.

The youth of today are unlikely to buck the trend. A recent study by K.N. Pandita, former Central Asian Studies Director at Kashmir

University, found that they had borne the brunt of the mental and emotional damage wrought by the conflict. Trauma, disorientation, frustration, unemployment, and other negative pressures of the lingering insurgency have in the last decade psychologically ravaged young Kashmiris, creating a lost generation tossed by forces beyond its control. Many have turned to drugs, militancy, or crime, others to fundamentalism. Very few have found their creative side.

Hamdani foresaw a dark future.

"It's going to be very difficult for this Institute to survive," he said. "Full-fledged status is the most important thing now."

Long seen as a panacea in the halls of the Institute, full-fledged status as a department of Kashmir University finally appears within reach. The arts college is only loosely affiliated with KU, which administers exams and confers official degrees. Governor S.K. Sinha, who also serves as KU Chancellor, and Vice Chancellor Abdul Wahid made an assessment visit in May.

"They have a very good faculty, very good students - I was deeply impressed," Wahid said of the visit. "We thought it would be in the best interest of the Institute if we can help them by offering to take over."

Wahid is currently preparing a letter describing the specifics of the handover for Chief Minister Ghulam Nabi Azad, which he plans to send in early October. He expected a final response from Azad, who controls both education and cultural academy funding, by December.

"We want very sincerely to help this Institute," said Wahid, who pointed out that some of the Institute's professors were not fully qualified, that the college did not own its own building, and that it had a sizable non-teaching staff. "If we decide to take over we must take over these liabilities also. The University cannot afford to finance the whole activity, so we need this financial support from the state."

Approval would mean double the Institute's funding, additional infrastructure, its own building, and likely UGC moneys down the road.

"Something is really cooking," said Hussain, confident of state approval by the end of the year. "Everything would be changed."

Not everything, according to Hamdani.

"Our society doesn't realize the importance of culture," he said. "When people visit a place they don't look at the house you live in or the car you drive, the food you eat or the clothes you wear. They look at the civilization, what type of things we've created, imagined, and built.

"I'm not a pessimist," he clarified. "I hope things will get better. But the first thing we need is freedom, and that we don't have."

Ahmad hoped to eliminate the mental and emotional imprisonment.

"That is the main point of my paintings: to address why we can't express these things," he said, standing next to three of his gory works, including "October 22," which commemorates the massacre. "My work is not finished yet."

For the students of Kashmir's Institute of Music and Fine Arts, the work has just begun.

☐

JAGDISH MEHTA PASSED away in 2016, and the photography studio on the Bund soon followed. Today, Mahatta is a cafe, and the Mehtas' time-capsule photos hang on the walls, drawing curious diners. But the Mehta sons, Dushyant and Hemant, have moved the studio out of Kashmir — another cultural touchstone lost.

☐

Nearly 90, Mahatta Photo Keeps On Clicking

(KO report)

November 11, 2006: On a recent afternoon, a walker down that faded glory of Srinagar, the Bund, dodged hanging power lines, feisty stray dogs, and baksheesh-begging bums. Although overgrown brambles and a rusty chain-link fence obscured the river view, a distinctly sewage-like aroma still wafted over from the mud brown Jhelum below. Despite such deterrents, a local merchant strolled effortlessly down a spruced up memory lane.

"I remember when the Bund was clean and beautiful, so alive with people and full of life," a smiling, white-haired Jagdish Mehta said recently, squinting into bright sunlight from his Bund storefront. "I remember having to put a tie on so I'd look nice, like everyone else. In the evenings everybody was out here walking…Oh, it was lovely."

Like their 21st century counterparts, that bygone era's natty pedestrians would come upon a deep brown wood facade with intricately carved eaves just east of the Polo View shikara stand. "MAHATTA & CO." the signage read, the place for captains and kings.

"All of the British came here," said Jagdish, 63, grandson of the store's founder and proprietor for nearly 40 years. In the back-room studio he pointed out portraits of a white-suited Hari Singh and eagle-eyed Tyndale-Biscoe. "We had viceroys and generals, and of course the Maharaja, too. We were the official state photographer for some time."

Sturdy survivor of an historical roller coaster ride, the Valley's oldest photography shop and studio is an eloquent reminder of what Kashmir has lost in recent decades, and to what it still holds fast. Although other aged photo shops still operate and even flourish, none have survived as long as Mahatta, none ever grew as prominent, and none spawned the love of photography that has inspired four generations of Mehtas to devote their lives to the work, and to rescue bits of a long-vanished Kashmir from oblivion.

It all began when Amarnath Mehta and his younger brother started a little business.

"They opened a humble photography studio in a houseboat on the Jhelum in 1918," said Jagdish. "The clients were predominantly British, and they had difficulty pronouncing Mehta correctly. So Amarnath went instead with Mahatta."

The name stuck, business boomed and after a short-lived move to Lal Chowk, Mahatta Photo settled in the early 1920's into its Bund location, where it continued to flourish. By the late 1930's the brothers operated a miniature photographic empire, with six stores across the area, including outlets in Gulmarg, Pahalgam, and Rawalpindi. Business tailed off with the departure of the British and the Mahatta kingdom retreated to its Bund redoubt.

Today that shop is a place where colors recede as the decades telescope. On top of a black and white checkered floor stand row upon row of wood-accented glass display cases. Dust-covered antique cameras and dark leather carrying cases complement dozens of sepia-toned picture postcards of Kashmir in the middle of the last century.

Like the blown-up landscape and portraiture prints near the ceiling, the postcard photos are the work of Jagdish's father Ram Chand Mehta, whose studio childhood made a deep impression and ultimately altered the legacy of Mahatta.

"Ram Chand made the shop more about Kashmir because of his interest in photography," acknowledged Jagdish.

Wasim Showkat Wani, whose exhibition of hundreds of Valley photos from the past 150 years will go up for public viewing on November 8th at Kashmir Haat, highlighted the value of Ram Chand's photos.

"They mean everything to Kashmir," said Wani, whose show will include over 100 Mehta pictures. "Ram Chand Mehta did something unique – he returned to places where photos had been taken 50-60 years before his time, in the late 19th century, and retook them from the same spot. So you can see how Kashmir has changed over time… how people have changed, how the landscape has changed, how the quality of life has changed."

Like the glorious old Bund, Ram Chand's Kashmir is a relic with which a young Valley resident might be unfamiliar. In parallel flatboats on a glass-like Dal, two fishermen scan the water with cocked spears. A braided, bright-eyed, and jewel-bedecked Gujar girl smiles warmly. As it bends in front of the stark white face of the old palace, shikaras plying its edges, the calm, broad Jhelum conjures Venice. A lone, skull-capped boatman hunts on an empty, sun-dappled Wular Lake, twenty-foot long blunderbuss gun in hand.

Jagdish's son Dushyant, 35, is all too familiar with a very different Kashmir.

"The Bund deteriorated a couple decades ago and from the late 80's to the late 90's there was no business," he said. "The conflict was the problem."

Still, with Dushyant, a documentary filmmaker, and his brother Hemant, 36 and a photographer, the Mehta legacy seems in good hands. The two own and operate one of India's largest online photographic clearinghouses from offices in Delhi. Founded in 2002, India Picture (www.indiapicture.in) boasts a catalogue of 60,000 photos and works with 140 photographers around the country. The website also offers for purchase a large chunk of Ram Chand's Kashmir portfolio.

"We are adding new shots at a rate of 5-7,000 per month and regularly selling to publications abroad and ad agencies in India," said CEO Dushyant. "And we are just opening an office in Bombay."

Like his great grandfather, Dushyant is slowly building a Mehta empire. Both originated at that little shop along the Bund, a burbling photographic spring for over three quarters of a century. And with business picking up in the Valley in the last few years, the younger generation has been considering a return.

"It's always been in the back of our minds to get back to Kashmir but one thing has led to another and the political situation has been a big detriment," Dushyant explained via phone from Delhi. "It's never normal over there, something bad always happens. And the pace of doing things in Kashmir is still sluggish – people are not yet confident, they are getting it back but not fully yet."

Jagdish appeared confident, that the business still coursed through the family blood, that customers would continue to materialize, and that the Bund studio would soldier on.

"Business is okay, so I have no plans to shut it down," he said as he surveyed the store for what might have been the ten thousandth time.

"I'll probably do this as long as I can, as long as I can stay on my feet," he added with a smile before pausing. "What else would I do?"

□

The below ran alongside the article "Kashmiris Close the Book"

The Neglected Glories of SPS Library

November 12, 2006: Making one's way into Srinagar's State Central Library is no easy task. Get through the soldier-manned checkpoint across from the Jhelum River in Rajbagh, stroll past three wooden wagon-wheeled cannons near the museum entrance, hop down a flight of stairs, pop over to your left, climb a few more stairs and – whew! – you are inside Sri Pratap Singh, Kashmir's largest public book repository.

Established by Maharaja Pratap Singh in 1896 as part of the State Museum, the library has seen better days. Yet with attractive new hard-covers lining one wall, the latest newspapers scattered about the long, welcoming reading tables, and warm rays of sunlight filtering through the south-facing windows, the reading room is undeniably pleasant. But continue onward, brave explorer, into either of two almost-identical and identically misused backrooms, which speak volumes about the efficacy and utility of Kashmir's Directorate of Libraries and Research.

"This is an old building; the colors are fading, it needs cleaning," said Chief Librarian Zaheeda Bano as four employees lounged nearby in plastic chairs, chatting in the afternoon sun. "Tell the government to send people; they are not very helpful."

Still, squinting through the darkness and dust, a backroom visitor could be struck dumb by the lush papier-mâché. Deep, sensuous reds, lively blues and greens and bright shining whites mingle in gorgeous swirling patterns. Long, flowery shapes dance around arched doorways and window sills, shimmy up the walls and toward the ceiling, where new shapes and patterns emerge. The drawings cover every inch of the 20-foot high space: a rich and immersive design experience and a potent illustration of Kashmir's dwindling artistic heritage.

Over a century later the colors remain vibrant, but much of the work has been obscured by dirt and grime, run-ins with various pieces of furniture, and perhaps most damagingly, the ravages of time and neglect. Yet even if these artistic treasures had been taken care of, one would be hard pressed to enjoy them. Bulky wooden bookcases topped with four to five-foot stacks of newspapers, large desks and filing cabinets, cardboard boxes and stacks of folders, mop buckets and various other tools and supplies block the walls from view.

Masood Hussain, an instructor at the Institute of Music and Fine Arts, highlighted the appeal of the papier-mâché work yet was not surprised about its neglect.

"It's good, very nice workmanship," said Hussain, adding that the work reminded him of beautiful centuries-old papier-mache works in Zadibal and Shalimar that had recently been lost. He realized that the same thing might happen to these works if the new SPS Library were ever built. [The foundation stone was laid in early 2004 but due to financial difficulties constructing never began, as detailed in Kashmiris Close the Book.] "Who is going to take care of this?"

Hussain considered having his students pitch in to maintain and restore the walls.

"They could do that, sure, but who is going to take the initiative?" he wondered, dubious of winning approval from the Archives Department. "Nobody really bothers about these things; it is definitely being neglected."

Dr. S.M. Fazlullah, Director of Libraries, disagreed.

"These are not being neglected," he said. "Owing to bad circumstances in the state, militancy and other things, and circulation was so bad and things were disturbing, we have not been able to renovate everything, things have gone down in the libraries, but now we are picking things up again."

Traffic in the backrooms of SPS has not picked up at all, so these hidden riches go unappreciated as another fragment of Kashmir's cultural legacy is lost to governmental and popular inertia.

"There are a lot of monuments in Kashmir and they've destroyed everything," said Hussain. "They are not aware of these things. Everything is vanishing."

□

Liberation from the Inside Out

(KO report)

May 15, 2007: The inaugural International Film Festival of Kashmir unspooled at Tagore Hall this past weekend. Screening more than a dozen features, documentaries, and shorts from a handful of countries over three days, the Experimental Moving Image and Theatre Association (XMITA) event was a godsend for local cinephiles and an opportunity for one and all to experience varied and valuable points of view.

Despite a turnout hamstrung by the weekend's political rallies and traffic jams, and technical glitches that marred early screenings, the mood was upbeat.

"This is just the first one," said festival organizer Aarshad Mushtaq, a local filmmaker and theatre director. "We plan to do this every year, and hopefully each one will be bigger and better than the last."

Many of the films commented directly or indirectly on the conflict in Kashmir. *Temporary Loss of Consciousness*, a short by Monica Bhasin, analyzed the legacy of Partition, while Anand Patwardhan's two-part *Father, Son, and Holy War* dissected communalism through the efforts of India's majority Hindu community to launch a baby boom as a means to overwhelm Indian Muslims. *Paradise on a River of Hell*, by Abir Bazaz and Meenu Gaur, shined a light on the havoc and destruction wrought by the violent struggle in Kashmir.

Amidst the rabble, one gem gleamed: *Amandla*, a feature-length documentary from Lee Hirsch. The sleek, professionally-made film reveals how Black South Africans used enduring traditions of music and dance as primary tools in their decades-long struggle for freedom. In doing so, the film celebrates the indomitable nature of the human spirit and highlights an ingenious undermining of an oppressive regime.

Apartheid, the social and political system in which an elected white Afrikaaner government segregated and subjugated black South Africans, began officially in 1948. A charismatic black leader named Vuyisile Mini emerged soon after: political figure, actor, poet, composer and singer, he spread the message of the freedom movement through song. His most lasting tune was "Look out, Verwoerd," which warned Hendrik Frensch Verwoerd, known as the "architect of apartheid" and South Africa's prime minister from 1958 to his assassination in 1966, that the blacks were coming to get him.

Buoyed by an endemic song-and-dance culture, Mini sparked a trend that came to define the black South African movement. Starting in the mid-70's, Radio Freedom, the propaganda wing of the pro-black freedom African National Conference, brought the songs, ideas, and energies of the movement to a large and hungry audience, even as its propagators courted arrest. As the years passed and the suffering deepened, no rally, protest march, funeral, or public gathering would pass without group singing of freedom songs old and new.

"I want to join your revolution!" renowned American jazz musician Dizzy Gillespie is said to have told one of the better-known South African musicians in the 1960's. "Everybody's always singing and dancing."

This movement expressed in song succeeded mainly for two reasons. Firstly, group song and dance is inherently appealing, with pleasing rhythms and smiling faces, and was thus allowed and even supported by the authorities. Second, the songs were written and sung in a language — predominantly Zulu — unfamiliar to the oppressors, and thus went unnoticed for years. Celebrating life as it denounced oppression, the music encapsulated a quest for freedom even as it freed a people.

"It wasn't liberation music," explains Abdullah Ibrahim, a musician, composer and activist forced into exile for almost 30 years. "It was a part of liberating ourselves."

In the last couple decades Kashmiris have failed to do the same. Admittedly, Kashmiris are not a people that breaks into song or dance at the drop of a hat. But Kashmiri history does include cultural touchstones capable of serving a similar purpose. Sufiana is the most analogous musical form, mournful and spiritual; Kashmiris have embraced its soothing tones for centuries. It also represents a form relatively unfamiliar to their oppressors.

An even better alternative might be bhand pather, a respected yet slowly dying dramatic art. Alternatively comic and pathos-filled, pather is perfectly tailored for expressing, exaggerating, and satirizing oppression, and in fact many of the traditional tales make light of or point up Kashmiri suffering at the hands of various historical tormentors. This artform could have been dusted off and polished for a new era, used in the service of a new and more intense struggle. Instead, most outspoken Kashmiris embraced victimhood, and when independence seemed nigh, turned to violence.

[Black South Africans also took up the gun, in the 1980's, and experienced the most violent period of their struggle as a result. But as an underground movement it was never widely embraced. Also, no "friendly" neighbor offered a helping hand.]

The road to freedom has been a long, torturous and winding one for Kashmiris, but it seems the long-suffering people of the Valley have finally set aside the gun. On top of a considerable decline in violence and militancy of late, recent signs suggest Kashmiris are beginning to liberate themselves, as Mr. Ibrahim put it.

Plays about disappearances and fake encounter killings have been well-received, a major screening of a lively pro-people film drew an animated crowd, and a Kashmiri-authored graphic novel about militancy has put the plight of Kashmiris in a vibrant and easily-digestible form.

Could it be too little too late? It's never too late to end needless self-destruction, but maybe Kashmiris have grown too comfortable with their sorrow.

"When we left the gravesites after a funeral we didn't weep," a South African freedom fighter says in the film. "We sang, because if you mourn for too long you start to lose hope."

Kashmiris have made mourning and victimhood a defining trait, thus rendering legitimate liberation antithetical to their way of life. Let's hope recent developments herald the birth of a new movement, one that finally brings true Amandla (power) to the people of Kashmir.

□

Artists flesh out Kashmiri torment

(KO report)

0In earth-toned oils a small, proud Kohi Sulaiman loomed over Srinagar with a deep red oval hovering nearby.

"That represents the situation in Kashmir through the state of the Dal," said Iftikhar Jaffar, an instructor at the Academy of Music and Fine Arts in Rajbagh, gesturing towards the oblong maroon moon in his painting. "All the blood; it's not just militants' or civilians' or security's, but all of humanity is bleeding, and it's flowing into the lake."

The suffering in Kashmir was the unspoken theme of an Art Festival held at the new Kala Kendra complex in Jammu last week. Forty-three artists from across India gathered in the winter capital's gleaming new gallery space to celebrate self-expression and comment on the bonds within Kashmir and between the state and the rest of the nation.

"This festival is intended to stretch a cultural fabric from the Centre to J&K State," said Dr. Sudhakar Sharma, Secretary of Lalit Kala Academy, New Delhi, which organized the event in conjunction with the J&K Academy of Arts, Culture, and Languages.

The largest artists' gathering in state history was originally slated for Srinagar last summer but a surge in violence forced organizers to reschedule and relocate. Although announced guests Chief Minister

Ghulam Nabi Azad and Governor S.K. Sinha did not attend, the festival, in which the artists were given six days to create two new works to be displayed on the final day, was widely viewed as a success.

"We would love to do another one in the future," said Sharma.

Some images from a stroll through the crowded grounds during Thursday's celebration: sad feminine eyes peer from a niqab, the only visible human features of a sculpture in douri stone; the face of a bright green man is blotted out by newspaper clippings of killings in Kashmir; blue-faced, half-veiled women shut their eyes to the world in two vibrant oil paintings nearby.

"I had Mary in mind when I was doing this," said Razia Tony, a teacher at Stella Morris College in Chennai and the painter of the blue women. "But then I realized that all suffering, all sorrow is the same, so I thought I'd do a series on Kashmiri women."

Akram Khan, from Reasi in Jammu province, said he has painted many images of the conflict but for the festival he depicted communal harmony.

"Although the sky is one," he said with a shy smile, "religion is many."

Not all of the works were connected to the struggle in the Valley. Anil Kumar Sinha, a painter from rural Bihar, painted a grinning, greedy-eyed man attempting to seduce an anxious, shapely young woman, a common scene in the tribal villages of his home.

"He's flirting with her," explained Sinha, looking over his work. "But she's innocent, doesn't know about the outside world."

A day before the opening, Rohit Verma dabbed lime green to his painting of a naked-woman floating over a geometrically-designed river.

"It is not reality," the Jammu Academy student reminded an observer. "It is a flight of the imagination."

Prakash Bhise came from Mumbai and presented warm, abstract works.

"They want a story, but I don't like that," he said. "I prefer something different — go with my inner flow."

For some Kashmiris that flow was considerably less pleasant.

Srinagar resident Mohammad Iqbal, the sculptor of the woman in the niqab, was the last to pick up his participatory scarf at Thursday's reception ceremony. When he accepted his tassled reward he did not smile. He nodded his head, returned to his seat, and stared toward the stage expressionless.

"They are not safe on their side and we are not safe on ours," said Aftab Ahmad, an Academy colleague of Jaffar and Iqbal, referring to his impressionistic work Insecure Fencing. "After 17 years of this it's gotten inside us all."

□

Chapter 7

Ravaged Infrastructure

"Anarchy is the stepping stone to absolute power."

— **Napoleon Bonaparte**[156]

INDIA HAS LONG sought to encourage development in Kashmir — its stated reason for the revocation of Article 370 — but a stunning lack of infrastructure has long hampered the growth of tourism and the broader economy. The road from Srinagar to Leh via Kargil and the Zojila Pass could serve as Exhibit A. Since ancient times, this artery has provided Kashmir a crucial link to the Silk Road and points east. Kashmiri scholars trod this path to bring Buddhism to Tibet. A millennium later Mir Sayyid Ali Hamadani went to Central Asia via Ladakh and brought artisans and scholars back to Kashmir.

In modern times, in contrast, National Highway 1A has mostly been a major obstacle. This 434-kilometer stretch represents an economic lifeline for the remote Ladakh region, which has only one other road connection, from Manali. Yet it is stunningly unsuited to the demands of 21st century transport. Officials will tell you that heavy winter snowfall at Zojila (3.528-meter altitude, or 11,575 ft) means the Kashmir-Ladakh link is open for just six months of the year. But nowadays, thanks to climate change, it's often much longer than that.[157] At its most twisty high-altitude sections, overloaded 18-wheelers and tourist buses make glacial progress. During the rainy summer season, landslides are frequent. Countless vehicles have plunged over the edge, which is why the Srinagar-Leh highway ranks among the world's most dangerous roads.[158]

For decades, locals and officials talked of repairing the road or even building a tunnel to enable year-round trade and transport. The insurgency had long put this on the back burner. But in 2018, Delhi announced plans for a two-lane, 14-kilometer tunnel from Sonmarg to Dras, in Kargil, that would skip Zojila and cut the drive time on that section from three hours to 15 minutes.[159] When work on the tunnel began in October 2020, the government acknowledged that the nearly $1 billion project was a response to "30 years of overwhelming demand" and that its completion, expected in 2025, would be a "landmark achievement" for India.[160]

The government also acknowledged that the tunnel is partially about national defense. New Delhi is surely responding to Beijing's Belt and Road Initiative investments in Pakistani-controlled Kashmir, which include an $8 billion dam in Gilgit-Baltistan and $4 billion in hydroelectricity projects along the Jhelum River.[161] China also plans to build a modern roadway from deep in Pakistani-occupied Kashmir to the Karakoram Highway, which runs to Islamabad.[162] Such Chinese investments increase the security threat to Indian-held Kashmir and fly in the face of India's long-standing goal of unifying all of Kashmir. That vision also includes China-controlled Aksai Chin, which borders Ladakh to the east. In mid-2020, at least 20 Indian soldiers were killed as Chinese and Indian forces clashed at multiple spots along the Line of Actual Control — the first deadly gun battle along this shared border in decades.[163]

Thus, the Zojila tunnel, which should put an end to bus journeys like the one I recount below, may be India's way of making its technologically advanced presence felt in an area encroached upon by two closely-aligned, nuclear-armed neighbors.

◻

Repair the Road Far Too Well Traveled

(KO report)

August 19, 2006: Last week I slipped out of Srinagar for the Independence Day lockdown and made a visit to Leh, where the stupas and international tourists are thick on the ground and the soldiers considerably less invasive. Eschewing the flight as well as my colleague's suggestion of a Sumo, I was by the next morning comfortably ensconced in the rear seat of a JKTDC Super Deluxe bus, ready for an extended pastoral passage.

Yet less than two hours later an irksome sensation arose in my nether regions, and, looking askance at my seat, my neighbors, and the road, I found the last to be at fault. We had been bouncing over grapefruit-sized rocks, into ankle-deep ruts, and through wheelbarrow-sized potholes for what seemed like eons. The burn was making headway and we still had 18 driving hours to our destination. Add to this the hundreds of hair-raising switchbacks edging thousand-foot sheer drops, unexplained stoppages of up to an hour, and Sahara-like stretches near Zoji-La and Lamayuru, where kicked-up sand swirled, stinging eyes, noses, and mouths, and you have the makings for a very long trip.

Our progress was glacial and, jostled among my fellow passengers, I slid out at Kargil some thirteen hours after departure like a martini out of a cocktail shaker. The announcement that all were to reconvene for a 5 a.m. departure the next morning was greeted with groans and glares. By the following evening, after another, similarly turbulent leg, several of us weary travelers agreed, "Never again."

All of which came painfully rushing back this week as word spread that the Shri Amarnath Shrine Board, led by Governor A.K. Sinha, had bypassed state laws and begun work on a macadamized road from Baltal to the Amarnath Cave. Everything must be done to attend to the needs of the lakhs of summer pilgrims, the board apparently surmised, and, unimpeded by previous legislative measures blocking the development, proceeded to finagle financing from the Central Road

Fund without ministerial approval. The countless Hindu tourists who visit the Kashmir Valley on pilgrimages to their beloved shrine should certainly be considered regarding development in that area, and the Baltal to Amarnath passage could undoubtedly stand some sprucing, especially if a smoother, safer road could save some of the over 40 yatri lives lost to the wintry conditions this year.

The construction of such a road, however, would be both an ecological disaster and of dubious value. Roads laid in similarly mountainous and tenuous ecosystems – such as the Banihal cart road and Pahalgam to Chandwari road – have adversely affected breeding, herding, hunting and migration grounds for a variety of large valley mammals and led to landslides and untold accidents, according to local experts. Further, the Baltal to Amarnath road would cut directly through a wildlife refuge. PDP General Secretary Tariq Hamid Qarra should thus be thanked for discovering and stamping out the Amarnath road construction on the grounds of ecological impropriety, and these suddenly unattached funds should be earmarked post-haste for the state's great highway disaster.

"It's a stupid decision to carve out road through a wilderness area," said Javed Ahmad, managing secretary of the Sumo Taxi Stand on Residency Road. "Instead the government should concentrate on the renovation of damaged roads, such as Srinagar-Kargil-Leh Highway."

The lone route connecting Srinagar, the state's most populous city, in the center of the Kashmir Valley, and Leh, the state's most popular tourist destination, towards the far eastern end of Ladakh, has undergone practically every form of natural and manmade torment since it was first paved some 50 years ago. From driving snow, hail, rain, and sandstorms, to voluminous flooding, jarring earthquakes and great mudslides, and from an endless stream of ten-ton trucks and overloaded passenger buses to constant herds of goat, sheep, and other mountain keep. The beating has taken a great toll, and where there once was once pavement now stretches mile upon mile of large, sharp rocks, concavities that could swallow hangul, and treacherous hills of shifty sand. To top it all off, the sadistic engineer that designed this integral J&K artery made space for only one, peril-fraught lane.

"The road to Leh is a single-lane all the way, resulting in very close calls and frustrating traffic jams for hours together," said Sumo driver Mohammad Ashraf Bhat, who plies the road regularly. "Besides, due to the heavy movement of army vehicles, the situation turns more chaotic the moment you're stuck in the jam."

Indeed, a driver able to deliver his cargo safe and sound from one end to the other deserves commendation, if not a psychological assessment.

Yet the problem is not just one of safety or mental well-being; the road is a key shipping route, a primary tourist passage and one of the more frequent hosts of military convoys, as Bhat can surely attest. During the four summer months it is open, the Srinagar-Leh road sees a steady stream of trucks, buses, jeeps, and cars, most filled to bursting with soldiers, commercial goods, out-of-state visitors, and state employees, and were it to be spruced up, the benefits would be manifold. The economy of J&K's northern regions, which rely heavily on the route, would be vastly improved. Travel times could be cut in half, cutting down on fuel and wages outlay and improving regional trade. For the Indian army, a more pliable road would mean less time in transport and more in training and improved response times in getting soldiers to various locations as needed. Communications and commerce between the famously distant regions of Kashmir, Kargil, and Ladakh would be vastly improved, simplifying state operations and coordinating various overlapping industries. Last but not least, this road cuts through varied and spectacular mountain scenery, and, were there actual pavement and some semblance of safety, it could very easily be remade into one of the great scenic rides of India, if not all of Asia, attracting tens of thousands of sightseers each year for its breathtaking mountainscapes, bringing additional untold crores into local coffers. Thus, the investment would be returned in spades.

"The road is in pretty rough shape," acknowledged taxi driver Ghulam Jeelani, who frequently ferries foreigners along the route. "Fixing up the Srinagar-Leh highway should be a top priority."

Because it would be in the interests of all – residents of the Kashmir Valley, Kargil, and Ladakh, tourists, area businessmen, crafts workers, drivers, state bean counters, and the Central government – and because a mountain road should inspire anticipation and awe, not all-consuming fear and debilitating body aches, the Srinagar-Leh highway must be fixed, the sooner the better.

□

AS OF LATE 2022, Kashmir had seen 415 internet shutdowns since 2013 — more than quadruple any other Indian territory in this period — with most occurring in the past five years, according to the leading online monitor.[164]

Electricity cuts are also more chronic today, and longer lasting, than they were in my time in Kashmir. This is particularly true during the frigid winters, when demand goes up due to increased demand for heat and light.[165]

□

Power outage: Dancer in the Dark

(KO report)

August 6, 2006: Power outages are common throughout India, some due to weak or faulty lines, some scheduled as a means to control overall demand, and still others due to acts of nature or negligence. As a result, most Indians have learned to take such small hurdles in stride. No shrieks of terror or cursing at unseen demons – mostly they continue with what they were doing, provided it does not involve the use of electrical devices, confident the nuisance will be remedied in good time.

I recently had a chance to witness this sang-froid firsthand. I was interviewing Ajaz Rasool, the Superintending Engineer for the efforts to preserve and conserve Dal Lake (LAWDA), in the tiny sitting room of the *Kashmir Observer* offices. We sat on opposite sides of a small wooden table, upon which we had been served tea. Two feet to my left were three windows thrown open to the dark and fresh Srinagar night and the mountains beyond, where a thunderstorm was brewing.

A bronzed and hefty Kashmiri, Rasool is able to talk at length on various technical minutiae. After about an hour of his verbiage I was finally able to ask him why, if LAWDA had been doing all of this great work he'd been recounting, had the High Court come down so hard in its ruling the previous week?

"I'll tell you what happened there," he responded sharply, winding up for another long delivery as rain began tapping at the window. "They were saying that we'd only done part of the job. You see Dal Lake..." and then the power went off without warning. I blinked and looked up at the ceiling and started to apologize, but he went on undeterred, "...is a shallow lake, and it has its own species of flora and fauna. There are so many varieties here that..."

I could not see six inches from my face, except when the lightning flashed, and this government official is sitting four feet away from me talking as if we're under a sparkling noontime sky. "As a result, we have prolific growth of weeds and various reeds and other beds of various sorts..."

I smiled and almost giggled: how could I take notes?[166] Now the storm has blown closer, the wind is whipping in through the open window and the lightning flashing every few seconds, lighting up his face and his hands, which he is employing as a complementary communicative tool, and his eyeglasses, which reflect my stunned face and the wondrously ridiculous scene back at me. Still he takes no note, on and on he continues...

"And this growth creates a sea of aquatic fauna, so thick that it blocks the light of the sun and slows photosynthesis." To a neophyte this seemed a contradiction, but there's no way I was about to interrupt. "The reed belt in the northern part of the lake can just get out of control, and that's why we have reed management, which is very difficult, and delicate."

By now my eyes had adjusted somewhat and I could see just how much he was using his hands to carry his shovel-fulls of BS across the small wooden table and into my field of vision, my notebook, and hopefully my article. His arms moving up and down, over his head and between his legs to accentuate points and possibly wave planes into their assigned gates at Sher-e-Kashmir airport ten kilometers away.

"Just because the judge cannot see any difference in the underwater growth above the surface," – the lights flickered on again — "doesn't mean we're not making any headway."

Rasool leaned back and smiled broadly, pleased not only with his finely calibrated performance, evincing as it did his mastery over both the inadequacies of man and the power of nature, but also with that final punctuation mark, a viable defense for millions of souls trying to prove they're accomplishing something, anything, yet lack sufficient evidence.

□

This Page Can't Be Displayed

(KO report)

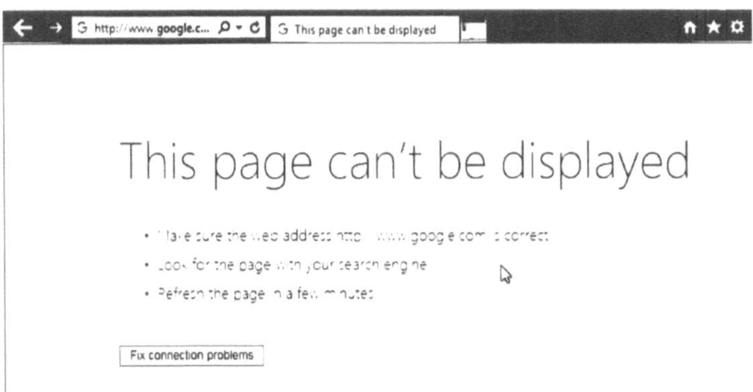

April 6, 2007: There's no point denying it: the above is my favorite webpage. It's the first site I visit when I get up in the morning and the last page I peep at night. It's my email service, my news update, and my online store, even my chill out and entertainment hotspot. Rarely do five browsing minutes pass without a visit to PCBD, as I like to call it, and I regularly linger for an hour or more. Without this page I wouldn't have much of an Internet at all, in fact, and therein lays the rub.

I'm a journalist, and my work requires reliable access to the Internet, preferably a version with more than one mind-numbing page. Reporting a worthwhile story demands considerable research – familiarization with related issues and an update of the latest developments across the region, even the world. Without online inputs my work is little better than the average citizen's daily observations. Nothing against the average Javed or Joe, but a respectable journalist should offer something more, a little added value. Sans Web I'm a baker without flour; I could whip something up but it's unlikely to satisfy.

So among my myriad concerns when I moved to Srinagar about ten months ago was what sort of archaic Internet access might be available in such a remote, under-developed Himalayan valley. Semaphore and smoke signals came to mind, but I was pleasantly surprised to learn of General Packet Radio Service (GPRS), a deal offered by the government-run communications network that allows the subscriber to use a mobile phone to connect to the Internet via Bluetooth. My employer signed me up and pretty soon I was wading hip-deep into the information ocean wherever and whenever, from home, from the office, even from a cozy tourist hut in Gulmarg.

But after a few months the service turned unreliable. Once or twice a week I couldn't connect at all, for a few hours or even a couple days. And more often than not I was able to connect but the link would be practically nonexistent, as if some fool were attempting to shove a crystal ball through a kitchen funnel. From the narrow end I could discern distant, shimmering glimpses of infinity, but no hard evidence was forthcoming (it was around this time that PCBD and I started getting intimate). As a result I was mostly unable to check my email without visiting the Internet café – and even there the connection was unpredictable: down for a day; up for two; then down again. As the winter leaned into its stretch run my favorite news sites – the *New York Times*, BBC, *the Hindu*, et al – were regularly reduced to mirage and catching up with friends and family and trolling for freelance gigs became nigh impossible.

Thus I slowly lost touch, which many Kashmiris would argue is the very intent of the Indian government. In fact, there is a good reason the Centre controls communications services: money. But in the disputed state of Kashmir there is also a second justification: control. The poor Internet connectivity of the Valley is analogous to the occasional passability of the Jammu-Srinagar National Highway, famously called Kashmir's only link to the outside world and frequently in disrepair. From February 1st to March 25th the road was open a total of 10 days, and for the entirety of winter the link was passable for just over 40 days. For much of the cold season tens of thousands of locals were stranded in Jammu, along with various supplies and vital food stuffs such as eggs, mutton, chicken, milk and vegetables. Kashmiris also face unreliable mobile phone networks; area mobile users seethed last week as networks crashed and calls and SMS's failed.

Kashmir's virtual and physical links to the world beyond the Valley, then, remain tenuous, even as India soars into the 21st century. But unlike some of my friends and co-workers I can't with any certainty say these failures have been foisted upon us by design. Call me a skeptic, but I think it overestimates the managerial skills of Indian bureaucrats and politicians to believe them capable of scheming to keep our road and Web connections unreliable and then actually executing the plan to perfection. After all, it took the Centre around three decades to realize that Sheikh Abdullah was doing his damnedest to be on their side. That lethargic, oft-corrupt administrators are simply unable to maintain reliable connections is a great deal more believable. Poor infrastructure probably plays a part. Perhaps incompetent or ill-trained employees. A lack of governmental know-how and support, too.

Two BSNL employees offered conflicting theories.

"I myself have been dealing with problems, too" admitted Anwar, my neighborhood GPRS troubleshooter. "It's because the routing is not correct – the information has to come here and then to Jammu and then back to Srinagar."

A higher-up was slightly more convincing.

"We have had media problems the last few months," admitted one Mr. Daeshmu, GPRS supervisor for BSNL. "There was an optical cable breakdown between Jammu and Kashmir, and now with weather difficulties and landslides and all that the problems have become more frequent."

Not being able to catch up on the latest from the US' war on terror or scan the scores from the Cricket World Cup is no great tragedy. And toughened by decades, even centuries of oppression, Kashmiris can easily go a fortnight without an omelet.

But they've had their whole lives to become acclimatized to inconsistencies and unreliability. More importantly, even when the Net is off limits and the highway blocked they have their friends and family close at hand, not to mention all the signposts of home. I've left my habits and loved ones behind to move halfway around the world, where the Web serves as ballast. Indeed, Daeshmu now represents one of my most consistent and positive human relationships in Kashmir: I call or text him to plead or complain; he replies in comforting tones; and shortly thereafter my quality of life improves, for a time.

Still, I've been wedded to a zippy, limitless 'Net for the past four or five years, and now when I'm most in need of its various uses I regularly find myself untethered. My work has suffered and my morale drooped, which subsequently leads to even poorer work.

In the time it took me to write this piece I've tried to open a Gmail from my girlfriend nearly a two dozen times. The message is unlikely to contain anything earth-shattering but still I like to think each word she sends is precious. I've clicked the link and hit "Refresh." I've disconnected, reconnected, and screamed at the screen – all to no avail. On another browser my favorite webpage is taunting me with broken promises and vast emptiness.

I ring my new pal to get the lowdown. After again blaming the damaged cable he offers an optimistic big picture perspective.

"The traffic has increased in the last couple of months," Daeshmu confides. "We are expanding our sites and after one month or so it will be better."

I grumble, hang up, and cross my fingers. And then I realize: one month from now is precisely when the government will move back to Srinagar for the summer.

Chapter 8

Endless Violations

"In this world, shipmates, sin that pays its way can travel freely and without a passport; whereas Virtue, if a pauper, is stopped at all frontiers."

— Herman Melville[167]

"Truth never damages a cause that is just."

— Gandhi[168]

EN ROUTE TO Kashgar with a sizable caravan, British adventurer William Moorcroft visited Kashmir under Dogra rule in the early 19th century and noted how little value was attributed to the lives of locals, most of whom were Muslim.

"The murder of a native by a Sikh is punished by a fine to the government, of from sixteen to twenty rupees, of which four rupees are paid to the family of the deceased if a Hindu, and two rupees if he was a Mohammedan," he wrote in 1822, adding that such murders appeared rather common. "The body of a stout young man, whose throat had been cut, was lying close to the road on one part of this day's journey, and the only notice taken of it was by Mardan Ali, the Malik ["leader"], who ordered it to be covered with grass, that our porters not be frightened at the sight. Three other bodies were met with on the route."[169]

Kashmiri lives today seem to hold about the same value for India. Actually, 21st-century Kashmiris are more valuable dead. Since the early days of the insurgency, Indian security forces have offered their cadre a sizable financial reward for each Kashmiri militant killed. This policy has prodded more Machiavellian Indian troops to kidnap two or three innocuous Kashmiri men, kill them and then claim the "terrorists" had been killed in a shoot-out. An incident of this sort has happened every 4-5 months for the past quarter-century in Kashmir. In every conflict there will be chaos, and civilians sometimes pay the price. But the fact that one after another innocent Kashmiri is getting mowed down by the very people paid to protect them — who are then rewarded for their deceit — seems the ultimate dereliction of duty.

In July 2020, Indian army troops kidnapped and killed three Kashmiri laborers, planted weapons on them, stripped them of their identities and transformed them into terrorists. The army captain in the case has been charged with murder, kidnapping and conspiracy, and as of mid-2022 faced a possible court martial.[170] Most fake encounter cases, as they are known, never get anywhere near a court. In the rare cases when bodies are found, they tend to be burned beyond recognition. In the event that there is a court case, the decision tends to favor New Delhi. Indian security force members are rarely convicted of any crime and victims' families are often given hush money by the state, maybe 200,000 rupees. These funds are often rejected as "blood money," but they do represent a sizable improvement on two rupees.

□

Blame the System, Not the Sucker

(KO report)

February 06, 2007: Zero tolerance. It's a phrase Kashmiris have heard a great deal in the past couple of years. A promise of behavioral discipline on the part of Indian armed forces in Kashmir, made first by Chief Minister Ghulam Nabi Azad when he assumed his post in late 2005, and again six months later by Prime Minister Manmohan Singh.

They swore "zero tolerance for custodial deaths." But what is zero tolerance, exactly? What does it mean, in practice, in reality? Recent events demand we take a closer look.

Last week a routine Ganderbal police investigation uncovered a falsified encounter with militants that ended in the killing of Abdul Rahman Padder, a 35-year-old Kokernag carpenter who made the fatal mistake of trusting Farooq Ahmad Padder, his ostensible friend and a low-level SOG officer. In early December Farooq Ahmad, finding himself in possession of a cache of seized militant weapons, called Abdul Rahman in Batmaloo and told him to wait for him; apparently he had told his acquaintance that he could pay back the Rs 75,000 he had accepted from Rahman as pay for finding the carpenter a job. Instead, he snatched him up and brutally killed him, then hurriedly buried the young father and offered his superiors a few previously seized weapons as proof of his victim's (falsified) militancy.

Without any questioning or investigation, Farooq Ahmad and his fellow constable were immediately awarded Rs 1.2 lakhs each for the killing of an enemy of the state. Despite the fact that they had almost zero evidence to support their claim and that they had in truth committed pre-meditated murder on an innocent, law-abiding Kashmiri, a crime for which any one of us would be condemned and punished with the full force of the law, these two officers were rewarded handsomely. In the ensuing days, similar incidents were revealed. On Friday, the victim of another such encounter – a perfume seller that had gone missing a year ago from Lal Chowk – was exhumed and identified by his wife, and on Saturday three more victims of fake encounter killings were dug up. This is not zero tolerance, nor is it an isolated incident; this is a deeply flawed system.

As details of these horror stories spread the Valley has seethed, even as Chief Minister Ghulam Nabi Azad denounced the Ganderbal incident and called for a judicial inquiry into the Padder killing. Meanwhile, frustrated Kashmiris turned bloodthirsty; thousands of angry locals have attended the disinterments, throwing stones at military personnel and demanding that the guilty parties be hanged.

Indeed, it is all too easy to focus our rage and frustration on Farooq Ahmad and the other officers. If, as it appears, he was the mastermind of the gruesome and unjust slaying of Abdul Rahman, he is a liar and a murderer and a traitor to his own people, deserving of neither forgiveness nor sympathy. Yet Farooq Ahmad is no more than a sucker, a warped Manchurian candidate and the product of a demented security apparatus that degrades human life – Kashmiri lives, to be specific – to the point of negation. For Indian security personnel the line between good and bad Kashmiri was blurred long ago, ever since several soldiers opened fire on protesting civilians in Bijbehara in 1993, or even earlier. Under the Armed Forces Special Powers and Disturbed Areas Acts Indian forces have been killing Kashmiris on mere suspicion for nearly two decades, receiving not punishment but rewards and promotions as a result. According to a respected international rights group that released a detailed study of abuses in Kashmir late last year, such practices have become embedded in the culture of Indian security.

"Police and army officials have told Human Rights Watch that security forces often execute alleged militants instead of bringing them to trial," HRW wrote recently. "Most of those summarily executed are falsely reported to have died during armed clashes between the army and militants in 'encounter killings.' This is done with the knowledge of superior officers and has led to a culture where security forces feel they can murder persons in their custody for rewards and promotions."

Indeed, in September 2003 Abdul Hamid Gani was killed by officers of this same department – the Ganderbal SOG – because of a debt owed to an SOG officer by his brother Rashid. Afterwards, the perpetrators forced a local dentist untrained in autopsy to sign papers claiming the death had occurred in a gun-battle. A subsequent professional examination revealed torture and pointed towards a custodial killing, but over three years later no charges have been filed and the accused officers still hold the same jobs.

"'These people are like trained killer dogs,'" one senior police official told Human Rights Watch, referring to the SOG. "'Once unleashed, it is difficult to keep them in check.'"

So is it any wonder that Farooq Ahmad killed Abdul Rahman, and that fake encounters and custodial killings continue to occur with regularity? The Indian armed forces put the carrot out there long ago, for all to see. All Farooq Ahmad did was reach out and take a bite.

For his part, CM Azad has altered his tune, saying Thursday that the insurgency made maintaining zero level of human rights violations difficult. He then underscored his argument by pointing out the inability of the all-powerful U.S.A. to eradicate human rights violations in Iraq.

Although weak-kneed and incomplete, his point is well-made. With some 7 lakh security personnel patrolling the state, there will inevitably be some mistakes, some of which will be fatal violations of human rights. It's unfortunate, but it's also the nature of imperfect man; no matter how vigilant the Indian government, keeping watch over every soldier every hour of the day is simply not possible.

Keeping this in mind, then, why not take the next step? Since individual soldiers can never be completely controlled, the system itself must be changed. Soldiers should not be rewarded for murdering Indian citizens, for instance, nor should they be able to kill, arrest, and harass with impunity. Not only because it is morally and socially wrong, but because these practices foster the very cycle of violence they are meant to stamp out; fake encounters and unjust custodial killings inspire Kashmiris to turn militant, precipitating further battles and Indian army deaths, thus justifying future rights violations by Indian security personnel, and so on.

Even so, the news from Kashmir had until recently been quite good. Both violence and militancy have decreased markedly; Indian armed forces have acknowledged a drop in cross-border infiltration in the past year, and the 2006 death count was about 1000, the lowest total since the conflict began in 1990 and just over one-fifth of the total killed as recently as 2001. Moderate APHC President *Mirwaiz* Omar Farooq called last month for an end to the violence, claiming the militants "have not achieved anything other than creating more graveyards." This week he urged the *mujahideen* to call for a "unilateral ceasefire" as a means to put the pressure on India. Coming from the leader of a separatist party, these are meaningful and unprecedented statements, signaling a potential sea change in Kashmiri sentiment vis-à-vis India. And on Friday Pakistani President Pervez Musharraf said that those who believed in using the gun to settle the Kashmir dispute "cannot be taken on board" in resolving it. Clearly, the political climate in Kashmir is changing for the better, and if the Central Government wants to foster any semblance of goodwill in the local populace it should alter its policies to reflect this cooling of hostilities.

And here, right on cue, is the perfect opportunity for Azad and Singh to keep their promise: a case – or several, apparently – in which, by all appearances, human rights were violated and a horribly unlawful custodial death was the result. The evidence seems clear: Farooq Ahmad's number on Abdul Rahman's mobile phone in the days and hours leading up to his early December disappearance; a quickie burial; and false claims of Pakistani origin and armed militancy. How should they proceed? Get the DNA results, investigate the crime with an open and transparent judicial inquiry, and, if the findings merit it, punish the perpetrators of these crimes: put them on trial and send them to prison or death, whatever is deemed appropriate. Saturday's arrests, of the SSP Ganderbal and the Deputy Superintendent of Police Operations, were undoubtedly encouraging signs.

But more importantly, revamp the system. Zero tolerance is not just a penalty to be meted out after the fact; it is as much about prevention as punishment. The culture of operating above the law, of killing Kashmiris for reward, must be altered. The Central Government must use its security apparatus to display its intolerance towards these offences and violations, towards unlawful kidnappings, abuse, and custodial killings. In light of a less violent, more diplomatically engaged political climate in Kashmir, the Centre should be capable of making concessions to Kashmiris, who have for a generation suffered grave losses and been understandably unsure of their loyalties. End the black laws. Disband the unruly Special Operations Group. If rewards must be handed out, they should be offered only when foreign rebels are killed on Indian territory and after concrete proof – more than mere weapons – has been confirmed.

For until zero tolerance is actually enforced – until the state-sponsored perpetrators of these vile acts face justice and the Indian security forces' contemptible culture of falsifying killings and rewarding murder is eliminated – peace in Kashmir will be no more real than the militancy of Kokernag carpenter Abdul Rahman Padder, may he rest in peace.

□

Once Again Justice Prepares For Its Vanishing Act

(KO report)

April 1, 2007: Chief Minister Ghulam Nabi Azad stepped to a podium in South Kashmir's Kulgam town this past week and swaddled a throng of agitated locals in the downy-soft blanket of his dulcet words.

"I will fight any oppressor to save innocent lives!" he declared in reference to the victims of the recent encounter killings. "I wield a sword for militants but I am butter for innocent civilians."

Azad neglected to mention that he is also butter for Indian security forces, and that two months after the encounter killings discoveries raised hopes of a conscientious occupying force, justice in Kashmir remains a distant dream.

The trial of seven-accused Ganderbal SOG officers is currently stayed at Jammu & Kashmir High Court in Srinagar. Claiming her husband could never receive a fair trial in the Valley, the wife of lead defendant and alleged mastermind SP Hansraj Parihar wants the trial to take place in Jammu.

"This is definitely a way in which the defense wants to delay the case, but they may be justified in saying that 'we are not getting legal aid,'" said S.M. Afzal Qadri, Kashmir University Law Professor. "I feel that this is a delaying tactic; they think they may get the case transferred to Jammu."

Legal analyst Sheikh Showkat Hussein saw a silver lining, which he quickly dulled.

"The prosecution needs to build their case during the stay, but they are not serious," said Hussein. "These public prosecutors are part of the police administration, so why should they punish their own people?"

Good question. But Azad had no time for petty concerns.

"Human rights violations from either side won't be tolerated," he said, adding that there had been only five encounter killings during his tenure but 433 for his PDP-led predecessor. "I never remained silent when any human rights violations came to my notice."

Yet last year the all-but-defunct State Human Rights Commission filed a report documenting 44 disappearances from March to April 2005 alone. Perhaps Azad doesn't remember these findings because he never did anything about them: fed up with the body's impotence, former Chair Justice J.A. Mir resigned from the commission last August claiming "not a single recommendation of the Commission was implemented by the government".

Today the SHRC is without a Jammu office and its Valley staff recently sold their computers via public auction.

The way Azad and his government fight oppression and human rights violations in Kashmir is not only pitiful but also contrasts strongly with the Indian army's recently released Sub-Conventional Operations Doctrine. The document advises "scrupulous respect for Human Rights, [and] upholding laws of the land" and outlines a soft-gloved counter-insurgency strategy: "Such a campaign demands that all military operations are people-centric and conducted in a manner that generates a groundswell for peace...It must always be remembered that the populace constitutes the centre of gravity of such operations and, therefore, winning of their hearts and minds is central to all our efforts during conflict management and resolution."

The state and central governments, along with the security forces themselves, have acknowledged that fake encounter killings are no way to win hearts and minds. Yet none dare denounce the state's hypocritical two-step: promising justice but delivering smoke and mirrors.

"This trial serves mainly to portray to the EU and other international organizations that India has a legitimate judiciary - it might make a lot of noise, but few convictions," said Hussein, recalling that several officials accused in the recent sex scandal case have already been reinstated. "Inevitably the case will fail."

And it's not just the trial. Days after the exhumation of Padder's body, Azad announced the creation of a High Court-level judicial inquiry into the killings. Two months later the probe exists only in name.

"These commissions are just to pacify the people and keep the pot boiling," said Qadri, pointing out a similar probe slated to investigate the army's Pathribal killings that never came to fruition. "They are political games, political gimmicks; until Azad names a judge we will doubt his sincerity."

Last week the state government announced that the High Court was unable to appoint a judge because of a Supreme Court ruling that forbids sitting justices to head such commissions. The government report claimed a search is underway for a retired High Court judge to lead the probe.

"There are a number of retired justices that fit the bill," said Qadri, citing Justice Mir and several other candidates off the top of his head. "It's a matter of approaching them and asking. However, if the judges' feel that nobody will listen to their recommendations they might not want to accept this role; it is a question of political views."

So the victims' families wait, along with countless others with absent loved ones, their livelihoods compromised and their lives a constant struggle. Some have accused the authorities of harassment, even while the state is legally bound to protect and rehabilitate them.

In its defense, the government has offered jobs to the family of Abdur Rehman Padder, the Kokernag carpenter and the first victim exhumed.

"I want to remind the Chief Minister of his promise," responded Ghulam Rasool Padder, father of Abdur Rehman. "I surrender the government job he had given to my daughter; I just want to see the killers hanged."

Qadri feels such punishment would be legally justified in this case.

"The conscience of the nation, the sentiments of the whole community, have been destroyed with these gruesome acts," he said. "In 'the rarest of rare cases,' the death penalty must be considered; with such cold-blooded murder, the death penalty is the only alternative."

On this point Azad appeared to be in agreement.

"They will be dealt with more harshly,"' claimed the Chief Minister, referring to the accused. "This is a big step in the history of the state, as it has never happened before."

Sadly, gross injustices have happened before, repeatedly, and will most likely happen again. Indeed, one strains to imagine what justice in Kashmir would look like. Certain elements would surely be part and parcel: the lifting of the Armed Forces Special Powers and Disturbed Areas Acts; the implementation of a security forces monitoring group; and the creation of a Truth and Reconciliation Commission, to review not only the recent fake encounter killings but all the custodial killings, disappearances, and incidents of rape, torture, unjustified detention, and abuse in the last 17 years. If the Centre wants Kashmiris to accept Indian dominion it must first give them back their humanity.

"Justice is like the kingdom of God," George Eliot wrote, "it is not without us as a fact, it is within us as a great yearning."

Do Azad, the state, and the Central Government have that yearning? Only time will tell, but the early signs are not encouraging.

□

'We are evolving a culture:' Human Rights in Kashmir

(KO report)

November 10, 2006: Srinagar-based lawyer Parvez Imroz has for two decades endeavored in a highly dangerous, generally thankless, and likely Sisyphean task: defending the human rights of Valley residents.

Born and raised in Kashmir's summer capital, Imroz was recently awarded the world's highest honor for human rights lawyers, the Ludovic-Truriex International Human Rights Prize, the first of which was given to Nelson Mandela in 1985. The prize is to be conferred on October 13 in Bordeaux, France, at a special ceremony Imroz is unlikely to attend. Despite the efforts of several international right organizations such as Amnesty International, the Indian government has yet to give up Imroz's passport.

In a small sitting room at his office along the Bund near Lal Chowk, the activist-lawyer received a pleasant surprise from *Kashmir Observer* correspondent David Lepeska during a wide-ranging conversation that touched on the dangers of his work, the prospects for peace, and the fate of Afzal Gooru, among other issues.

DL: How did you first get interested in defending human rights?

PI: I was a lawyer by profession, with the High Court Bar, and before the militancy even started I was already working on human rights on minor violations. But after the conflict began, then it really became a very full-time engagement. Right from the start I had to be very careful in those days – I had to leave my house and stop the work and so forth.

After some time I again started the work and soon realized it was better for me to be independent. In 1994 I started a monthly gazette documenting the human rights on a monthly basis. In 1998 the organization for disappeared persons was started (APDP). And in 2000 there was a request that there should be some cooperation between Indian civil society groups and us. I approached some groups and we had a meeting and after some problems with some people we reconstituted in 2001 as the Jammu and Kashmir Civil Society.

DL: What is the mission of this organization?

PI: Civil Society is not for power and does not have any affiliation with any political party. It is meant to galvanize the civil society to evolve a public opinion regarding the issues being confronted by the people here, whether it is human rights violations, disappearances, or other political issues: all such issues that affect life in Kashmir. To deliberate upon the issues which people are concerned about, that's the first thing. Second, find out the ways and means of responding in a non-violent, peaceful way. This is mostly done by consensus. And then lastly we endeavor to build public opinion. Besides that we are in a process to have alliances with international civil society groups.

I believe it was *The Economist* said that in the 21st century there are two superpowers: the US and global civil society. With globalization, particularly in conflict areas, local society has to be linked with the global civil society... alongside an independence movement there should be a strong civil society. You have to out-administer the government, you cannot outgun the state. Let them de-legitimize their own efforts.

DL: What was your reaction to the recently released Human Rights Watch Report on Kashmir? And has the human rights situation in Kashmir improved?

Human rights violations are still going on, in the rural areas nothing has changed. In Srinagar we have a bit of space. But security forces are still acting with impunity. Disappearances have gone down, but there's still no commission, no response, no relief to the families of disappeared.

First problem with the HRW report was the terminology. "Islamic militants," they wrote, and said it's become "a Hindu-Muslim conflict." Why are they not called a Hindu army? Also, some of the data was not correct. And the elections, we as well as Indian groups found they were not free, fair, and inclusive, only 28 percent involvement. (HRW Asia Director Brad) Adams told us he would fix it up, and we hope he does because the J&K; Civil Society has been named as a source.

DL: Were you aware of the Ludovic-Trurieux International Human Rights Prize before you were informed that you had won the 2006 award?

PI: I had heard of it, yeah, a few years ago. In fact I was once in Holland, and the lawyers there had applied for me but I didn't win it that year.

DL: The prize includes a good-sized financial award. What do you plan to do with that money?

PI (Looking confused, surprised): I don't know... Is there any money also?

DL: Yes, almost Rs 3 lakh rupees. ($11,000 US at the time)

PI: This is the first time I've heard of it.

DL: The cash prize is right there in the Ludovic-Trurieux regulations and procedures – available on their website.

PI: I don't know. I'm getting first time from you. My wife asked me and I said there's no award.

DL: Well, there is.

PI: If that money's there, it'll be used in the Civil Society. It'll definitely be used in a new project which I will tell you in one or two months. I'm working on something new. Ask again in one or two months.

DL: Because the panel of judges is comprised solely of prominent lawyers, the prize is highly regarded by human rights defenders around the world, as it reflects the respect and honor of peers. What does it mean to you? I assume it is a real honor.

PI (Smiling): Not for the government of India.

It was good for me, yes. Exposure is the best opportunity to change the situation here. Civil society groups can further build alliances with international groups in the West – moral support from that side is very important to us. It's also a chance to display the lies the government of India feeds us to the people over there. But more important for me are the security implications. For me personally, for my group here – the legitimacy of the award gives us some sort of security.

DL: Speaking of security, four of your colleagues have been killed in the last decade. You yourself have been shot several times and were most recently targeted this past April. Do you still feel threatened? And do you ever consider quitting?

PI: There's no such thing as the bulletproof human rights defender. Honestly speaking you still feel like you're walking in a minefield. But you have to take risks. Take risks and become critical. Otherwise life will be very boring. (Chuckles lightly)

DL: The government of India is as of this writing still refusing to handover your passport, breaking international law to which it is a signatory. Do you think you will be able to travel to France and receive the award?

PI: What can you do, man? What can you do? I've been to the IGP's office and requested it. They said they would call me on telephone. They did not. Many people are campaigning: lawyers, human rights organizations, the French Bar Association, several sent letters to the Prime Minister. One lady from Srinagar said she spoke to someone at the consulate and told me that the passport decision must be made at a high-level meeting. "Prepare your bag and get ready to go," she told me. She's too optimistic.

DL: A slew of recently released studies and reports have found the emotional and mental damage wrought by the conflict to be skyrocketing, perhaps endangering future generations and society as a whole. Does your work provide any insight on these developments?

PI: We have mentioned that in our recent report, an increase in cases of PTSD (Post-Traumatic Stress Disorder) and trauma. There are the visible problems, like killing and that. But then there are the invisible problems, like torture, most of which nobody knows about. Many people die of the torture, they go unnoted, how does that affect the whole family, the children? So the whole generation is involved.

Additionally, militarization itself. It's a huge subject. Huge subject – what is the impact of militarization? Unfortunately we do not have the resources to accurately gauge it. My daughter, for instance, goes 8 kilometers to school every day, goes by all these soldiers with guns. What is the effect? How does it affect the day to day life of every Kashmiri individual, not only in urban but also the rural areas? The rural areas are probably worse – forced labor, human shields and that. But my organizations are not covering all of this – how much can we cover? Our monthly dossier covers maybe 5-10 percent of the difficulties, of the violations. The Human Rights Commission of Pakistan does much more thorough work because they have the resources – the financing, the offices, the people, the access.

But I do know that fear is the main obstacle, because it's being used as a weapon of war by the government and the conflict area becomes ruined. Even the militants are using it – they are also using fear.

DL: Even after the recent attacks in Srinagar, violence and death are way down on the year, continuing a trend that started in 2001. Could the insurgency be on the wane? Have you detected any legitimate progress towards peace?

PI: Unfortunately not. I would be happy if I were wrong, but no. The confidence building measures have not made a difference. Look at Sri Lanka, and at the Northeast of India – forward and back like here.

Kashmir is something very problematic, and sensitive also, in this case peace is totally unlikely. They must contain Pakistan, and the US has pushed Pakistan to stop militancy. But it is only meaningful once there is a reciprocity from India. What are you doing? On that count there is no reciprocity from Indian side. Second is what happens to the militants is all connected to the Middle East, Palestine and other places.

DL: Last year you said, "Any peace has to come with justice." What did you mean by that?

PI: When we are talking about peace, peace is a positive peace, not a negative peace. India, for instance, wants peace in the status quo. You see when Germans were in France they also wanted peace there in France. And if a lion eats a zebra after that time the lion also wants some peace, too. When we are talking about peace it has to be based on truth and justice. If you go with a negative peace it will collapse. Negative peace will always collapse. You have to resolve the sources of the conflict. Those have to be addressed. That is the reality.

DL: Is this what you and the Coalition are trying to achieve?

PI: We want to build institutions which will evolve a culture of dissent, enlightened dissent, evolve a culture which will promote democracy, which will promote internationally recognized democratic rights, build institutions which will protect an individual's rights. Because if we don't do that right now and the Kashmir issue is resolved, it will be worse. It will be worse. Because the history is that people fighting a monster become monsters themselves. So you have to build institutions that protect these rights. Also to question their methods, accountability, transparency, what is happening – what are you doing?

DL: How has the work gone so far?

PI: It has been more successful than our expectations. We are not an NGO, we are a civil society. We are part of civil society. We don't have the offices. A large number of young people really are so frustrated, they are so fed up looking from the fences, watching what's going on. They want to do something. They don't go to political parties. They want to contribute somewhere where they know there is trust and they are needed.

We believe that public opinion is stronger than violence, we are in a process to give people space here. Space to evolve a culture, to continue something in a peaceful way. Because we believe that you have to give resistance, and one of the keys to resistance is speaking truth.

We now have about 100 workers and I'm really very optimistic that many young people are coming and it is getting institutionalized. Success is if one person doesn't become indispensable. That is a failure. If people keep coming it will become a mindset.

DL: What are your thoughts on the impending execution of Afzal Gooru?

PI: First of all he was not given a fair trial, according to Amnesty International. India broke these international laws and he was deprived that. Secondly the judgment announced by the court is that he was convicted as only a facilitator. For the facilitator it is a very disproportionate punishment. Death is disproportionate. Third, there was a "media trial," and once he was arrested, as a Kashmiri, he was all but convicted.

It's another attempt to discredit the movement – perpetrated by "Islamist militants," full of "massacres." It's a deliberate attempt to stifle the process and it's already provoking people. Was the government of India seriously considering the consequences? I don't think they were anticipating this type of reaction (referring to protests). If it keeps going it will build. If he goes to the gallows it'll create a deep wedge. The moderate leaders that have been engaged in dialogue – can it continue? Also, it will strengthen extremist groups here.

The government of India is painted into a corner. This has again mobilized the people. Will it last? Kashmiri politicians are not that organized but this could well be sustaining. Our work is part of this. (A petition created by the Coalition garnered nearly 10,000 signatures in only three days and was just sent to the UN Secretary-General and the Indian President. With the help of the Coalition, three local colleges attempted to hold silent protests on their campuses last Saturday but we're stopped by school administrators.)

We are evolving a culture; the process will take some time.

□

Earthquakes, Sensitive Areas, and Successful Operations

(KO report)

October 7, 2006: This article was supposed to be about the great Kashmir earthquake. On the first anniversary of that devastating disaster I had planned to deliver an in-depth look at recovery, aid, and rehabilitation, with a focus on the hardest hit and the most neglected, those without homes and still struggling to put their lives back together, as well as those admirable souls lending a helping hand. With a little reportorial luck you would have been moved nearly to tears by firsthand glimpses of the lives of victims in the tiny Uri village of Dedkote, whose twenty-six households lost thirty-one inhabitants, and Tangdar tehsil's Teetwal, snug up against the Line of Control and structurally and emotionally eviscerated by last October's temblor.

Sad and hopeful, illuminating and inspiring, a testament to the strength of the Kashmiri spirit that would goad officials into action: the article might have been all this, but for the Indian army. Due to the current zero-exceptions-no-foreign-nationals-allowed-into-sensitive-areas policy of the Defence Ministry, security forces stopped a colleague and I enroute to Uri on Tuesday. On Wednesday, an hour after we had received a soon-to-be-meaningless pass from the very helpful Senior Superintendent of Police in Kupwara, checkpoint officers again halted our advance, this time about 20 kms short of Tangdar.

Returning to Srinagar that afternoon stewing in frustration, my journalist's heart jumped when I heard of the Budshah Chowk shootout with militants, which had evolved into a standoff just down the street from where we disembarked. If not the earthquake at least there would be a story to cover, I thought to myself, and perhaps a potent one. Although my colleague, a Kashmiri all too familiar with such encounters, was indifferent, I forced the issue and we hustled over to my first live military engagement, which would turn out to be a lesson in lethargy.

On Budshah Kadal we passed no less than seven armored and attack vehicles and at the eastern end came upon nearly 100 loitering soldiers. Some wore khaki uniforms and berets, others camo outfits with caps; all had shiny black weapons slung over a shoulder. They leaned against the bridge railing in a haphazard queue, crossed and uncrossed their arms and talked on mobile phones. Across the broad, paved square the beige façade of the Hotel Taj bore the scars of countless bullets. (The Standard Hotel, where the *fidayeen* were hunkered down a couple buildings over, was not visible from our vantage of the horseshoe-shaped commercial hub.) A faint smell of gunpowder and tar lingered but the gathering seemed no tenser than a bridal wazwan. The traffic congestion, vehicle exhaust, and choking dust that define Budshah Chowk during daylight hours were pleasantly absent and the unusual calm lent the open space a serenity that was shattered every ten or fifteen minutes by gunfire. Photojournalists and cameraman commiserated along a protected wall and two dozen soldiers positioned themselves behind sandbags three stories overhead. High-ranking officers conferred in small groups while nearby inferiors fingered AK-47's, chatted amiably, and occasionally smiled for the camera.

Two incidents spurred the milling soldiers to purposeful action during my two-hour vigil. The first occurred about twenty minutes after our arrival, when a militant bullet slammed into the side of a baby blue armored vehicle - whap! - about five meters from where we stood. The CRPF men who had been standing near the vehicle broke off their conversation with a start and pointed out the bullet hole before ordering the vehicle moved and ushering fellow soldiers and journalists out of what had suddenly become harm's way. The second was the sinking sun, which in heralding the approach of iftar sent a dozen low-ranking soldiers scurrying over to Lal Chowk. They returned minutes later to swarm the recently-arrived SSP Srinagar Afad-ul-Mujtaba with apples and dates, bread, bananas, and water. He and several officers enjoyed a small feast on the trunk of his shining white Ambassador as the rest of us contented ourselves with hand-outs or nothing at all. Across Budshah Bridge the western sky peacocked pink, scarlet, then violet and the two besieged militants punctuated the daily breaking of fast with the occasional gunshot.

The Indian soldier may be well-versed in serving his superiors and herding Kashmiris with the expertise of a Sonmarg Gujjar, but when it comes to engagement he has a few things to learn. When all was said and done Thursday afternoon seven security men, two militants and a civilian had died in the Budshah battle, which J&K; DGP Gopal Sharma termed "a successful operation." Militants also likely view the almost four to one favorable death ratio as successful. I offer my condolences to the seven soldiers who fell at Budshah Chowk, as well as to the other deceased, but a more disciplined, organized, and focused operation could have saved lives.

As we left Budshah Chowk and headed towards Residency Road I recalled recent reports that the rural areas had become a breeding ground for militancy in recent years. The same rural areas in which, this past Friday, villagers protested harassment and beatings from government troops in Baramulla and the unexplained arrest, torture, and release of four youths in Nowgam. The same rural areas from which I'd been denied entry that very day.

If the Central government had a little more sensitivity to these rural areas they might not be so sensitive. International observers would be welcome to visit, to record and report back to Kashmiris, Indians, and the international community not only on earthquakes but also that the security situation is indeed improving, both in Srinagar and further afield. And maybe, just maybe, fewer frustrated and angry young men would turn to militancy, and incidents like Budshah Chowk would become a thing of the past.

Now that would be a successful operation.

■

Chapter 9

Cracking Up

"Either the well was very deep, or she fell very slowly, for she had plenty of time as she went down to look about her and to wonder what was going to happen next."

— Lewis Carroll[171]

WHEN TEACHING HIS drama class, Pulitzer Prize-winning playwright Ayad Akhtar advises students to make the middle section of the narrative as long as possible. "The middle is when we still don't know the outcome," he says.[172] "That's when we care the most about what's happening." Kashmiris have all but given up caring because the middle ended long ago. They have little doubt about the outcome — and that is an impossible burden.

Thus far I've detailed Kashmir's abysmal infrastructure, corroded culture and system of education, limited free speech and absence of human rights. The insurgency has rippled into and hollowed out every element of life in the Valley. Put it all together, add in the endless violence and the ubiquitous Indian troops, and you've got an entire population with severe emotional and mental distress. The revocation of Article 370 has brought still more. Within days, more than 7,000 civilians, including politicians, activists and civil society figures, were tossed in jail. Then came the pandemic-driven lockdowns, enforced by fines and the use of force, with no social media or Netflix to turn to thanks to the internet blackout. In April 2020 the New York Times described the situation in dire terms:

Eight months after India revoked Kashmir's semi-autonomous status and brought the region fully under its authority, doctors here say a state of hopelessness has morphed into a severe psychological crisis. Mental health workers say Kashmir is witnessing an alarming increase in instances of depression, anxiety and psychotic events. Hard data is difficult to come by, but local medical professionals say they are seeing a rise in suicides and an increase in already disturbingly high rates of domestic abuse.[173]

This is nothing new for Kashmir. According to a 2016 report by Doctors Without Borders, close to half of all adult Kashmiris (1.8 million, or about 45%) had some form of mental disorder, while 9 out of 10 have experienced conflict-related trauma.[174] Every resident of Kashmir has had a family member killed, faced detention and interrogation, hidden from a shoot-out, been struck by some sort of police projectile or dealt with the disappearance or major injury of a loved one. This list does not include the irregular crackdowns, which can occur at any time, day or night, driving all able-bodied men into the street with their ID card to face the Indian military sniffing out militants and their associates.

Not all non-militant Kashmiris are wholly undeserving of some measure of state justice — some have aided militants; others have injured riot police with stones. But even those actions mainly attest to the great mental and emotional pressure they face daily.

☐

The Trouble with Asif

(old blog post)

September 7, 2006: I first met Asif at the office, like most of my co-workers. He shuffled in silently without my noticing while I sat at a computer, and then, just behind my left shoulder, said in a soft, purposeful baritone, "Hello."

I turned and took him in, a lanky man with a thick salt and pepper beard and curly, similarly streaked hair. He was wearing, as always, an ironed button-up shirt and khakis. He stood stock still with his right hand extended, just the hint of a smile on his lips, and what struck me was his presence, or lack thereof, his very lightness of being. Here before me was one of Kashmir's countless living victims, a man not fully there, a wraith, a phantom, with the shock of some great horror still in his eyes, which were wide open but emotionless, as if he were seeing the world through a dark veil and it took a Herculean effort to make out the proper shapes and images, faces, facts.

Rallying the severely weakened force of his combined energies, Asif had willed himself into that office, driven himself to greet a new colleague as if everything he believed in had not some long ago day been consigned to oblivion. With a birthday candle breath I could blow him out of the room.

"Hi," I said, trying to sound comfortably pleasant and giving his hand a firm shake, which he returned wanly while endeavoring to make his smile foreigner-worthy.

"Asif here is a great writer, Dave, a really great writer," said a nearby Farooq, stressing those adjectives as only he can.

"I used to be a writer," Asif corrected sluggishly, glancing at me but focusing on the floor.

Sajjad pointed out that I was sitting in Asif's seat, using his computer. I noticed that he was still at my shoulder, sort of shuffling in place unsure what to do, not wanting to make any requests on the new big shot but also desirous to get down to the business of getting lost in his work.

He was soon able to do just that, and, as I would learn over the next few weeks, it entailed sitting at that very seat to Sajjad's left, poring over endless pages of newswires written in Urdu and translating them oh so meticulously into English while chain-smoking Gold Flake cigarettes. He rarely made a peep, except when asked by Sajjad or Hamid about some language clarification for a headline or a news story. From 5:30 p.m. until whenever the paper was done, Asif sat and worked, gripping the pages with long, slightly unsteady fingers, reading with his golf ball eyes, and typing slowly, steadily, with great focus and determination.

For weeks I've been trying to pull him out of his shell, to get him talking and laughing and generally joining the living. About a week after I arrived he had complimented a story of mine and I asked about his writing. We came to the subject of why he had stopped.

"I have sinned," he intoned, smiling thinly in an attempt to play it off as a joke.

It sounded more like a mantra than an honest response, and I dared not go further. Then last week Asif and I fell into an amiable conversation and again I felt like digging a little deeper.

"So why did you stop writing?" I asked, knowing I was heading down a dark corridor.

"A long time ago," he responded, deeply, ominously. "I did something."

"What?" I asked, hoping, yet worried, he might tell me. "What did you do?"

"Something very bad," he answered, staring into me with his gentle brown eyes wide as saucers, then letting them droop slightly and turning away slowly. "Very bad."

□

The Right Man at the Right Time

(KO report)

August 26, 2006: Six days a week from early morning until after dark, a slow-moving stream of patient locals snakes up a creaky staircase off a dusty road in Hazratbal, winds through a bright red door and down a hallway to a smallish, nondescript physician's office. The queue is filled with victims of mental and emotional turmoil, some minor, others requiring serious medical attention, but all happy to wait for the services of Dr. Mushtaq Margoob.

"He's the best doctor in Kashmir," said a woman on line who would not give her name. "He's very smart, he's very observant, and he really helps people."

One man believed it was divine intervention.

"He's a gift from Allah."

Whether Margoob and his contributions to Kashmir are a supernatural occurrence or within the bounds of human capacity, his protean output is extraordinary. Since garnering an MD in psychiatry from Kashmir University on his first attempt in 1985 - all his schooling was local, he likes to point out - Margoob has labored indefatigably to study and improve the emotional and mental state of Kashmiris.

His personal practice, housed in a two-by-three-meter shack for much of the 1990's after his regular clinic was burnt down, today sees over 400 patients a week. He teaches at the Government Medical College and is closely mentoring six future psychiatrists, adding to the dozens that have come before. Writing late at night, he guest edited the most recent volume of JK-Practitioner, a quarterly journal, which details the results of nearly a dozen psychological studies - on post-traumatic stress disorder (PTSD), trauma occurrence, children in local orphanages, and much more - all of which he spearheaded. As if that weren't enough, he has raised two young daughters to follow in his footsteps, one studying clinical psychology at the renowned Institute of Human Behavior and Allied Science in New Delhi, the other a respected research neuroscientist and biotechnologist.

"I'm just getting started," a vigorous Margoob, 52, said during a recent interview at his office. He spoke energetically, gesturing often with his hands, and recalled his decision to study psychology.

"From an early age my teachers felt I had a holistic view of human nature," said Margoob, whose father taught literature at Kashmir University and won awards for his Kashmiri poetry. Margoob committed to psychology "body and soul" around 18 years of age and soon after, he said, "People felt I was well suited to understand medicine as both art and science."

That he settled into his calling during the insurgency-riddled 1990's and early 21st century was fortuitous, coinciding as it did with an explosion of mental and emotional difficulties for residents of the Kashmir Valley. From an average of about 1300 mental patients throughout the 1980's to 1700 in 1990, the sufferers have skyrocketed, to 48,000 in 2002 and over 62,000 in 2004. And, because of the harsh social stigma associated with mental problems, Margoob believes these numbers are just the tip of the iceberg.

Now the numbers may be nearing a dangerous tipping point.

"The truth is that everybody here experiences mental and emotional adversity because of the present conditions," he said, referring to the conflict. "And the majority suffer horrible trauma."

Indeed, Margoob believes he is in a pitched battle for the future of Kashmiri society. One of his studies in the Practitioner found that nearly sixty percent of all Kashmiris will be exposed to major trauma at some point in their lives, and another found that one of every six Valley residents will suffer from PTSD in his lifetime.

Margoob estimated that over one-third of Kashmiris will suffer from a medication-necessitating psychological disorder, the impact of which is difficult to fathom. As an example he cited a case from 2003 in which the family breadwinner, a man, was killed in a grenade attack. The mother-in-law went into complete denial and after going months without medical attention or counseling as her family struggled to survive, she settled into morbid depression, with suicidal tendencies. The wife of the victim became bitter and the two children withdrawn and fearful.

"That is a very big problem because with the men gone, the women are greatly needed," said Margoob. "These are the kind of cases where children are shipped to orphanages and the entire family is essentially destroyed. At the same time, the emotional and mental problems are passed to the next generation to resolve."

Thus, the crisis mushrooms.

"Because we lack the appropriate psychological support systems, this is happening on such a vast scale," warned Margoob. "It will significantly weaken our sense of community in Kashmir and radically alter behaviors in a negative way, endangering society as a whole."

The best solution to this epidemic would be an end to the conflict, but short of that, Margoob had several recommendations. He would like to build up disaster and trauma response systems, eliminate the stigma associated with mental disorders, and increase awareness on the part of all concerned parties: doctors, nurses, pharmacists, counselors, public figures and the immediate caregivers - friends, family, and the patients themselves.

Still, Margoob, who offered additional comments via phone while en route to a conference in Chandigarh, where he is to deliver a lecture today, felt invigorated by his patients. He was pleased with the work of his clinic and the progress made in the last few years at the Government Medical College, which he said is experiencing a new openness.

"You have to give, and give, and give, and not consider what you might want to take for yourself," he said. "I see whole families in tears, just destroyed by some trauma, and then by that third visit they are smiling brightly, asking 'Doctor what can we do for you?'"

He paused before completing his thought.

"These are the things that keep me working, and there is so much more to be done."

□

It's Nothing. Really.

(old blog post)

September 28, 2006: Leaving home for work yesterday morning on my motorbike I had to stop in the alley leading to the main road because two men were blocking my path, chatting amicably as one straddled a gun-metal grey Vespa. Angry shouts suddenly rang out from behind. A fiery-eyed young man wearing green pants sped around the corner on his Vespa and stopped nearly on the gray Vespa driver's shoes. He shouted in the smaller man's face accusatorily — condemning, cursing as he grabbed his collar and shook him.

Just as I squeezed past, green pants cocked his right arm, once twice, then let fly a punch into his offender's jaw. Grabbing each other's shirts and pulling every which way, the two clambered off the scooters and started to wrestle, still shouting. This drew men from nearby doorways and alleys, some trying halfheartedly to separate them and others watching with concern, interest, indifference. At one point green pants was getting the better of the other and the two were separated as they spit venomous words across the meter-wide divide.

To my surprise, a smallish oval was cleared and the inflamed duo were left to their passions — a street fight given the locality's blessing. The two danced unpredictably in the dirt for a few seconds then pounced simultaneously, twisting and grimacing. Finding a free arm, smaller black shirt got in a couple good shots to the face from close range, enraging green pants.

An older gent stepped into my peripheral vision, then came close, amiably, as if we were at the zoo. "Hello, Sir! And where are you going?" he smiled broadly, gesturing towards my bike.

"Uhh," I responded, grasping now the meaning of the word desensitized. "What are they fighting about?"

"Huhnph?" he queried, completely unaware to what I had referred. "Oh, this." He smiled the smile of the older and wiser. "Oh, it's nothing. Where are you from?"

By this time green pants had his black-eyed and bloodied opponent in a solid headlock and began to eye the brick wall, at which point saner heads stepped in. And from violence we swung to urgent diplomacy, the two men breathing heavily with reddened faces and rent clothing. Green pants incensed about some great offense and black shirt embarrassed to have been so thoroughly thrashed and, if his eyes were any indication, still intent on revenge.

The scene appeared to be calming when suddenly another young man flew in from nowhere – my right, actually, from whence green pants and I had come – and started punching black shirt, which sparked an entirely larger and more complicated ruckus. Suddenly there were four or five combatants, somebody's head was very nearly thumped into the wall, and a white shirted deviant picked up a softball-sized chunk of black pavement and bashed it into the head of black shirt. I stepped in and separated those two and corralled black shirt from behind to make sure he was OK, which he was generally, although woozy and with the eyes of a frightened animal, red molasses dripping from his dark curly hair. Stuck in survival mode, he wheeled to punch me but stopped short upon seeing my face.

Passions waned. Black shirt waved off aid and suggestions of the hospital. Green pants was led back to his waiting, prone Vespa, and the white shirted lunatic stared into and kicked the dirt in the face of a gentle talking-to from a white-capped older gentleman.

My new friend smiled. "It's OK, it's OK," he said. "This is Kashmir."

☐

In like a lamb, out like a lion

(old blog post)

April 24, 2007: When last spring I began to consider moving to and living in Kashmir for an entire year, I was told of bitter cold nights that lasted a lifetime, of entire villages buried in snow, of roads closed and power out for weeks on end – of the confounding trials of a frigid season in an under-developed, Himalayan region without indoor heating.

"You're staying there during the winter?" asked Rafiq Kathwari, a Kashmiri journalist and photo-documentarian who now spends much of his time in New York. "You will die."

But as September waned the days were still warm, and then October brought little change: the sun still shone nearly every day and even if the nights had grown chilly the daily rise of the mercury was as reliable as that of the sun.

Then in the early days of November the sun took regular siestas and that long, roomy overcoat-poncho, the Kashmiri pheran, became ubiquitous. By the time I'd arrive home from work after the ten-minute motorbike ride in the evenings my hands were nearly numb. One evening I saw a man maneuvering something unseen under his pheran. When I walked closely past I felt its warmth: a kangri!

The mythical earthenware pot that Kashmiris hold underneath their outer coverings during the winter months, it holds perennially burning coals and is generally a substitute for what the developed world all but ignores: heating. The slang term is winter wife, a phrase that sounds much more pregnant in Kashmiri. But feeling generally warm enough at home, I shrugged off the arrival of fall and girded myself for what lay ahead.

A few days later, just before dinner, as a wet and chilly day turned misty evening then bone-chilling night and I buttoned a heavy wool cardigan over my hoodie, winter arrived. As I finished my meal and shut the doors to keep out the chill, I saw it. Right there in front of my face as I opened a book; hovering and vaguely opaque. It looked like smoke but I wasn't smoking. And then it hit me: it was my breath.

So I began to understand. In Kashmir the winter is not the one with which we Westerners are familiar. Yes, in New York temperatures drop below freezing, great snow storms interrupt normal life, and ice mocks us on the roads. We bundle up against the cold, and plagues of flu can temporarily lay low entire towns. But no matter how cold the temperature, no matter how hard the wind blows or the snow falls, like an ill-mannered neighbor, winter can be dismissed with a simple shutting of the door and pulling closed the windows. The furnace clicks on and our home or office or wherever we happen to be – and we are mostly indoors during this season – becomes a womb of one's own. We forget the world outside, the time of year, the cold, and go about our lives.

But in Kashmir winter is a season just like any other, and when it comes it's everywhere, in our kitchens and bathrooms, our parlors and our bedrooms, and until it recedes we must pile on the layers, grin and bear it. For the last four months plus I had done just that. Indoors I've been wearing 4-5 layers at all times, often with a hat and gloves (fingerless, so I'm able to type). And with regular electricity cuts, I often bathe in ice cold water. Still, the infamous blizzards never came. The legendarily frigid cold mostly stayed away. And then in early March – right about the time my patience had worn thin – the season started to roar: a sanity-sapping fortnight of snow and rain, wind, chill and incapacitation.

First, three days of fat flakes buried Srinagar under more than a foot of snow. The Srinagar-Jammu National Highway, Kashmir's unreliable link to the outside world, was closed to traffic. For days the Valley was without eggs, chicken, mutton, milk and most vegetables. Schools were closed for a week. All flights in and out were cancelled. The power went out for three days and for the next week flicked on only intermittently. The snowstorm would've been the last straw if it hadn't been so beautiful.

And then just when Srinagar had dug itself out and the snow had mostly melted, we were walloped with three days of nonstop rain. The roads of my Rajbagh neighborhood flooded, along with many others. Schools closed again, as did the National Highway. Meals consisted of breadstuffs and rice and pre-made packaged curries. Mobile networks and Internet connections were woefully inconsistent; cross-town friends might just as well be in Bangalore. And without power, again, I couldn't work.

Of course, people are suffering through vastly worse days, weeks, even lives, across the globe. But after the long cold winter it was enough to drive a man, at least this man, half batty. I was short-fused and fussy for most of March. I hated Kashmir, the government, my computer, the Internet, my phone, my colleagues, even my local market vendor. The longer the harsh weather lingered, the more I growled.

And then, without warning, April rose up like a dream. I looked out the window and praised Allah, Buddha, and Jesus – ten days of off-and-on precipitation and the 100-odd hellish days that preceded it had apparently come to an end, at long last. Today the sun is shining and children are playing cricket in muddy open squares. Women are out chatting and shopping in twos and threes. Men stand laughing at tea stalls and snack shops. The mynahs are singing. Kites and pigeons are getting amorous on rooftops. Grass is greening, buds are sprouting; spring is aswing in Kashmir.

And I'm still here. Slightly shaken, perhaps, a bit stirred, but alive and well. Take that, Rafiq.

❑

Chapter 10

Pandit Problems

"Do not differentiate between a Hindu and a Muslim, For He who created them all is watching you everywhere."

— Lal Ded

"It is really difficult for me to distinguish between a Hindu Kashmiri and a Muslim Kashmiri. You people speak one language and have one culture. While the rest of the country burns in communal fire, I see a ray of hope in Kashmir only."

— Gandhi, during Partition[175]

IN HINDU MYTH, the two heads of the bherunda bird, Garuda and Upagaruda, ensure their eternal security by sleeping at different times to guard against predators.[176] But one day, Garuda finds a delicious flower and gobbles it down while Upagaruda sleeps. The two share a stomach, so upon waking Upagaruda realizes what has happened. Seeking revenge, he finds a poisonous flower, furiously eats the whole thing and both die.[177] So it is with the Hindus and Muslims of Kashmir, except that each has been eating the poisonous flower over and over again. It's an imperfect analogy, because where are the foreign oppressors in all this? And which is Garuda and which Upagaruda? Still, it's useful, in part because the united bherunda was said to possess incredible strength — echoing the famed communal harmony that originated during the Kashmiri sultanate.

The cracks began to appear about two centuries ago, when Dogra Maharajas appointed Pandit deputies who lorded over the Muslim peasantry. Over the next hundred years the Pandits solidified their position as the Kashmiri elite while the majority Muslim population barely scraped by.[178] Whenever socio-economic strata are divided on religious identities, and particularly when a minority population persecutes the majority, resentment is sure to fester. Though Sheikh Abdullah, in taking the mantle of Kashmiri Muslim leadership in the early 20th century, repeatedly stressed communal harmony and the power of *Kashmiriyat*, his calls often went unheeded, particularly after the 1947 Pakistani-driven invasion. With a series of land reforms in the 1950s through the 1970s, Sheikh Abdullah handed great swathes of Kashmiri farmland to the Muslim majority, frustrating many Pandits with his "Land to the Tiller" campaign.[179]

In 1984, the Pakistani government launched Operation Tupac. The brainchild of the country's Islamist president Zia-ul-Haq, the plan sought to draw waves of frustrated Kashmiri youth to Pakistan for training, then send them back to Kashmir to attack the Indian military. The scheme succeeded, abetted by the fraud in Kashmir's 1987 elections (see Introduction). "The Kashmiri youth were brainwashed and weapon-trained to indulge in large-scale subversive activities and succeeded in creating an atmosphere of terror in the Kashmir Valley and forging divisions in the name of religion, thereby blurring the ethno-religious identity of Kashmir," argues the European Foundation for South Asian Studies.[180] This in turn led to the communalism seen in the Babri mosque destruction, the driving out of Kashmiri Pandits, the Gujarat riots and beyond.

Modi and the BJP's approach to Kashmir echoes their view of India's 200 million Muslims, which make up just under 15 percent of the population. Before accepting his position as home minister, Amit Shah described India's Muslims as "termites". In 2010, Shah was charged with extortion and murder in connection with the murder of a Muslim man falsely accused of plotting Islamist terror.[181] Modi, too, has been linked to that series of fake encounter killings in Gujarat. In December 2019, the Modi government pushed through an amendment that fast-tracks citizenship for Hindu, Sikh and Buddhist immigrants from neighboring countries, but not for Muslims. Shah has proposed a national citizenship registry that would require documentation of place of birth and residence, which many poorer Indians lack. This could leave countless Indian Muslims stateless and at risk of being put in proposed migrant detention camps, as appeared to be happening in Assam in mid-2020.[182] Residents of a mainly Muslim neighborhood in New Delhi launched a sit-in to protest the citizenship amendment and proposed registry, holding up banners advocating harmony and fraternity. The BJP depicted them as "traitors" and "anti-nationals".[183] Muslims in at least three Indian states — Uttarakhand, Uttar Pradesh and Madhya Pradesh — can be arrested and face up to five years in prison for falling in love with a Hindu, with more BJP-controlled states likely to follow suit.[184][185] Police in Uttar Pradesh, the first state to propose the law, started raiding weddings in November 2020, halting the ceremonies midway and arresting the bridegrooms. Unsurprisingly, these communal tensions have spilled over into Pakistan. In December 2020, Pakistani police arrested more than a dozen people after fire badly damaged a Hindu temple in the northwestern province of Khyber Pakthunkhwa.[186]

Pro-government voices tend to view the revocation of Article 370 as a precursor to the Pandits' return. "The return of Kashmiri Hindus to their homes and their resettlement with full dignity, honor and safety is a must, otherwise the whole purpose of abrogating Article 370 will be defeated," nationalist commentator Seshari Chadri wrote in July 2020.[187] Modi appeared to confirm this view speaking to parliament a few months prior, when he said Kashmir's identity had been destroyed in January 1990, when Pandits started to flee. "Who made Kashmir's identity only about bombs and guns? Can anyone forget that dark night of January? In reality, Kashmiri identity is closely linked with harmony," said India's leader.[188] In early 2022, The Kashmir Files, a fear-mongering anti-Muslim screed masquerading as a history of the Pandit exodus, emerged as India's top-grossing film in years.[189]

In August 2020, Modi laid the foundation stone for the Ayodhya Ram Temple on the former site of Babri mosque.[190] The next month a special court acquitted 32 top BJP figures, including LK Advani, of their role in the 1992 demolition of the centuries-old Babri mosque, which sparked rioting that killed some 2,000 people. The court ruled that the mosque's destruction had not been pre-planned and that the accused had tried to stop it.[191] As if that weren't enough, in July 2022 authorities arrested leading rights advocate Teesta Setalvad, who has worked tirelessly for years to bring charges against those behind the 2002 Gujarat riots, including Modi.[192] Weeks later, a review committee of the Gujarat violence overturned the life sentences handed down to 11 men for the gang rape of BilkisBano and murder of her young daughter, and let them walk free.[193] A BJP legislator on the review committee suggested their high-caste Brahmin status helped secure their release.[194]

□

Goodbye to All That: Kashmir and the Problem of Pandits

(KO report)

December 17, 2006: *Union Home Minister Shivraj Patil's announcement this week that the security situation in Kashmir had improved enough to accommodate the return of the Pandits brought to mind all the thorny issues related to that unfortunate rupture as well as how murky the historical record had become. Kashmiri Observer reporter David Lepeska will attempt to illuminate these matters, beginning with today's recollection of the events of the past and concluding later this week with an analysis of the Pandit plight as it stands today.*

"Kashmiris, and in fact all Indians, have rather a bad habit," R.L. Bhat, a Kashmiri Pandit and a leader of the political forum Jammu Kashmir Vichar Manch, said recently. "They become cognizant of a fact but then proceed to willfully ignore or even disbelieve it, as if that will make it untrue."

In the frenzied, rebellious, and terror-filled early months of 1990, the Pandits reluctantly packed up their belongings and headed south, taking with them the harmonious Kashmir of legend — a now-mythic place where Hindus and Muslims shared neighborhoods, religious celebrations and seasonal traditions, even customs and meals.

Yet nearly 17 years later mystery continues to swirl around every aspect of the exodus of the Kashmiri Pandits, who had called Kashmir home for thousands of years. Had there been a long, creeping rise in communal tensions post-1947 or was it merely a single, three-month explosion of frothy Muslim nationalism? Was it a case of ethnic cleansing or just intelligent Pandit decision-making in a time of vast paranoia and clear danger? How many Pandits left - over three lakhs or around 1 lakh? And who, after all, was to blame - Governor Jagmohan Malhotra, gun-toting Muslim militants, devious, foot-dragging national and state politicians, or possibly the high-minded Pandits themselves?

Kashmir's Hindu community was for eons one of its defining features and the living, breathing link to the Valley's origins. Thus, their departure is a black spot on the heart of Kashmir, and will remain so until all sincere and legitimate efforts have been made to enlist their return.

"One cannot imagine a Kashmiri culture without Kashmiri Pandits," said Kashmir University History Professor Farooq Fayaz. "Not only are they intelligent and well-educated, but more importantly, they generally have a deep sense of tradition and culture, a clear connection with their roots, their history - which is partially our roots, our history - so their absence has created a great gap, without question."

The Pandit refugees have been biding their time in camps near Jammu, in Delhi, and points beyond. Very few have forgotten their Valley home, and efforts to return have been ratcheted up in recent months as Chief Minister Ghulam Nabi Azad has created a working group and the Supreme Court weighs a Public Information Litigation requesting a high-level inquiry into the events that led to the mass exodus.

Like any tale of war, the Pandit exodus has many strands, each containing some truth and some fiction, and looking for a straight line in the jagged arc of recent Kashmiri history is like looking for clean water in the Dal. What follows is an attempt to employ a variety of voices and views to paint a lively, relatively accurate rendition of the events leading up to and including that tumultuous season 17 years ago.

"The whispers started in the 60's," said the president of the Panun Kashmir Movement Ashwani Kumar, who grew up on the banks of the Jhelum in Habba Kadal. "We were made second-class citizens."

Srinagar's political record bears out this last statement. The majority-Muslim J&K State Legislative Assembly restructured constituencies in which Ashwani believed Pandits had a decisive vote. With mal intent or not, from three seats in the 1950's and '60's the Pandit presence fell to one in the 1970's and beyond.

Dr. S. N. Dahr, a World Health Organization fellow who recently founded an institute to research Kashmiri Heritage, is a well-regarded Pandit physician who remained in Kashmir in 1990, and even after being kidnapped by militants two years later. He spoke about the Pandits' changing socio-cultural landscape as the latter half of the 20th century wore on.

"There was some alienation, particularly in the economic and political communities," said Dahr, who is 68. "Sometimes it was difficult for Pandits to get what they deserved."

He listed a litany of hurdles for his community.

"It probably started with Sheikh Abdullah's 'Land to the Tiller' because Pandits, who had owned much of the land, were affected... An increasing squeeze for jobs, opportunities, and resources; because of affirmative action, merit was sacrificed. So it was a bit of corruption, coupled with nepotism," he said. "All these things together meant heartburn for the Pandit."

But because they had called Kashmir their home for thousands of years, most failed to see the writing on the wall. One, however, did not.

"It is time they realize the stern reality," Prem Nath Bazaz wrote of the Pandits in 1954. "The internal conditions of the state can in no way improve; indeed they will deteriorate and some day something might happen which will jeopardize the life of this community. It is therefore wise and sagacious to take the time by the forelock and prepare the community psychologically and otherwise for the inevitable."

So, as perhaps any minority might when faced with a rising majority, the Pandits began shuffling towards the door. In a 1995 essay, former Indian foreign secretary M. Rasgotra found that the Pandit population was near one million at the turn of the last century and that a steady trickle had begun to depart after a deadly Hindu-Muslim riot in July 1931, only to grow stronger in the decades after accession.

"The Kashmiri Pandit was out-and-out Indian," said Dahr. "Whether he liked India, that is another concern, but he believed in the broad outline. He was secular and his secularism began to clash more and more and more with the ideology of separatism and the new Islamisation that was happening."

Along with political divergences, cultural differences started to appear, explained Dahr.

The proliferation of the *salaam alaikum* greeting, for instance.

"You are the same, but you are not the same," he said. "Kind of a glass wall, an invisible wall was being built, and as a result our value system and culture are a little bit undermined."

Requesting anonymity for safety reasons, a Kashmiri Muslim political analyst who was in the chief minister's security detail throughout the 1980's had a different perspective.

"There wasn't any obvious communal tension at all," he said. "This was not an individual thing; even the Anantnag riots had political motivations."

In February 1986 several temples were burnt and a number of Pandit houses and shops were destroyed by rioters in that southern district. The analyst was convinced that a leading politician, angling for the chief minister's office at the time, was behind the mayhem and that ultimately it was politics that undid the Pandits in Kashmir.

"The Pandits were ultimately the victims of a big political game," said the analyst.

Jagmohan as fall guy is a common argument among Kashmiri politicians. National Conference patron and former Chief Minister Farooq Abdullah stated this as "the gospel truth" on a national news station earlier this month. Yet that same week hardline Hurriyat leader Syed Ali Shah Geelani admitted that Muslim militants had killed Pandits during this time, calling them "not true Muslims."

Of course, no single person or group can be blamed; everyone is at fault. "Jaghmohan, the militants, Kashmiris themselves," the analyst said. "But Jagmohan engineered the departure to a certain degree."

He pointed out that the Union-appointed state governor bought tickets and rented trucks to help the Pandits get out of the Valley. "He wanted the Central government to see that it was a communal conflict and bring in more force on the Muslim," the analyst added.

Most agree that the period of dread began with the September 1989 militants' killing of Tika Lal Taploo, an outspoken Hindu leader well-liked in his Habba Kadal community.

"He was very much liked by Muslims," said Dahr. "So that sent a shiver and produced a bit of terror."

Then the hammer fell with the January 1990 reappearance of Jagmohan rule.

"By 1990 there was essentially no government, the militants had taken over and a fear psychosis had begun to grip Kashmir," the Kashmiri political analyst said.

Killings became regular and unpredictable, with Pandits in the crosshairs.

"A lot of killings occurred," said Dahr. "But more important, the Pandit killings were all selective, targeting the community, brutal and advertised, and word was spread."

Estimates range from as few as 50 to as many as 1000 Pandits killed from late 1989 to April 1990. Regardless of the true total, the situation created awesome fear.

"It was meticulously well-organized, a campaign of terror that ultimately forced us to flee," Ashwani recalled. "What did the Centre and State Government do? Nothing. One of two things would've happened to us had we stayed: we'd all be killed or all become Muslims."

The analyst echoed these sentiments.

"Nobody felt completely safe," he said. "But if I were a Pandit I would have left, too; when there is paranoia from all sides, there is no other option."

Dispute still rages regarding the number of Pandits that left the Valley, with most turning to possibly inaccurate census numbers to gauge the Hindu population at that time.

"There was a trickle happening since the '50's, but not this 60 percent." said Dahr, referring to official population figures that put Kashmir's Pandit community at one third of its 1947 total by the 1980's.

Dahr and Rasgotra argue, as have many Pandits, that Muslim officials had long skewed the Kashmir census numbers and that the total number that ultimately left in 1990 was over 3 lakhs, as opposed to the 1.2 lakhs the records suggest. Some 56,000 Pandit families registered with the Jammu government following the 1990 uprising. At an average of 5-6 per clan, the real number of departed would appear to lean towards the higher estimate.

The tale of one such family, the Bhats, sums up a great casualty of the Kashmir conflict. By June 1990, Dr. Bhat had sent his wife and children to Jammu and was staying alone with his father.

"They came to kill me in the evening," he said of militants. "But a couple Muslim friends who had heard about the attack shifted me to one house, and then to another, and then they got me a taxi and I got out."

Bhat admitted that his Muslim neighbors had probably saved his life.

"It was a mass uprising, but it was not about personal or collective anti-Hindu animosity," he explained. "When we left there was no animosity, and there's no animosity even now. It is not a Hindu-Muslim conflict; we have no trouble with Muslims, we had very cordial relations with our Muslim neighbors. We can still have that kind of brotherhood."

□

Displaced and Abandoned, Pandits Face Facing Dream of Return

(KO report)

December 21, 2006: Ruby Raina has no plans to tell her two-year-old daughter Vinaji about her homeland.

"Kashmir?" said Pandit and former Anantnag resident Raina, 30, mulling a visitor's query. "We try not to think about it."

Standing outside her dilapidated brick and tin shack at the Muthi refugee camp near Jammu, the young mother furrowed her brow and pursed her lips.

"We don't want to live here," she explained. "But we are afraid to go back."

When to return? The question faces millions of peoples displaced by violence all over the globe, but for Kashmiri Pandits the pangs of nostalgia are particularly acute. After all, Kashmir's green valleys, burbling streams, and craggy, snow-capped Himalayan peaks nestled and nurtured their community for two millennia, until they were forced out with the onset of an armed revolt against Indian rule seventeen years ago.

The Pandits worry about what might happen were they to return to a changed Kashmir, even as they struggle to survive in strange, largely unappealing lands.

"Life there is not so good," Arun Kardar, 26, said of life in the Kathua camp, where he lives with his family. He was speaking in a Jammu cafe. "But living there the last 15 years, we have adjusted ourselves."

That's precisely what Pandit leaders were afraid of.

"We thought, let this be a tactical retreat," Panun Kashmir Movement Chairman Ashwani Kumar said of the 1990 departure. "We never thought it would last, but the government of India is still in deep slumber."

With Indian Home Minister Shivraj Patil last week urging the Pandits to return to new settlements and J&K Chief Minister Ghulam Nabi Azad creating a Pandit working group earlier this month, that government is trying to awaken.

"What has happened to the Pandit community in the Valley is a great national tragedy, I would say a great human tragedy," soon-to-be Prime Minister Manmohan Singh told a Pandit seminar in 2003. "Whatever can be done to relieve their pain and suffering is in the wider national interest...The long-term objective, of course, has to be to enable the Pandit community, and all those who want to go back to the Valley, to return and lead a life of dignity and self-respect. We have to find ways and means to create a secure environment."

Yet around three lakh Pandits still bide their time in temporary dwellings across India, many in just-tolerable conditions. The longer it lasts - the more the Pandits accept their exile, the more the next generation loses touch with its Kashmiri roots - the less likely a return becomes.

Could the displacement of Pandits, and thus the loss of Kashmir's renowned culture of amity and cooperation, be a permanent condition? Only time will tell, but a return appears as far off as it's ever been.

"Life here is terrible," said Rajnath Malla, originally from Sopore, standing outside his 10-by-12-foot brick hut at the Muthi camp. "These conditions are not satisfactory for human or animal."

On a sunny morning earlier this month garbage was piled high and the stench of sewage was wince-inducing in certain sections of the Purkhoo camp. Cluttered, narrow alleyways and small courtyards linked the housing units, and if the Pandits were close before relocation, their lives are now lived one on top of another. Serious health problems such as cancer and tuberculosis have risen as a result. Depression and other stress-related health concerns are also frequent, and studies have shown that the fertility rate has sunk while mortality has spiked.

"It's very hot in summer and cold in the winter, with everyone getting sick," said Vinaji Raina from Kupwara, who has three children, a husband and her own mother under one thin tin roof at Purkhoo camp. "We have lots of health problems."

Sixteen-year-old Pooja Pandita, born shortly after her family arrived at the camp from Anantnag, was frustrated with her circumscribed life.

"We have difficulties with the electricity and the heating, the lights go off and I can't study during the night time," she said, adding that she was going for her 12th standard and that her grandmother had heart problems. "It's very crowded with five people here; my father, brother, mother come in and I get very distracted. This is a crucial year for my studies and I can't concentrate."

Pandit political group Panun Kashmir has urged the government to make three improvements for those living in the camps: a youth-oriented employment package; a special drive for sanitation, sewage, and health; and increased relief funds.

"There's no reason why the government can't do this," said Kumar. "It would improve their lives substantially, and these are things a government is supposed to do. It is their prime duty."

Despite the harsh conditions of the camps, many of the 18-20,000 displaced Pandits living in rented housing in Jammu sought to move to the camps. This is likely because there is no rent and the government gives each camp-dwelling family Rs 3000 per month, or about 100 rupees per day.

"This is not enough to live on, and the government is doing nothing," said Sanjay Seli, a 32-year-old from Habba Kadal who has a ten year-old son and lives in Muthi camp.

In fact, Patil announced last week that financial assistance was being bumped to Rs 4000 for families in Delhi and Jammu areas. After visiting the camps two years ago, Prime Minister Singh said the government would build two-room quarters in Jammu and Delhi, formulate a comprehensive rehabilitation plan, and create a ministerial team to assess the Pandit problem. None of that has happened.

"Singh started a project but the state squashed it," said R L Bhat, National Vice President of Jammu Kashmir Vichar Manch, a political forum for Pandits and peace in the state. "They are trying to sabotage it all. Very little progress has been made."

At Kheer Bhawani, Mattan, and Awantipora, among other places, governmental construction of over a hundred temporary tenements has indeed progressed, and last week Patil announced Rs 20 crore for the construction of 200 flats at Sheikhpora and Rs 10 crore to rebuild damaged Pandit homes and shrines.

Chief Minister Azad has put together a working group to address the hurdles related to the return of the Pandits and the Supreme Court is currently awaiting State and Central Government responses to a high-level inquiry into the events that led to the mass exodus.

"There has been no large-scale mass migration since 1990-91," Patil said last week, claiming the security situation in Kashmir had improved enough to accommodate the Pandits' return.

The majority of Pandits are reluctant, however, either because they would prefer their old homes to the settlement complexes or still fear for their safety. Many may find trusting Patil difficult because three years ago he called Kashmiri militants "our brothers and sisters".

Just last week militant group Hizb-ul-*Mujahideen's* supreme commander Syed Salahudin said, "the time was not ripe for the return of Kashmiri Pandits." Further, hardline Pandit group Panun Kashmir backed out of the working group because they felt it ignored their concerns.

"They only give us lip service, talk about returning Pandits with security, honor, and dignity," said Kumar. "But what does that mean? Being the indigenous people we should have a forum to speak. We have a legitimate, territorial claim."

Panun Kashmir (Our Kashmir) supports the carving out of a Pandit homeland, a Union Territory within Kashmir. The plan involves using the Jhelum as a border to partition part of southern Kashmir between a Hindu minority and a much larger Muslim majority, although the group says all law-abiding Kashmiris would be welcome in their state.

"Many years ago nobody thought of a Jewish state," said Kumar, although the proposed territory sounds more like the West Bank. "In politics nothing is final. The course of events makes events and places emerge. Our conviction is that there is no other way."

Other Pandits were less sanguine.

"This is an emotional slogan because they love this land so much and they want to be treated as equals," said S.N. Dhar, a respected Pandit physician who stayed in Kashmir despite the violence and fear, and despite being kidnapped for almost three months in 1992. "But some people are more equal than others in a democracy; it always happens."

R.K. Mishra, Chairman of the Observer Research Foundation, a think-tank that held a seminar on the Pandit problem in 2003, also poked holes in the homeland concept.

"People live in entangled relationships," he wrote in his 2005 book "Kashmiri Pandits: Problems and Perspectives". "These cannot be disentangled by political surgery. The Partition of India did not solve any problem. Similarly, a partition of this state will not solve any problem, neither of the Valley nor of Jammu and Ladakh, neither of Muslims nor Hindus and Buddhists."

Vichar Manch leader Bhat tried to find a middle ground.

"Why should we call it a homeland?" he asked. "These are unnecessary complexities; we want a space to live in Kashmir where we can live with reasonable assurance of safety, and the township plan is the only way."

Kumar was not having any of it.

"These constructions, it is all a facade," he said, waving off the settlement concept with an open hand. "It's all to get money from the Central Government. They have never consulted with us, never spoken to us about what we needed, they built it to get more money, and we're not willing to live in these cluster buildings."

Regardless of which plan one favored, considerable dispute remained regarding any possible return.

"My perception is that things are changing," said Kumar, who believes the world links Kashmiri militants with Al Qaeda and its ilk. "9/11 has done the trick: people in Europe, America, and other places, now see that yes, there is Islamic terrorism, there is a real threat in India. I don't think thousands of books and speeches could have done this."

Dhar didn't see that development as very helpful.

"The Kashmiri man on the street even today is not Islamicized," he said. "He just wants his bread buttered, preferably on both sides."

Did Dhar think the Pandits were any closer to coming back to Kashmir?

"It's a question of peace," he said. "When peace returns they will trickle back in."

Bhat, like many others, remained frustrated.

"All we want is to be able to return with an assurance of reasonable safety," he said. "But the government is single-mindedly closed to listening to our considerations. They are determined to not take our apprehensions seriously, and the state government is playing to lobbies in Kashmir."

Mishra viewed such complaints and conspiracy theories as part of the problem.

"Kashmiri Pandits, amazingly intelligent and clever people, do not appear to have moved out of the condition of paralyzing trauma," he wrote. "I cannot but observe as a well-wisher that like all Kashmiris, the Pandits also remain engrossed in blaming others. Not that others are not responsible, but the future of neither the Pandits nor of other sections of people in this state can be salvaged by blaming others."

Indeed, many Kashmiri Muslims are of two minds regarding the Pandits' plight. An entry at *Kashmir Observer*'s online forum, which is popular with the Kashmiri diaspora, summed up this perspective.

"If Kashmiri Pandits are suffering so are Kashmiri Muslims, Sikhs and other minorities in Kashmir, but they - unlike the Pandits - decided to stay in Kashmir no matter what happens to them," a Kashmiri named Hussain wrote recently. "We all have been suffering in Kashmir... thousands of our youth laid down their lives for a Cause and we will achieve that."

As the debates and blame games continue, the next generation of Pandits is growing up far away from their Valley home.

"They don't remember Kashmir at all," Purkhoo resident Kudesh Koul said of her three sons, aged 22, 20, and 18 and all born in Kashmir.

She laughed bitterly at the thought of a place now foreign to her.

"I don't remember, how could they?" wondered Koul, whose husband works in a fruit market to pay for the boys' schooling. "I have forgotten each and every thing about Kashmir."

Pukhoo resident Pandita had a similar problem.

"We don't talk about Kashmir because we don't know what that life is like," said the sixteen-year-old. "Also I am afraid to go there because militants killed my uncle not so long ago."

He was killed in the Nadimarg massacre, in March 2003.

"They do not see Kashmir as realistically as we do," Kumar said of the younger generation. He has a 13-year-old son who has never been to the Valley. Kumar has not visited since he left in 1990, and rarely speaks Kashmiri.

"They are losing the language and culture because they don't have the overall Kashmiri environment," he added. "The homeland is a dreamland for them."

Koul echoed these sentiments.

"I've never been back to Kashmir," she said. "We can't bear to go; why go there? There is nothing for our children in Kashmir."

At least one Pandit saw things differently.

"I remember each and every thing about Kashmir," said Kathua resident Kardar, who visited Kashmir in 2004 and would love to return permanently. "It was a beautiful place, we had apple orchards and walnut orchards, and when I was a kid I used to run here and there."

Kashmir University History Professor Farooq Fayaz also recalled a distant Kashmir.

"Kashmiri history, if we look at its composition, there has always been an element of heterogeneity there, a wealth of different types of people in terms of race and culture and language and tradition," he said. "With the departure of Pandits that has disappeared, and it has created a great gap in our society."

In his award-winning 1997 collection *Country Without a Post Office*, Kashmiri poet Agha Shahid Ali slyly prophesied the end for communal harmony in Kashmir.

At a certain point I lost track of you.

You needed me. You needed to perfect me:

In your absence you polished me into the Enemy.

Your history gets in the way of my memory.

I am everything you lost. You can't forgive me.

I am everything you lost. Your perfect enemy.

Your memory gets in the way of my memory.

There is nothing to forgive. You won't forgive me.

I hid my pain even from myself; I revealed my pain only to myself.

There is everything to forgive. You can't forgive me.

Still, Arun Kardar held onto the dream. "I am not a political guy. I keep myself away from these things because I think this is nonsense," said the young Pandit. "All I know is that I'm a Kashmiri and I want to go back."

☐

THE DAYS-LONG SPASM of bloodletting that gripped Gujarat in 2002, which is the subject of Raj Kamal's Jha's novel *Burning Down Our House*, may, at first glance, seem like the distant past. But in fact it remains a powerful part of India's present.

Look no further than the BBC's 2023 documentary *The Modi Question*, which investigates whether the state's chief minister at the time, current Prime Minister Narendra Modi, is to blame for the pogrom. Immediately upon its January release, the Indian government barred social media platforms, including Twitter, from sharing the film.[195] Soon after, authorities raided the BBC's offices in Delhi and Mumbai, apparently sending a message about criticizing the government and its leader.[196]

More than two decades later, Gujarat remains an incredibly touchy subject in India.

❑

Burning Down Our House: Book Review

(KO report)

June 28, 2007: On a chill, late February evening five years ago, a gang of marauders stopped and then torched a nearly full Sabarmati Express near Godhra, about 150 kms from Gujarat's capital city of Gandhinagar. The case filed later by the police claimed several Muslims conspired to burn the train and its passengers, but two subsequent court decisions were inconclusive. Either way, the deaths of 59 Hindu passengers – including several returning from Ayodhya, where they had been campaigning to build a temple in place of a mosque destroyed ten years prior – sparked an unprecedented communal conflagration across the state. The deliriously violent five-week spree of fire and rioting destroyed 25,000 shops and homes and resulted in over 1000 mostly Muslim deaths.

Award-winning novelist Raj Kamal Jha covered the carnage for Indian Express, where he is executive editor. Sifting through the detritus of Ahmedabad's Gulbarga Housing Complex, which had been torched with residents still inside, he came upon a child's workbook. The cover was singed but inside were several pages of exercises and a number of surprisingly mature poems. One stunningly relevant verse stopped the author in his tracks and inspired him to pen a fictional account of the tragedy, one that could encompass all of the horror and the guilt, the suffering, fear, and denial that pierced the heart of India in the winter of 2002.

The result is *Fireproof*, one Ahmedabad man's fantastical, fearsome hurtling through the anxiety-drenched first days of violence and a visceral fever dream of a book readers will find hard to put down and impossible to shake. Although occasionally stomach-churning, Mr. Jha's new novel is not only a crackling good read – a thrilling bullet train of mayhem, mystery, and magic realism – it is also a wake-up call.

The book opens with the protagonist, Mr. Jay, at the hospital. Due to a difficult delivery his wife is unconscious and his newborn son horribly deformed: wrapped in dark, burnt-looking skin; without arms and legs; and with a slit for a mouth, a two-holed bump for a nose, and a soft, lumpy head. Only the eyes are like other babies', allowing him to keep watch as events unfold. Flummoxed by his progeny, Mr. Jay dubs the baby Ithim, a mash-up of "it" and "him."

While waiting to see his child he spies a woman standing in a window across the hospital courtyard. She scribbles "HELP ME" on fogged-up glass then vanishes along with the words. That night, after Jay has taken Ithim home, he receives a call from the mysterious woman. Miss Glass tells him to meet her the following afternoon at an undisclosed location a few hours outside the city. She says she can fix Ithim. After some indecision Jay acquiesces, leading to a riveting journey through which he begins to fully appreciate the horrors that have gripped his city.

A Greek chorus of soon-to-be-killed bit players delivers a warning shot in the Prologue, making readers aware, right from the start, that this will be no walk in the park. And indeed, tongues are cut from mouths, women raped and killed in front of their children, and bodies rain from the sky. The brutality and gore are presented with such forthrightness the reader finds himself riveted even as the steady drumbeat of death appalls.

"Then they rape the daughter-in-law. They strangle her with a towel. They slit her throat. They wait for her to die. They slit her stomach, all the way down. From her breasts to her pubic bone. They take her baby out. They throw up, at the sight of unborn flesh. And, of course, the blood. They throw up on the kitchen countertop, over the vegetables she was peeling. Then they set the house on fire."

The above is from one of three lengthy eyewitness accounts attached to an email Miss Glass sends to Mr. Jay providing directions for his journey. In these tales the witnesses and victims have names but the perpetrators are simply called A, B, C, and D. And between each chapter a member of the chorus of the dead – Head Nurse, for instance, or Taxi Driver – recounts his or her fiery end at the hands of a similarly nameless, faceless gang. The acts of violence remain vivid but anonymous, for now.

And the gruesomeness of these literary body blows is intended. Gujarat was vile and indefensible – over a month of jaw-dropping communal murder on a vast canvas – and Jha is attempting to recreate the aura of shock and disgust, danger and fear that swallowed the state like darkest night. THIS REALLY HAPPENED, he is reminding us, and such matter-of-fact recounting of horrors – Jha keeps the prose mostly plain rather than purple – rings more of history than fiction.

In an audacious and hilarious set piece at the railway station, however, Jha looses his pen. Jay is awaiting his escort to Miss Glass when a dwarf named Bright Shirt appears. Waltzing through a puddle of trousers, shoelaces, and a lengthy black and white-checked scarf, the stubby one freezes Jay in bemused awe:

"He was running, on the spot, stomping and stamping in this puddle, his clothes flapping like giant tropical birds perched on his body. He was jumping up and down, his elbows and knees jerking back and forth, restless, impatient, like a player limbering up before a game...

'Forgive my looks, for I am just a clown,

My job is to cheer you up, Whenever you are down.

You look very tired, sir, you look quite beat,

So let's sit down for a while, and get something to eat?'

Then he turned, with a flick of his heel, a stamp of his foot, like a soldier in a parade, and was off. He walked as if there was no crowd, barging right into people, banging against their suitcases and their bundles, almost knocking his head against their knees. This strategy of his seemed to work, though. For the crowd was parting for him, easily and spontaneously, and he was walking, running, jogging, as if this were a playground and he were a child."

The comic relief is short-lived and serves mainly as a bridge between the atrocities of the book's first two-thirds and the surreal fantasyland of the finale. Here we find dead families swimming in water-filled homes, books and towels doing stand up, and juggling, singing fire-wielders. With the last fifty pages Jha floats to heights of silly surreality and stoops to somewhat reductive social commentary. The clash with what has come before is jarring, yet in the cacophony a potent message rings true.

Even as Gujarat burns and hundreds die, this is a story about Jay. We never meet his wife, and in a way we never meet Ithim, either. All of the lesser characters end up dead. There are clear echoes of Kenzaburo Oe's piercing novel Bird, in which the titular deformed son reflects a physically and psychically scarred post-WWII Japan. But in Fireproof it is the protagonist, not his misshapen offspring, who stands in for a devastated Asian nation.

Once upon a time Gujarat was just one of 28 Indian states. A pleasant enough spot snug up against Pakistan and the Arabian Sea; unremarkable, perhaps, but with decent beaches and Asia's lone lion preserve, it kept up appearances. Today the word describes not only India's stubby most-westerly appendage but also a time and place one would prefer to forget.

Five years later the violence has waned but tensions have yet to ease. Some 30,000 of the 200,000 Muslims made homeless by the pogrom still live as refugees in 81 relief camps across the state. Afraid of inciting violence, Gujarat's theatre owners regularly refuse to screen controversial films: last year *Fanaa* was banned because of Aamir Khan's controversial political stance and just last month it was Naseeruddin Shah starrer *Parzania*, in which parents search for their young son, one of the countless lost in the madness. And it appears a lack of political will is as culpable as lingering communal animosity: as of June 2006 only 10 convictions had been made in over 4000 criminal cases originally filed by the police in connection with the carnage.

Gujarat, then, is the great national nightmare from which India has yet to awake. With *Fireproof*, Mr. Jha endeavors to ring the alarm.

□

Chapter 11

Slouching Toward Disaster

WHEN I RETURNED to Kashmir in 2006 it was with great anticipation, mainly to see how mistaken I'd been — or whether I'd been mistaken at all — to fear for my life during my first visit, seeking refuge from Delhi's hellfire heat back in 1998.

It's been a quarter-century now, so the memories are patchy. I remember long afternoons on the roof of St. James Palace, my Nagin Lake houseboat, reading, relaxing and watching kingfishers hover, dive and emerge from the water with their wriggling catch. The all-encompassing mist over Dal Lake in the morning. Being the only tourist on the muddy streets of Srinagar, the object of countless blank stares while taking in the aged wooden homes. The shikaras stopping at my houseboat landing every few hours, a kindly, desperate merchant offering shawls, souvenirs, sweets. The fantastic curry dinners my host Muhammad Ali's wife would prepare (his family stayed in a smaller boat tied to the St. James, where I presume they lived when there were no guests) and the haunting blue-green eyes of his 15-year-old daughter, who would steal glances my way while doing the wash.

Most of all I recall a trek in Pahalgam, during which we stumbled upon a family living in a hut carved into the mountainside. I followed two toddlers into their stone home to find a black and white television playing a Bollywood movie, which, on the side of a Himalayan mountain, literally miles from anything resembling civilization, struck me as impossible. After that trek, Muhammad Ali pressed me every morning, every afternoon, to go on another, to Gulmarg or Sonamarg. "They are even more beautiful," he would say. "You can stay overnight, and sleep among the stars." His persistence, and the way he said it, with a thin smile, unnerved me.

I thought of my Indian friend's warning and the kidnapping of those Westerners. They had been trekking when they were nabbed. Then there was this: I had booked a week-long stay, but on the seventh morning no boat arrived to take me away. Even if a boat had come, I wasn't sure where I'd be going. I had no ticket for a return flight or a bus headed south. In my overheated state, back in Delhi, I'd never pondered what might come afterward. Or even that there would be an afterward. But what sort of innkeeper lets their guest stay additional nights free of charge and makes no mention of the extension? I was enjoying my leisurely days on a houseboat, in no great rush to depart, but after an eighth day came and went with no sign of a shikara, it dawned on me that my host seemed acutely interested in getting me on an overnight trek yet surprisingly uninterested in clearing me out and readying the place for his next guest.

Looking to take matters into my own hands, I noticed that the stern of the boat, like a handful of other neighboring houseboats, was tied to a thin strip of land, sort of an earthen pier, maybe two meters wide. In one direction it receded into the lake. My view of the other end was obstructed, so I hopped off the St. James for a closer look and found that it ran to the shore, ending next to a rice patty. I made my way through the paddy and found myself in a leper colony. It's still there today, some 25 years later: the Leper Hospital on Google Maps. I strolled through, waving to a few patients taking some air, then up a hill and onto a dirt road lined with impressive homes tucked behind red brick walls topped with shards of glass — the Kashmiri equivalent of barbed wire.

A man operating a roadside stand, selling cigarettes, sweets and chai, told me a minibus stopped every 20 minutes or so, and it all came together. I packed my things that night, woke before dawn on the 10th day — three nights free, if you're able to check out! — and crept off the boat as quietly as I could. The minibus took me to Srinagar's main bus station, where I hopped on a full-sized bus to Jammu, where I boarded a train to Pathankot, and from there a bus to Dharamsala. As that bus approached the home-in-exile of the Dalai Lama and the Tibetan government, I noticed, even in my exhaustion, commotion along the side of the road. I blinked and took a closer look. Monkeys. Dozens of them. At last. After nearly two weeks in-country I'd found the India I'd come looking for.

The next morning I finally had a chance to catch my breath. Just days after I desperately fled Delhi, I hurried out of Kashmir, stealing away in the still-dark morning. I was pretty sure traveling didn't generally involve fleeing from one place to the next. Had I begun to see Kashmir as a dangerous place filled with jihadis? My friend, an Indian with some familiarity with that part of the world, held such a view and feared I'd be in grave danger in Kashmir. His view then influenced me, and led me to see my host as a potential captor and plot an escape. Western views of Kashmir have been similarly shaped by media coverage, such as my Economist article on Asiya Andrabi, and those 1995 kidnappings.

That incident might have ended quite differently. As detailed in *The Meadow*, a 2012 book on the kidnappings, escaped hostage John Childs, the lone American, wanted to immediately lead police to the kidnappers' hideout, where the others were still alive. Instead, his American handlers whisked him out of India.[198] In the end, he was the only one to survive. If the Americans had allowed Childs to lead Indian authorities to the hideout, perhaps none of the kidnapped foreigners would have died. Setting aside the insurgency, Kashmir might never have gained a reputation as a dangerous place for Westerners, my Indian friend would probably not have warned me to stay away and I would never have rudely slithered away from St. James Palace under cover of a misty dawn, without a thank you or goodbye.

And yet, one unsettling winter night at my Kashmir home points toward another reality. Were they planning to kidnap me and demand a ransom payment? That's my best guess, and locals concurred. Had I been a tad lucky to be out of town when they dropped by? Unfathomably so. So fortunate that to this day I wonder if it were more than mere coincidence.

□

The Night They Came for Me

(old blog post)

December 26, 2006: "Where are you?" Sajjad asks when I call after returning from Gulmarg.

"I'm back in Srinagar, Lal Chowk," I tell him. "Just arrived."

"Oh, OK," he says. "I was just at your house."

"Oh, too bad I missed you."

"Yes, I was talking to Iftikhar," he says. "There is something we should discuss."

"Oh, yeah, what is it?" I responded, wondering what it could be.

"No, no, I will tell you later," he said, sounding serious.

"OK, we'll talk tomorrow."

"Yes, tomorrow morning," he agreed. "Alright, fine."

In the five months I've worked for him, Sajad has never once told me that we needed to talk, so this little conversation sets the wheels spinning. He has said several times how he is tired and would like very much to quit the paper and retire. Could this be it, the end of

Kashmir Observer? Could I be unemployed by tomorrow? It seems unlikely, but I count it among the possibilities.

Another is that it has to do with Hussain, mine and Iftikhar's servant. Dissatisfied with his work of late, Iftikhar had a few weeks ago told Hussain that he (Iftikhar) would be letting him (Hussain) go at the end of November. Sajad and I spoke and decided that we would try to settle the matter so that Hussain would continue to work as my cook — for which Sajad and I would share the payment of his salary — and as Iftikhar's gardener in return for housing. Perhaps some new development had occurred on that end.

These were the thoughts bouncing around my head when Sajad came online later that evening and I asked him what was up. He said that it was important and that it concerned all of us, but that it was nothing to worry about and that we'd discuss it tomorrow.

The next day I got to the office and was waiting, waiting, waiting. Finally he arrived at about 2:30 p.m. and we went into the sitting room to chat.

"OK," he begins, in his that slow drawl of his. "There were some visitors to your house on Friday night. Three men. Armed. Militants."

He looks at me sharply and I move not a muscle. He continues.

"Apparently they knocked on your window first," he says. "You were gone and they received no response, of course. Then they knocked on Hussain's window and he woke up and they told him they wanted a place to sleep."

I was shocked. Sajjad went on to say that the militants did spend several hours in Hussein's little room before departing, and that I should talk to my servant to learn more. A few hours later I returned home and found Hussain in the kitchen cooking my dinner.

"So we had some visitors, I hear," I say, hoping he gets the drift.

"What?"

"Sajjad told me about the militants that were here, Friday night?"

"Oh, yeah!" he said, screwing up his face and sticking a ladle into the pot.

"Tell me about it. Did they knock on my window first?"

"Yeah, they knock your window and I hear something and look out. I see them and they come over and ask for place to rest for a while," he said. "I let them inside and two of them fell asleep. But the other, the commander, he stayed awake."

"The Kashmiri?" I asked, trying to get a sense of who was in charge, what might have been their mission.

"The Kashmiri was sleeping first!" he shot back. "He out right away. Nooooo, commander big, strong Pakistani. Like this," lifting up his shoulders and arms like a gorilla.

"He told me that it was bad that I was working for this man, as a servant. Asked me why I'm not fighting for my home. I told him I working!" Hussein continued. "He said that I should join the movement. Told me if I ever needed anything I should give him call."

"He gave you his phone number?" I asked.

"Yeah, his mobile number."

This seemed a breach of militant etiquette.

"They had so many guns — big, militant guns and six pistols!" Hussein resumed, getting jumpy. "But next time they come, I killing them!"

My home away from home suddenly seemed less homey. Initially I had thought maybe these militants had just found themselves in our neck of the woods for whatever reason late one night. Not having any friends or acquaintances in the area, they snuck into a sizable compound thinking they might find an empty space to rest until morning. What seemed unlikely before I spoke to Hussein, his recollections made even more so. It's possible that when the commander told Hussein he shouldn't be working for "this man" that he meant Iftikhar, who is Shia. Much more likely is that he meant me, the Westerner, the Amrikan, on whose window he knocked first. Whether they wanted to kidnap or straight out kill me is to some extent immaterial. The most reasonable conclusion to take from this episode is that Pakistani and Kashmiri militants know where I live, do not like me a great deal, and might return someday soon.

From that point on I felt less than comfortable bedding down in the dark mere feet away from the window to which large, armed militants had recently come a-knockin'. At Sajjad's suggestion, I hurriedly began looking for other lodgings, preferably somewhere closer to town, somewhere safer, and somewhere with 24-hour power supply. After a few days' search I found a too-large, too-expensive place in Rajbagh, a pleasant, army-infested neighborhood across the Jhelum from the *Kashmir Observer* office, and snatched it up.

Best of all, it has a hamam, which in this case is not a bath or sauna. A hamam is a domestic heating apparatus unique to Kashmir and going back to at least the 12th century writings of Kalhana. Under internal concrete flooring, a wood-burning fire is lit and controlled from a small external opening. Generally, the homeowner goes outside in the evening to build and light the fire. Once it's burning strongly he shuts the metal door and allows the fire to burn out on its own, which keeps the concrete floor warm throughout the night.

My hamam is warming my buns as I write on this fine, chilly Christmas night. And all is well again in Kashmir.

□

Thank you and goodbye for now

(KO report)

June 14, 2007: By the time you read this I will be safely ensconced on a jet plane en route to the United States, to my home in New York City.

My time with *Kashmir Observer* has come to an end, but before I go I'd like to say a sincere farewell, and offer a heartfelt thank you.

Three cheers to the Indian government, for your charming way of making a grand show of doing absolutely nothing. Transparent human rights commissions, Swiss-cheese probes, farcical trials and tribunals. Cracking good stuff.

To the Indian security forces, for countless human rights violations, suicides, fraggings, and most importantly, those pesky fake encounter killings. What would I do without you? Wait, don't answer that — it's rhetorical. But here's a real question: When will you be leaving?

To *Mirwaiz* Omar Farooq, for never saying or doing anything that merited any more than passing attention. You allowed me to focus on the important stories.

To Asiya Andrabi, Dukhtaran-e-Millat, and FASE, for giving journalists so much to write about and the good people of Kashmir an excellent rib tickling. But enough already, yeah? Stop being so damned silly.

To the average Kashmiri, for no longer reading books, attending the cinema, viewing art, worrying about your heritage, or making music. Without your lack of interest in culture I would have struggled to find subjects worthy of lengthy, in-depth feature treatment.

To SAS Geelani, for always offering good copy and continuing to stir the pot. One request: no more hartals, alright? You made your point.

To Dal Lake. They say you are world famous but if that's the case then how come the world is letting you die? My guess is that you are not as famous as they say, and that Kashmiris continue to do so only as a way of avoiding the painful truth: you will not be with us much longer. You will be missed and mourned, never forgotten.

To the teachers of the Waterhal school and other rural areas. Your hard work and determination to help students grow and learn despite harsh circumstances is impressive and admirable. It is also the very foundation upon which the future Kashmir will be built.

To Tagore Hall — without you we'd have no culture at all.

To Chief Minister Ghulam Nabi Azad. No man is as capable as this Jammu native at claiming one thing and proceeding to do the exact opposite. Time and again, Mr. CM, you have failed Kashmir. As a journalist, my cup runneth over.

To Agha, for some of the best evenings and conversations I had during my stay. (Could I please have my book back now?)

To Farooq Shah, for being my man Friday and encapsulating all that is wonderful and frustrating about Kashmiris.

To Dr. Mushtaq Margoob, Pervez Imroz, and many determined others who are fighting every day to improve the lives of Kashmiris.

To Salama, the best tailor in Kashmir, who provided good tea, better suits, and a comfortable and comforting sanctuary from the vagaries of Kashmir.

To Tao Cafe and De Linz, for making lunch the most difficult decision of my day.

To the Kashmiri print media, for accepting me and embracing me as one of your own. I will never forget your guidance and support.

To my editor and all the good people at *Kashmir Observer*. For hiring me and bringing me here to experience a new world. For helping me get my bearings in a difficult, dangerous, and complicated place and allowing me to learn on the job. For working so hard, often with little reward. I had no idea a newspaper could be put together by so few, with so little, in such difficult circumstances. KO's continued existence defies reason.

To the conflict, aka trouble in paradise on earth, aka the jugular vein of Pakistan, aka integral part of India. Without you I would never have come here. Without you journalists like me would have nothing to write about. Without you Kashmiris would not have faced so much suffering of late. You've had your fun, now please, bug off.

Thank you and farewell to all. And don't fret — I'll be back.

□

I MAY HAVE gotten swept up in the enthusiasm of my return to the Valley with this blog post, but thankfully, I'm far from alone in misjudging this troubled region. The history of Kashmir is littered with observers who viewed a momentary shift through rose-tinted glasses and envisioned a more hopeful future.

Looking back now, it all seems part of the desiccation cycle: Kashmir is constantly being reborn and crushed anew. It's Sisyphus, or the mythical phoenix stuck in a twisted *Groundhog Day* — eternally approaching something like progress before crashing down in flames and rising again from the ashes.

☐

Rebirth of Kashmir

(old blog post)

August 25, 2008: They came from Bandipore and Baramulla, Pampore, Rajbagh, Sonmarg, and Uri, three to a scooter, 60 to an overloaded minibus, on foot, by bicycle, truck, rickshaw and horse-pulled tonga. Aged 8 to 68, men and women, boys and girls, waving placards and posters, hoisting banners and waving flags, miles-long convoys coursed through the streets of Srinagar as lakhs of Kashmiris descended on Idgah last Friday for the most exuberant display of their favorite new pastime, the protest party.

The demonstration was called by leading separatist politicians, but you can tell it's a celebration because of the smiling faces, the sense of brotherhood, the confident glow of the righteous. The protesters are exuberant, unchained, shouting anti-India slogans and pro-freedom chants. Everywhere, Kashmiri men are starting impromptu performances of the two-step jig that's sweeping the Valley. Hands in the air, shoulders rolling, heads bobbing and right foot stomping an imaginary Indian flag, boys and men bounce in a misshapen circle, shouting, "Ragda! Ragda!" They look at each other, one to the next and again, grinning and soaking it in, almost unbelieving. They've been waiting for this day for years.

The origins of the ragda are a bit vague. Some say it began this spring when a Kashmiri hijra set an Indian flag out on the ground and, seeking a more fabulous way to denounce his oppressors, stepped on it and shouted, "Ragda! Ragda!" ("Stomp! Stomp!"). It's turned out to be contagious, and it's given this movement rhythm.

The police and Indian army troops, armed to the teeth and out in force earlier in the day, have melted away. How do you attack someone laughing and dancing joyously as he denounces you and your country?

Later on, separatist politicians would clamber up to the dais only to be lost in the din, like a drop of water trying to direct the tides. The masses would be too busy dancing and shouting and unburdening themselves in a grand group catharsis. Parties don't need to be told how to embrace the moment.

Yes, many protesters are vehemently denouncing their oppressor, India, and celebrating Pakistan and Islamist militant group Lashkar-e-Taiba. But these are less acts of allegiance, more expressions of Kashmiri unity, as separatist and Muslim.

Walking to Idgah, a smiling Mehrajudin Mattoo, 63, pauses to reflect on the sea change in Kashmir. "Those days, it was the gun, everywhere," the retired civil servant tells me, thinking back to the 90's. "But this is different. This is the real Kashmir and they can't stop us. We know what we want and we know the best way to get it."

Hilal Ahmad Bhat, 26, is standing in the back of a lorry with a few dozen like-minded new friends heading towards the protest grounds. He is a teacher at a government-run school and I ask why he's protesting the very government that pays his bills and feeds his family.

"It is not a question of our bread," he said. "It is a matter of our freedom, because the exploitation has gone too far. Amarnath was just a single issue, just a part of the larger struggle that's been going on for a long long time, and now we've had enough."

The tipping point was not the land transfer, but what came after. "The road blockade was the turning point," said businessman Rafiq Bhat, 40. "Kashmiris are sensitive about their land, but if you threaten to starve them, look out."

Still, that push has not prodded Kashmiris to embrace the violence that's been frequent further south. "Our protests are totally peaceful – not like Jammu," added Bhat, who stayed in school when the conflict was revving up in the early 90's. He didn't think the gun was the answer.

"We want a peaceful resolution to our struggle. India keeps telling the world about the militancy here, that we are terrorists. But look around, there is no violence here today. There are no terrorists. We are a peaceful people."

I spent a week in Kashmir in the late 90's, lived in Srinagar from mid-2006 to mid-2007 and have visited regularly since, and suddenly it's completely new. Still kind, generous and willing to talk through the night, most Kashmiris had lost family or friends in the last few years and been worn down by the conflict, despite the recent drop in violence. Depression and other mental illnesses quadrupled from 2001 to 2007. While Kashmir remained beautiful, the shadows of the past and a lingering threat darkened the days.

No longer. The floodgates have opened and Kashmiris are releasing two decades of pain, anger, fear, frustration and loss – the pent-up emotions of the conflict generation. It is not a revolution as much as an evolution. We are witnessing the rebirth of Kashmir. For now, the insurgency is over, giving way to a broad-based non-violent movement for azadi.

And for my money, this is how freedom arrives. Not from the barrel of a gun. Not with a knock at your door in the dead of night. But from a seething, jeering, bopping mass of one. I'm reminded of a well-known reggae protest song:

Ah, no ignorance he do it.
Ah, no brute force do it.
Your weapons can't do it.
So hear this!

Throw down your arms and come,
Throw down your arms and come,
Throw down your arms and come,
Drop them
Put them away, to stay.

Kashmiris have answered the call. With the United Jehad Council announcing it will refrain from violence to allow this mass movement to take its course, so too have the militants. Who's missed the bus? Delhi. Portraying the heavy, the Indian government has imposed a curfew and, as of 25 August, taken to shooting violators.

□

EPILOGUE

"He who learns must suffer. And even in our sleep, pain that cannot forget falls drop by drop upon the heart, and in our own despair, against our will, comes wisdom."

— *Aeschylus*[199]

WHEN TURKISH PRESIDENT Recep Tayyip Erdogan bemoaned to the United Nations' General Assembly in September 2022 that India and Pakistan had failed to reach agreement on Kashmir, and expressed hope for a "fair and permanent peace", I felt the last 15 years of my life telescope.[200] As mentioned in this book's Introduction, I was working at the UN when I first came across the *Kashmir Observer* and decided to move to Srinagar. A few months after arriving in Kashmir, I took a break from the grind of reporting in the Valley and met a friend for an extended weekend in Istanbul. It was my first visit to Turkey, and I fell hard for the old Ottoman capital — the swoon-inducing Bosphorus views, the pencil-thin minarets, the kebabs and *kahvalti*, the swirl of old and new and the fizz of a Muslim-led democracy in the early 21st century. Years later I moved there, and the city exceeded even my rosy memories. By early 2016 I was producing the best work of my career — on Syrian refugees, the suffering of Kurds, emerging authoritarianism — and had begun talking with a major publisher about a book centered on Istanbul, which I considered home.

That April, my brother, sister and I took our mother to Italy, a country she had long loved but hadn't visited in ages, in an effort to cheer her up following the death of her husband of 52 years. We had a glorious time in Puglia, but upon my return to Istanbul's Ataturk Airport I was stopped at immigration. They told me there might be a ban on my entry into Turkey and I needed to wait. One hour passed, then two. Waiting for me at home, my Turkish girlfriend urged me not to worry, everything would be OK. Another hour passed, and another. Finally they put me in a room with a couch. In the morning, security officials told me I could return to Italy or to my native country; I soon found myself being hurried onto a plane headed for Chicago. Today, seven years later, the Turkish government has yet to provide a reason for banning my entry and labelling me a national security threat, but it was most likely in response to my dispatch, published in *The Guardian* a few months prior, on Turkey's military aggressions and human rights violations against its Kurdish population in the southeast.[201]

The mission of a foreign correspondent, as I see it, is to move beyond one's origins and latch onto a new narrative. The fears and concerns of the local population become your own, to an extent. My goal was to see through their eyes, while maintaining my own perspective, so as to connect with readers back home. During the period of the reporting in this book, I had yet to appreciate the extent to which the lives of Kashmiris, and most of the world's disadvantaged, were shaped by distant, unseen forces. Today I too know what it is to have a life destroyed by the powerful. In a few hours I lost my apartment, my job, my girlfriend, many good friends and the city in which I expected to spend the rest of my life. A few weeks later I lost an unborn child. At age 42, I woke up one morning and had to start over again.

With this book, born amid the plague, my eviction from Turkey may have come full circle. I'm no longer a foreign correspondent, but simply a correspondent. It's all rather less foreign now. I would never claim to understand the suffering, nor the survival, of Kashmiris, Kurds, Black Americans or other persecuted peoples. Nor would I compare my suffering to theirs. But I can say I have a greater understanding of their predicament, how it may have shaped them and their view of the world, and how life, much like a seemingly endless insurgency, is often an arduous slog through the waist-high mud of loss.

Not only do I now have a much better understanding of suffering, I know that my country is just as desiccated as any other. I write this in late 2023 from Kyiv, Ukraine, where most locals choose to hold Russians collectively responsible for their leader's decision to invade and carry on with his war of aggression, which some have labelled genocide. I tend to disagree, arguing that the single mother of three in Irkutsk, say, should not be blamed for deciding against going out to protest and risking jail, or worse. But I wonder if this is an attempt to excuse myself or ease my conscience for failing to act or raise my voice as my country, in the 90s and 2000s, trampled upon the rights and freedoms of countless millions, as well as its own ideals, around the world.

∎

Acknowledgements

I stumbled into this book much the way I stumbled into Kashmir. COVID-19 and a poorly timed trip to the US robbed me of my Berlin home in spring 2020, so I was riding out the late summer lockdown with my brother and his family in the White Mountains of New Hampshire when word came that retired Kashmiri educator Agha Ashraf Ali had passed away at age 96.

The memories flooded back. From mid-2006 to mid-2007 I worked as a reporter for Srinagar-based English-language daily *Kashmir Observer*, for which I'd written a lengthy profile of Agha. In a series of interviews he had laid out the history of Kashmir and that of his own family, mostly avoiding the emotionally fraught subject of his poet son Agha Shahid Ali, the chronicler of Kashmiri suffering who died of brain cancer in 2001. Nearly fifteen years after I'd written about him, and almost exactly a year after India revoked the special status of Jammu and Kashmir state, Agha's passing seemed yet another sign of the evaporation of Kashmiri life and culture. I hadn't spoken to my old boss Sajjad Haider, *Kashmir Observer*'s editor-in-chief, in nearly a decade, but he soon reached out to tell me KO was planning a book series to mark its 25th anniversary, in 2022. He thought my KO writings would be a great place to start. I hopped aboard, began wading through my 60-plus articles and soon saw, like invisible ink shimmering into view, the intertwining strands of my story and that of Kashmir.

First and foremost I must thank Sajjad, for being a wise, calm and steadfast editor way back when, and for alerting me, much more recently, to the opportunity of this book. I should also acknowledge here that *Kashmir Observer* and I are partners on this book, and that KO will actually receive more of the revenue (60%) than the credited author (40%). The idea is to help support independent media in Kashmir, which has been under siege for decades, and I couldn't be more pleased to have this opportunity to do just that.

A hearty thank you to my dear departed friend Agha Ashraf Ali, without whom I may not have survived Kashmir. You were a mentor and a tonic and an absolute joy. I also thank my lovely KO colleague M. Farooq Shah, the Sancho Panza to my Don Quixote, always there with enthusiasm and support. He and Kashmiri journalist Shabir Hussain also provided invaluable insight on reporting in the Valley and the pitfalls of Kashmir's mediasphere.

I'm grateful to KO's fearless leader, Rasheed Shahid, my KO colleague Asif Rizvi, for his steely determination, and the sultans of Kashmiri journalism, Yusuf Jameel, Basharat Peer, and Muzamil Jaleel, who have over the years lent more guidance than they could know. A sincere thank you.

Four Americans, all of whom are writers in one way or another, were instrumental in the shaping and writing of the book's introduction and other present-day sections. I hope Peter Lepeska, Chad Gracia, Unmesh Kher and Julie Wernau don't mind if I thank them jointly. Without their sharp reviews and insightful recommendations, this book would have been much less than it is today. Thank you all for your time and assistance.

Back in my Brooklyn College days, my instructors Paul Moses and Eric Alterman laid the foundation of my approach to and understanding of journalism, while JoAnne Wasserman, my editor at the Brooklyn bureau of the NY Daily News, provided the best on-the-job training a cub reporter could ever have. I couldn't be more grateful to these mentors.

I'd be remiss if I didn't thank Kashmiri historian Khalid Bashir Ahmad for taking the time to review the manuscript for historical inaccuracies. I only hope my fixes are satisfactory.

Last but not least I would like to thank my literary agent, Lalitha Ravindran of First Forays, for her dogged determination in finding a home for this book. Without her efforts this book would never have seen the light of day. And I feel endless gratitude toward Vishal Soni, Nupur Jain and the fantastic team at Vishwakarma, for their consideration, commitment, and, most importantly, their courage.

Desiccated Land Glossary

Accession to India: Maharaja Hari Singh signed Kashmir's accession to India document in October 1947, enabling the Indian army to intervene against Pakistan-backed forces.

Afghans and Sikhs: Ruled Kashmir in the 18th and 19th centuries and oppressed the local Kashmiri population, leading to a sense of resentment and opposition to outside rule.

Akbar's Conquest: Emperor Akbar defeated the Kashmiri Chak Dynasty and brought Kashmir under Mughal rule in 1586.

Article 35A: A provision in the Indian Constitution that allowed the Jammu and Kashmir state legislature to define who is a permanent resident of the state and grant them special privileges and rights. The provision was revoked along with Article 370 in August 2019.

Article 370: Article 370 of the Indian Constitution granted special status to Jammu and Kashmir, including autonomy over several areas such as the state's constitution, flag, and residency laws.

Bilateral Talks: Indo-Pak talks to resolve the Kashmir dispute have focused on issues such as trade, travel, and confidence-building measures, but have not addressed the core issue of the status of Jammu and Kashmir.

Buddhism: A religion and philosophy originated in ancient India, Buddhism arrived in Kashmir in the 3rd century BCE thanks to Mauryan Emperor Ashoka. The region eventually became a center of Buddhist learning and pilgrimage.

Chak Dynasty: A Muslim dynasty that ruled Kashmir from 1554-1586 CE, the Chaks are known for their patronage of the arts and their promotion of Persian culture in the region. Chaks were the last indigenous rulers of Kashmir.

Communication Restrictions: The gags that have been imposed over the region time and again - making it difficult for journalists to report on events and developments in real-time. This has often resulted in a delay in reporting and the spread of misinformation.

Dogra Dynasty: A Hindu dynasty from Jammu that ruled the region from 1846 to 1947. It was founded by Gulab Singh, a Rajput chieftain who was appointed as the Raja of Jammu by the Sikh Empire.

Farooq Abdullah: A prominent Kashmiri politician who has served as the Chief Minister of Jammu and Kashmir multiple times and is the President of the National Conference party, which has been a major player in the politics of the state.

Hari Singh: The last king of the princely state of Jammu and Kashmir, Hari Singh ruled from 1925-1947 and is known for his decision to accede to India following the partition of British India in 1947, spurring lasting conflict.

Insurgency: Starting around 1990, this continuing guerrilla campaign against Indian rule in Kashmir is characterized by violence between Indian armed forces and Pakistan-backed militants seeking Kashmir's independence or merger with Pakistan.

International Mediation: The global interest and involvement in the Kashmir dispute has yielded little success as New Delhi maintains that the dispute is a bilateral issue and has rejected any third-party mediation.

Kalhana: A 12th-century CE historian and poet who wrote the Rajatarangini, a chronicle of the kings of Kashmir from ancient times to the 12th century.

Kangri: Traditional Kashmiri firepot used to keep warm during the winter months. It is kept in wicker and contains smoldering coal.

Kashmiri: 1. Part of the Dardic language family, Kashmiri is spoken by the people of the Kashmir valley and surrounding areas and written in the Perso-Arabic script. 2. A person from the Himalayan region at the northern tip of the Indian subcontinent, an area claimed by India, Pakistan, and China.

Kashmir Architecture: Characterized by its blend of Islamic, Hindu, and Buddhist influences, the architecture of Kashmir include the Mughal gardens, the Grand Mosque and Khanqah-e-Maula in Srinagar.

Kashmiri Art: Known for its vibrant colors and intricate designs, Kashmiri Art is heavily influenced by the region's natural beauty and cultural diversity.

Kashmir Festivals: Marked by feasting, dancing, and other cultural activities, the festivals celebrated by the people of Kashmir include Eid, Navroz, and Lohri.

Kashmir Folk Dance: A traditional dance form of Kashmir, it includes the rouf, hafiza, and bhand pather. It is usually performed during festivals and other cultural events.

Kashmiri Handicrafts: Known for their intricate designs and high quality, the handicrafts of Kashmir include pashmina shawls, carpets, wood carvings and papier mache.

Kashmiri Literature: Known for its cross-cultural literary influences, the literature produced by the writers of Kashmir includes works in Persian, Kashmiri, Urdu and English.

Kashmiri Media: Leading local news outlets include Greater Kashmir, Kashmir Observer, Kashmir Images, Kashmir Times, Rising Kashmir, and others. Most have offices in and around Srinagar's Press Colony at Lal Chowk.

Kashmiri Music: The music of Kashmir is characterized by haunting melodies and soulful lyrics and made with traditional instruments like the santoor, rabab, and tumbaknari.

Kashmir Press Club: An association of journalists in Jammu and Kashmir that served as a platform for journalists to discuss issues related to their profession.

Kashmiri Shaivism: A school of Hindu philosophy that emerged in the 8th century CE in Kashmir, it emphasizes the importance of direct experience of the divine and the unity of the individual soul (atman) with the universal soul (Brahman).

Kashmiri Shawl: Famous and luxurious textile that is made in Kashmir, it is made from the wool of the pashmina goat and is known for its softness, warmth, and intricate designs.

Kashmiri Shawl Industry: The industry that provided a significant source of income for the region and helped to support its artisans and craftspeople, dates back to medieval times.

Kashmir Weddings: Known for their grand and elaborate affairs, the wedding ceremony in Kashmir involves rituals and customs, such as the mehndi, baraat, and walima.

Kehwa: Traditional Kashmiri brew, it is made with green tea leaves and spices such as cinnamon, cardamom and saffron. It is often served with Kashmiri breads such as sheermal, kulcha or baqerkhani.

Khanqah-e-Maula: An ancient hospice located on the banks of the Jhelum River in Srinagar, it was built in the 14th century CE by Mir Sayyid Ali Hamadani, a Sufi saint who is credited with bringing Islam to Kashmir and introducing Kashmiris to the crafts and sciences of Iran which it is now famous for.

Lalitaditya Muktapida: A king of the Karkota Dynasty who ruled Kashmir from 724-760 CE is known for his military campaigns, including an invasion of Tibet, and for his patronage of the arts and architecture.

Line of Control: The de-facto border between India and Pakistan over divided Kashmir land came into being following the Indo-Pakistan War of 1947-48. It was earlier called a ceasefire line.

Martand Sun Temple: An ancient temple dedicated to the Hindu deity Surya, is located in the Anantnag district of Kashmir. It was built by King Lalitaditya Muktapida in the 8th century CE and is known for its impressive architecture and elaborate carvings.

Mehbooba Mufti: A Kashmiri politician who served as the first female Chief Minister of Jammu and Kashmir. She is the leader of the Peoples

Democratic Party (PDP) and played a significant role in the politics of the state.

Mirwaiz Umar Farooq: A Kashmiri separatist politician who is the chairman of the All Parties Hurriyat Conference. He is also the hereditary religious leader of the Kashmiri Muslim community from Mirwaiz dynasty.

Mufti Mohammad Sayeed: A Kashmiri politician who served as the Chief Minister of Jammu and Kashmir twice and was the founder of the Peoples Democratic Party (PDP) and played a significant role in the politics of the state.

Muslim Rule: Muslim rule is the period when Kashmir came under the command of the Sultanate of Delhi in the 14th-15th centuries, the Mughal Empire in the 16th-18th centuries, and the Durrani Empire in the late 18th century.

Neolithic Age: A prehistoric period (c. 4000-2500 BCE) characterized by the development of agriculture, domestication of animals, and the use of stone tools, Kashmir's Neolithic Age surfaces in the form of the ruins at the Burzahom archaeological site.

Omar Abdullah: A Kashmiri politician who served as the Chief Minister of Jammu and Kashmir from 2009 to 2014. He is the son of Farooq Abdullah and has been a prominent member of the National Conference party.

Pheran: Woolen Kashmiri garment worn during the winter months, it covers the body from the shoulders to below the knees and is often paired with a headscarf.

Plebiscite: A referendum in which the people of a region vote on whether to join a particular country or become an independent state. The issue of holding a plebiscite in Kashmir was proposed by the United Nations in 1948, but has not been implemented due to disagreements between India and Pakistan.

Press Council of India (PCI): A statutory body in India established to maintain and improve the standards of newspapers and news agencies in the country. It addresses complaints and issues related to the freedom of the press.

Press Information Bureau (PIB): A government agency responsible for disseminating information about government policies, programs, and initiatives to the public and the media.

Sheikh Abdullah: A prominent Kashmiri politician and leader of the National Conference, Sheikh Abdullah played a key role in mobilizing masses for democracy in the 20th century. He served as the first Prime Minister of Jammu and Kashmir from 1948-1953, and was later imprisoned for advocating for Kashmir's independence from India.

Shikara: Wooden Kashmiri boat propelled by an oar, it is used for leisurely rides in Srinagar's Dal Lake.

Shimla Agreement: The 1972 Indo-Pak Agreement, which established the LOC as the de facto border between the two countries and committed both sides to resolving all disputes through bilateral negotiations.

Sultanate of Kashmir: A Muslim kingdom that ruled over Kashmir from the 14th-16th centuries, it was established by Shah Mir, a Muslim adventurer who claimed the title of Sultan after conquering Kashmir.

Syed Ali Geelani: A Kashmiri separatist politician who advocated for the merger of Kashmir with Pakistan. He was the chairman of the All Parties Hurriyat Conference, which is an umbrella organization of separatist groups in Kashmir.

Threats And Harassment of Journalists: The phenomenon of subjecting journalists to threats, harassment, and violence by both state and non-state actors. It has resulted in a difficult and challenging environment for journalists to work in.

Treaty of Amritsar: The treaty that transferred the region to Dogra control in exchange for a payment of 75 lakhs rupees was signed between the British East India Company and Gulab Singh in 1846, following the First Anglo-Sikh War.

United Nations Resolutions: A number of resolutions passed by the United Nations between 1948 and 1957, called for a plebiscite to be held in Jammu and Kashmir and allowed the people of the region to choose their political future.

Wazwan: Traditional multi-course Kashmiri meal served on special occasions, such as weddings and festivals. It consists of a series of meat dishes, often as many as two dozen, and is typically served around large, shared copper platters of steamed rice.

Yasin Malik: Kashmiri separatist and chairman of the Jammu and Kashmir Liberation Front (JKLF), which advocates for Kashmir's independence from both India and Pakistan. He has been an influential figure in Kashmiri politics since the 1980s.

Zain-ul-Abidin: A king of the Shah Miri Dynasty who ruled Kashmir from 1420-1470 CE, he is known for his patronage of art and architecture, including the construction of the Shah Hamdan Mosque in Srinagar and the restoration of the Martand Sun Temple.

Endnotes

1   Boochani, Behrouz. (2019). No Friend but the Mountains: Writing from Manus Prison. Anansi International. p30-31.

2   First Chief Information Commissioner of India and former chair of India's National Commission for Minorities. He served in several lead roles in Kashmir in the 1980s and 90s, and today is chair of India's Commonwealth Human Rights Initiative.

3   James Baldwin vs. William F. Buckley. February 1965 debate at Cambridge. National Educational Television Network. https://www.youtube.com/watch?v=5Tek9h3a5wQ&ab_channel=AeonVideo.

4   Munshi, Sadaf. (2020). Azadi. https://sadafmunshi.com/2020/08/15/az%c9%99di-freedom/.

5   1957-1963 American sitcom about an ideal suburban family in the post-war boom: https://en.wikipedia.org/wiki/Leave_It_to_Beaver

6   I mostly pumped out research papers for college students, who agreed not to turn them in as their own before doing precisely that. Morally questionable work, sure, but also a fast track to the "10,000 hours" of writing needed for mastery.

7   Many Kashmiris do not subscribe to this theory of the birth of Kashmir, and that's fine. It's just a myth.

8   Kumari, Ved, translator. The Nilamata Purana.https://www.wisdomlib.org/hinduism/book/the-nilamata-purana.

9   Bamzai, PNK. (1994). Culture and Political History of Kashmir, Volume 1. p4-5.   https://books.google.com.ua/books?id=1eMfzTBcXcYC&pg=PA54&redir_esc=y#v=onepage&q&f=false

10   Snedden, Christopher. (2015). Understanding Kashmir and Kashmiris. Hurst. p18, Kindle edition.

11   Swain, Ashok. "How the Himalayan region became a major climate hotspot." Gulf News. Sept. 6, 2022: https://gulfnews.com/opinion/

op-eds/how-the-himalayan-region-became-a-major-climate-hotspot-1.90352234& Khambete, Arti Kelkar. "The fast disappearing glaciers of Kashmir." India Water Portal. Sept 11, 2020. https://www.indiawaterportal.org/articles/fast-disappearing-glaciers-kashmir

12   The word "Himalaya" is Sanskrit for "dwelling place of snow".

13   Dhar, Somnath. (1945) Kashmir: Eden of the East. Intro by Jawarhalal Nehru. https://www.amazon.com/Kashmir-Eden-East-introductory-Jawaharlal/dp/B0007JDMHC.

14   Mughal Emperor Jahangir is widely credited with saying, of Kashmir, "If there is paradise on earth, it is this, it is this, it is this." But columnist and author Rana Safvi appeared to prove conclusively in her 2019 book Shahjahanabad that the line was written by Amir Khusrow, who never set foot in Kashmir. This is detailed here: https://scroll.in/article/942273/who-really-wrote-the-lines-if-there-is-paradise-on-earth-it-is-this-it-is-this-it-is-this.

15   Grover, Amar. "Postcard from Kashmir, Still a Hotspot." Financial Times. Feb 3, 2012. https://www.ft.com/content/9abef77e-4819-11e1-b1b4-00144feabdc0.

16   Livings, Jack. The Art of Fiction No. 186: Salman Rushdie. The Paris Review Issue 174. Summer 2005. https://www.salmanrushdie.com/the-art-of-fiction-no-186-from-the-paris-review/

17   Singh, Upinder. (2017) Political Violence in Ancient India. Harvard University Press. p241. https://books.google.com.ua/books?id=t6A4DwAAQBAJ&pg=PA241&redir_esc=y#v=onepage&q&f=false

18   Much scholarly research has revealed the dubious nature of the term "Kashmiriyat". This book makes no claim about its origins, but merely uses the word to refer to the region's reported religious and social harmony. Whether or not the term was used way back when, or is today misused, is better addressed elsewhere.

19   Kaw, Mushtaq A. (1996). Famines in Kashmir, 1586-1819. The policy of the Mughal and Afghan rulers. The Indian Economic and Social History Review. v33. https://journals.sagepub.com/doi/abs/10.1177/001946469603300103?journalCode=iera

20   European Foundation for South Asian Studies, Amsterdam. A Memory of Religious Plurality in Jammu and Kashmir. https://www.efsas.org/publications/study-papers/a-memory-of-religious-plurality-in-jammu-and-kashmir/.

21   Moorcroft, William. Trebeck, George, and Hayman, Horace. (1841). Travels in the Himalayan provinces of Hindustan and the Panjab; in Ladakh and Kashmir; in Peshawar, Kabul, Kunduz, and Bokhara.J. Murray, London. p294-5. https://archive.org/details/

travelsinhimala00trebgoog/page/n308/mode/2up.

22   Jaleel, Muzamil. "New land laws put all of Kashmir up for sale." The Kashmir Walla. Oct 30 2020. https://thekashmirwalla.com/2020/10/new-land-laws-put-all-of-kashmir-up-for-sale/.

23   Khajuria, Manu. "Why we must not forget J&K forces who fought World War I." Daily O. Nov 7, 2015. https://www.dailyo.in/politics/world-war-i-dogra-regiment-sikh-battalion-jammu-and-kashmir/story/1/7215.html.

24   I'm no historian, and Kashmir's political and social history are detailed in much greater length and breadth in many fine works, such as Sumit Ganguly's The Crisis in Kashmir, Kashmir in Conflict by Victoria Schofield, Understanding Kashmir and Kashmiris by Christopher Snedden, Ramachandra Guha's India After Gandhi, Basharat Peer's memoir Curfewed Night, Malik Sajad's graphic novel Munnu, Mirza Waheed's The Collaborator, and the essay collection Kashmir: The Case for Freedom. For the purposes of this book, a cursory background will suffice. But this account leaves out a great deal of useful detail and perspective and I urge the reader to avail herself of more historical, political and native works.

25   Ahmad, Khalid Bashir. (2012). Kashmir, Looking Back in Time: Politics, Culture, History. Atlantic. p 225-26

26   If only. — "Nehru's First Speech on Kashmir." Kashmir Life.https://kashmirlife.net/nehrus-first-speech-on-kashmir-165556/.

27   The party of Gandhi and Nehru is of course still today led by Nehru's descendants, who are rather conveniently named Gandhi as well, after his daughter Indira married an MP with the same surname as the country's founding father.

28   Hussain, Altaf. "Kashmir's flawed elections." BBC. Sept 14, 2002. http://news.bbc.co.uk/2/hi/south_asia/2223364.stm.

29   Mir, Hilal. "The Kashmiri novel: Tales in a lost tongue." Hindustan Times. Nov 26, 2016. https://www.hindustantimes.com/books/the-kashmiri-novel-tales-in-a-lost-tongue/story-2PqYE6Y4iSJviPJsCVGlyL.html

30   "Full text: bin Laden's 'letter to America'". The Guardian. Nov 24, 2002. https://www.theguardian.com/world/2002/nov/24/theobserver.

31   Smucker, Philip. "Al Qaeda thriving in Pakistani Kashmir." The Christian Science Monitor. July 2, 2002. https://www.csmonitor.com/2002/0702/p01s02-wosc.html.

32   Ibid.

33   Weiner, Tim. "History to Trump: CIA was aiding Afghan rebels before the Soviets invaded in 1979." Washington Post. Jan 7, 2019. https://www.washingtonpost.com/outlook/2019/01/07/history-trump-cia-was-

arming-afghan-rebels-before-soviets-invaded/.

34   Naeem, Raza. "Revisiting Manto's biting letters to Uncle Sam, Part 1." The Express Tribune. Jan 18, 2020. https://tribune.com.pk/article/93119/revisiting-mantos-biting-letters-to-uncle-sam-part-1.

35   Sprung, Andrew. "Did the US 'abandon' Afghanistan in 1989?" The Atlantic. Dec 17, 2009. https://www.theatlantic.com/daily-dish/archive/2009/12/did-the-us-abandon-afghanistan-in-1989/192860/

36   Coll, Steve. (2005). Ghost Wars: The Secret History of the CIA, Afghanistan and bin Laden. Penguin. p149.

37   Ibid, p221.

38   Hersh, Seymour M. "On the Nuclear Edge." The New Yorker. March 3, 1993. https://www.newyorker.com/magazine/1993/03/29/on-the-nuclear-edge.

39   May 14, 2002, terrorist attack near the town of Kaluchak in Jammu. Three Kashmiri militants disguised as Indian soldiers boarded a bus headed from Manali to Jammu. They shot and killed the driver, then opened fire and killed 6 more people. Then they entered the family area of the nearby Indian army base and killed 23 people, including 10 children. More detail here: https://en.wikipedia.org/wiki/Kaluchak_massacre.

40   "President Bush and President Musharraf of Pakistan Discuss Strengthened Relationship." The White House, Office of the Press Secretary. March 4, 2006. https://georgewbush-whitehouse.archives.gov/news/releases/2006/03/20060304-2.html.

41   Lavoy, Peter R. "Pakistan's Kashmir Policy after the Bush Visit to South Asia." Strategic Insights, vV, i4. April 2006. Center for Contemporary Conflict, Naval Postgraduate School.

42   Reynolds, Maura. "Bush says U.S. must spread democracy." Baltimore Sun. Nov 7, 2007. https://www.baltimoresun.com/news/bal-te.bush07nov07-story.html.

43   Coll, Steve. "The Back Channel." The New Yorker. Feb 22, 2009. https://www.newyorker.com/magazine/2009/03/02/the-back-channel.

44   Sanger, David E, and Dugger, Celia W. "Bush Intervenes in Effort to Stop a Kashmir War." The New York Times. June 6, 2002. https://www.nytimes.com/2002/06/06/world/bush-intervenes-in-effort-to-stop-a-kashmir-war.html.

45   Fisk, Robert. (2005). The Great War for Civilisation: The Conquest of the Middle East. Knopf Doubleday. Kindle Edition.

46   Evans, Lawrence. "Hegel on History." Philosophy Now. 2018. https://philosophynow.org/issues/129/Hegel_on_History.

47   Bielenberg, Aliosha. "Teleology, Hegel, and King." Feb 10, 2019.

https://alioshabielenberg.com/teleology-hegel-and-king/.

48   Mead, Walter Russel. "Decline Helps to Propel Us Forward." Guest on Wisdom of Crowds podcast. https://wisdomofcrowds.live/decline-helps-to-propel-us-forward/.

49   McBride, Frank. (2011). Frank Capra: The Catastrophe of Success. University Press of Mississippi.

50   Capra, Frank. (1971). The Name Above the Title: An Autobiography. Da Capo Press.

51   "Why We Fight: Prelude to War." (1942). Department of Defense. Department of the Army. Office of the Chief Signal Officer. US National Archives. https://www.youtube.com/watch?v=wcAsIWfk_z4&ab_channel=USNationalArchives

52   Frum, David. "Is America Still the 'Shining City on a Hill'?" The Atlantic. Jan 1, 2021. https://www.theatlantic.com/ideas/archive/2021/01/is-america-still-the-shining-city-on-a-hill/617474/.

53   Cohen, Michael. "Obama's great dilemma: to be or not to be the world's policeman." The Guardian. Sept 13, 2014. https://www.theguardian.com/commentisfree/2014/sep/13/obama-american-foreign-policy-isis-iraq.

54   Levin, Dov H. (2020). Meddling in the Ballot Box: The Causes and Effects of Partisan Electoral Intervention. Oxford University Press.

55   Kessler, Glenn. "The Iraq War and WMDs: An intelligence failure or White House spin?" The Washington Post. March 22, 2019. https://www.washingtonpost.com/politics/2019/03/22/iraq-war-wmds-an-intelligence-failure-or-white-house-spin/.

56   Purkiss, Jessica, and Serle, Jack. "Obama's covert drone war in numbers: Ten times more strikes than Bush." The Bureau of Investigative Journalism. Jan 17, 2017. https://www.thebureauinvestigates.com/stories/2017-01-17/obamas-covert-drone-war-in-numbers-ten-times-more-strikes-than-bush.

57   Gilmore, Jason, Sheets, Penelope, and Rowling, Charles. "Make no exception, save one: American exceptionalism, the American presidency, and the age of Obama." Communication Monographs. 2016, v83, i4. https://www.tandfonline.com/doi/abs/10.1080/03637751.2016.1182638?journalCode=rcmm20.

58   "Full Transcript of President Biden's Speech in Philadelphia." The New York Times. Sept 1, 2022. https://www.nytimes.com/2022/09/01/us/politics/biden-speech-transcript.html.

59   Beinart, Peter. "Biden wants America to lead the world. It shouldn't." The New York Times. Dec 2, 2020. https://www.nytimes.com/2020/12/02/opinion/biden-foreign-policy.html.

60   Vitali, Ali, Hunt, Kasie, and Thorp V, Frank. "Trump referred to Haiti and African nations as 'shithole' countries." NBC News. Jan 12, 2018. https://www.nbcnews.com/politics/white-house/trump-referred-haiti-african-countries-shithole-nations-n836946.

61   Smeltz, Daalder, Friedhof, Kafura, and Helm. "Divided We Stand: Democrats and Republicans Diverge on US Foreign Policy." Chicago Council on Foreign Affairs Survey.Dec 2020. https://www.thechicagocouncil.org/sites/default/files/2020-12/report_2020ccs_americadivided_0.pdf.

62   Krastev, Ivan, and Leonard, Mark. "The crisis of American power: How Europeans see Biden's America." European Council on Foreign Relations, Policy Brief. Jan 19. 2021. https://ecfr.eu/publication/the-crisis-of-american-power-how-europeans-see-bidens-america/.

63   Verma, Nidhi. "Russia's share of India's June oil inputs surges to record." Reuters. July 11, 2022. https://www.reuters.com/business/energy/russias-share-indias-june-oil-imports-surges-record-2022-07-11/& Mackinnon, Amy. "Sanctioned Russian Ships Are Still Doing Business with India." Foreign Policy. Sept 3, 2022. https://foreignpolicy.com/2022/08/03/sanctions-russia-ships-business-india/.

64   "Fault Lines: Global Perspectives on a World in Crisis." Open Society Foundations Survey. Sept 2022. https://www.opensocietyfoundations.org/publications/fault-lines-global-perspectives-on-a-world-in-crisis.

65   Index. Harper's. June 2022.

66   Abrahms, Max. "Why Terrorism Does Not Work." International Security. Oct 1, 2006. https://cisac.fsi.stanford.edu/publications/why_terrorism_does_not_work.

67   Akhtar, Ayad. (2020). Homeland Elegies. Little, Brown and Company. Kindle Edition. p50-51.

68   Barber, Lionel, Foy, Henry, and Barker, Alex. "Vladimir Putin says liberalism has become 'obsolete'." Financial Times. June 28, 2019. https://www.ft.com/content/670039ec-98f3-11e9-9573-ee5cbb98ed36.

69   "New report: The global decline in democracy has accelerated." Freedom House. March 3, 2021. https://freedomhouse.org/article/new-report-global-decline-democracy-has-accelerated

70   Filkins, Dexter. "Blood and Soil in Narendra Modi's India." The New Yorker. Dec 2, 2019. https://www.newyorker.com/magazine/2019/12/09/blood-and-soil-in-narendra-modis-india&Jaffrelot, Christophe. "How Narendra Modi Transformed from an RSS Pracharak to a Full-Fledged Politician and Hindu Hridaysamrat." The Wire. Aug 24, 2021. https://thewire.in/politics/

narendra-modi-rss-pracharak-politician.

71   Schmall, Emily. "Kashmir Votes, and India Hails It as Normalcy in a Dominated Region." The New York Times. Dec 22, 2020. https://www.nytimes.com/2020/12/22/world/asia/kashmir-modi-election.html.

72   Masoodi, Ashwaq. "States of Kashmir." N+1. Aug 17, 2019. https://nplusonemag.com/online-only/online-only/states-of-kashmir/.

73   "PM Modi urges film industry to shoot in Jammu and Kashmir, Ladakkh." Deccan Chronicle. Âug 9, 2019. https://www.deccanchronicle.com/entertainment/bollywood/090819/pm-modi-urges-film-industry-to-shoot-in-jammu-and-kashmir-ladakh.html.

74   Fareed, Rifat. "India's Modi promises investments on Kashmir visit." Al Jazeera. April 24, 2022. https://www.aljazeera.com/news/2022/4/24/modi-throws-open-tunnel-connecting-kashmir-to-mainland-india.

75   Ibid.

76   D'Mello, Sandhya, and Sankar, Adjana. "Emaar to develop shopping mall in Srinagar." Khaleej Times. Jan 3, 2022. https://www.khaleejtimes.com/business/emaar-to-develop-shopping-mall-in-indias-srinagar.

77   Bhattacharya, Ananya. "The 550-day 4G blackout cost Kashmir's economy \$4.2 billion." Quartz. Feb 9, 2021.

      https://qz.com/india/1970363/the-550-day-4g-blackout-cost-kashmirs-economy-4-2-billion/.

78   "Here's the truth about BBC, Al Jazeera, Reuters reports of protests in Soura, Kashmir." News Laundry. Aug 14, 2019. https://www.newslaundry.com/2019/08/14/the-truth-about-bbc-al-jazeera-reuters-reports-of-unrest-in-soura-kashmir.

79   "Indian-administered Kashmir cut off from the world." Reporters Without Borders. Aug 6, 2019. https://rsf.org/en/indian-administered-kashmir-cut-world.

80   "Jailed Kashmir rights activist Khurram Parvez in Time's 100 list." Al Jazeera. May 24, 2022. https://www.aljazeera.com/news/2022/5/24/jailed-kashmir-rights-activist-khurram-parvez-in-times-100-list. I spent some time with Khurram during my stay in Kashmir and I can confirm that he is one of Kashmir's most dedicated activists, having worked tirelessly for decades, as well as an amiable and insightful conversationalist. I wholeheartedly hope that by the time you read this he is a free man.

81   "India: Repression Persists in Jammu and Kashmir." Human Wrights Watch. Aug 2, 2022. https://www.hrw.org/news/2022/08/02/india-repression-persists-jammu-and-kashmir.

82   "India: Kashmiri Journalist Held Under Abusive Laws." Human Rights Watch. Feb 8, 2022. https://www.hrw.org/news/2022/02/08/india-kashmiri-journalist-held-under-abusive-laws.

83   Hussian, Bilal. "India Cuts Off Government Advertising to Over 20 Kashmiri Outlets." Voice of America. Jan 25, 2021. https://www.voanews.com/press-freedom/india-cuts-government-advertising-over-30-kashmiri-outlets.

84   Hassan, Aakash. "Kashmir's vanishing newspaper archives." Coda Story. Nov 23, 2021. https://www.codastory.com/rewriting-history/kashmir-vanishing-newspaper/.

85   Ibid.

86   Shah, Fahad. "India's Militant Pipeline." Foreign Policy. Dec 18, 2019. https://foreignpolicy.com/2019/12/18/jailed-stone-throwing-join-terrorist-militant-group-kashmir-radicalization/.

87   Dulat, AS. "Kashmir looks ahead at a winter of discontent." Deccan Chronicle. Dec 27, 2020. https://www.deccanchronicle.com/opinion/columnists/271220/kashmir-looks-ahead-at-a-winter-of-discontent.html.

88   "Datasheet: Jammu and Kashmir." South Asia Terror Portal. https://www.satp.org/datasheet-terrorist-attack/fatalities/india-jammukashmir.

89   Kapur, Roshni. "A New Phase of Militancy in Kashmir: Challenges for India." Middle East Institute. Feb 17, 2022. https://www.mei.edu/publications/new-phase-militancy-kashmir-challenges-india.

90   Nanda, Showkat. "India is Arming Villagers in One of Earth's Most Militarized Places." The New York Times. March 8, 2023. https://www.nytimes.com/2023/03/08/world/asia/kashmir-village-defense-committees.html.

91   Zargar, Safwat. "Shadow militants: Why a policeman's killing has shaken a battle-hardened Kashmiri village." Scroll. Aug 16, 2022. https://scroll.in/article/1030081/shadow-militants-why-a-policemans-killing-has-shaken-a-battle-hardened-kashmiri-village.

92   Ur-Rehman, Zia, and Masood, Salman. "Religion-Fueled Mobs on the Rise Again in Pakistan." The New York Times. March 20, 2022. https://www.nytimes.com/2022/03/20/world/asia/pakistan-blasphemy-religious-violence.html.

93   "I see Kashmir from New Delhi at Midnight." Agha Shahid Ali. https://jaddeyekabir.com/2014/05/19/another-reposting-of-an-agha-shahid-ali-poem-i-see-kashmir-from-new-delhi-at-midnight/.

94   Buchan, James. "Kashmir." Granta. April 1, 1997. https://granta.com/kashmir/

95   Bhasin, Anuradha. "Modi's Final Assault on India's Press Freedom

Has Begun." The New York Times. March 8, 2023. https://www.nytimes.com/2023/03/08/opinion/india-kashmir-modi-media-censorship.html.

96 "Hindu monk in India charged over call for 'genocide' of Muslims." Al Jazeera. Jan 18, 2022. https://www.aljazeera.com/news/2022/1/18/india-hindu-monk-yati-narsinghanand-genocide-muslims-haridwar.

97 Guha, Ramachandra. "India at 75." The Telegraph. Aug 13, 2022. https://www.telegraphindia.com/opinion/india-at-seventy-five-free-nation-unfree-people/cid/1879871.

98 "Pankaj Mishra and Mirza Waheed on the Deadh of India's Liberal Self-Image." The Wire. Jan 5, 2020. https://thewire.in/rights/pankaj-mishra-mirza-waheed-kashmir-caa-india.

99 Filkins, "Blood and Soil."

100 "Did someone make a fool of me, 'fore I could show 'em how it's done?" — Neko Case, Middle Cyclone.

101 Zakaria, Fareed. "After often-gloomy Davos, I'm still optimistic about the future." Washington Post. Jan 19, 2023. https://www.washingtonpost.com/opinions/2023/01/19/davos-optimistic-world-future/.

102 Wani, Maknoon. "Kashmir is bleeding. So is its economy." Al Jazeera. Feb 4, 2023. https://www.aljazeera.com/opinions/2023/2/4/kashmir-is-bleeding-its-economy.

103 Basit, Abdul. "A Peshawar Bombing Reveals Pakistan's Worsening Terrorism Predicament." Newlines. Feb 10, 2023. https://newlinesmag.com/argument/peshawar-bombing-reveals-pakistans-worsening-terrorism-predicament/.

104 Kathju, Junaid. "U.S. arms left in Afghanistan are turning up in a different conflict." NBC News. Jan 30, 2023. https://www.nbcnews.com/news/world/us-weapons-afghanistan-taliban-kashmir-rcna67134& "US Puts Onus of Talks On India and Pakistan." https://kashmirobserver.net/2023/01/24/us-puts-onus-of-talks-on-india-pakistan/.

105 "Surveillance concerns as India issues new digital IDs in Kashmir." Al Jazeera. Jan 26, 2023. https://www.aljazeera.com/news/2023/1/26/surveillance-concerns-as-india-issues-new-digital-ids-in-kashmir.

106 See opening of this Introduction, page 8 of this book.

107 Powell, Michael. "Sundance Liked Her Documentary on Terrorism, Until Muslim Critics Didn't." The New York Tiomes. Sept 25, 2022. https://www.nytimes.com/2022/09/25/us/sundance-jihad-rehab-meg-smaker.html.

108 Malcolm, Janet. The Journalist and the Murderer. (2011). Vintage

Reprint edition. p1.

109 Schmall, "Normalcy."

110 Most of the SUVs that ferry passengers from one town to another are Sumos made by Tata Motors.

111 "Desiccate" definition. Merriam-Webster online: https://www.merriam-webster.com/dictionary/desiccate.

112 Snedden, p27.

113 Snedden, p20.

114 "Key Buddhist Site Said to Be Found in Kashmir Valley." The New York Times. June 20, 1971. https://www.nytimes.com/1971/06/20/archives/key-buddhist-site-said-to-be-found-in-kashmir-valley.html.

115 Snedden, p27.

116 Snedden, p28-29.

117 "A Memory of Religious Plurality in Jammu and Kashmir." European Foundation for South Asian Studies. June 2020. https://www.efsas.org/publications/study-papers/a-memory-of-religious-plurality-in-jammu-and-kashmir/.

118 Hasan, Mohibbul. (2005). Kashmir Under the Sultans (Reprinted ed.). Delhi: Aakar Books. p80.

119 These generally happen at night, so no children or teachers are in danger. No group claims responsibility for such attacks, so we're left with speculation about why this is done, or by who. Pro-India voices tend to argue that pro-independence leaders encourage the burning of schools so that young Kashmiris, with no education and nothing to do, turn to militantism. There's no proof of this. Source: Fareed, Rifat, and Essa, Azad. "Who is burning down Kashmir's schools?" Al Jazeera. Nov 11, 2016. https://www.aljazeera.com/features/2016/11/11/who-is-burning-down-kashmirs-schools.

120 Wani, Fayaz. "47 schools came under arson attacks in Kashmir." New Indian Express. Dec 7, 2016. https://www.newindianexpress.com/nation/2016/dec/07/47-schools-came-under-arson-attacks-in-kashmir-1546672.html.

121 Ali, Agha Shahid. "The Country Without a Post Office." Posted online by Mara Ahmed: https://maraahmed.com/wp/2010/08/11/the-country-without-a-post-office-by-agha-shahid-ali/.

122 Shakespeare, William. "Henry VIII", act 3, scene II. https://www.litcharts.com/shakescleare/shakespeare-translations/henry-viii/act-3-scene-2.

123 Waheed, Mirza. "How to award a posthumous sedition award to a poet." Scroll. Feb 26, 2016. https://scroll.in/article/804163/how-to-award-a-posthumous-sedition-award-to-a-poet.

124 Kapoor, Manon. "The Country Without a Post Office." Boston Review. Aug 30, 2019. http://bostonreview.net/arts-society/manan-kapoor-country-without-post-office.

125 Ali, Agha Shahid. (1998). The Country Without a Post Office. W.W. Norton promotional page: https://wwnorton.co.uk/books/9780393317619-the-country-without-a-post-office.

126 Kapoor, "Post Office."

127 Ecevit, Bulent. "Visiting Turk Says of Americans: Even Angels Can Go Wrong." Sunday Journal and Sentinel. Jan 9, 1955. http://ecevityazilari.org/items/show/1427.

128 Knight, Sam. "Rory Stewart, the Insurgent Candidate for British Prime Minister, Soars Up and Out." The New Yorker. June 19, 2019. https://www.newyorker.com/news/letter-from-the-uk/rory-stewart-the-insurgent-candidate-for-prime-minister-soars-up-and-out.

129 "Press Release." Nobel Peace Prize 2009. Nobel Prize Organization. https://www.nobelprize.org/prizes/peace/2009/press-release/.

130 Purkiss and Serle, "Obama's covert drone war."

131 Feroz, Emran. "Death by drone — the Unites States' vicious Afghan legacy." Qantara English. June 5, 2020. https://en.qantara.de/content/war-crimes-on-the-hindu-kush-death-by-drone-the-united-states-vicious-afghan-legacy.

132 "Transcript: President Joe Biden delivers foreign policy speech." Nikkei. Feb 5, 2021. https://asia.nikkei.com/Politics/Transcript-President-Joe-Biden-delivers-foreign-policy-speech.

133 Wright, Robin. "The World Likes Biden But Doubts the U.S. Can Reclaim Global Leadership." The New Yorker. Feb 5, 2021. https://www.newyorker.com/news/our-columnists/the-world-likes-biden-but-doubts-the-us-can-reclaim-global-leadership.

134 Stewart, Rory. "Lord of misrule." Times Literary Suppllement. Nov 6, 2020. https://www.the-tls.co.uk/articles/boris-johnson-tom-bower-book-review-rory-stewart/.

135 Wintour, Patrick. "Boris Johnson to visit India in January in bid to transform G7." The Guardian. Dec 15, 2020. https://www.theguardian.com/world/2020/dec/15/boris-johnson-to-visit-india-in-january-in-bid-to-transform-g7.

136 Hall, Rachel. "Tory party's lurch to the right 'painful' to watch, says Rory Stewart." The Guardian. Aug 6, 2022. https://www.theguardian.com/politics/2022/aug/06/tory-partys-lurch-to-right-painful-to-watch-says-rory-stewart.

137 Elias, Norbert, and Scotson, John. (1995). The Established and the Outsiders. SAGE publications, 2nd edition.

138   Quran, Surah Fussilat 34, 41:34. https://www.islamawakened.com/quran/41/34/.

139   Bose, Sumantra. "Kashmir: An Uneasy Jewel in the Indian Crown." Open. Sept 15, 2016. https://openthemagazine.com/essay/kashmir-an-uneasy-jewel-in-the-indian-crown/.

140   Bhardwaj, Ananya. "Asiya Andrabi: Kashmir's first woman separatist who also dreamed of marrying a mujahid." The Print. Dec 10, 2018. https://theprint.in/india/governance/asiya-andrabi-kashmirs-first-woman-separatist-who-also-dreamt-of-marrying-a-mujahid/160138/.

141   Ibid.

142   "Asiya Andrabi Case: NIA Summons KO Reporter to Delhi." Kashmir Observer. July 14, 2018. https://kashmirobserver.net/2018/07/14/asiya-andrabi-case-nia-summons-ko-reporter-to-delhi/.

143   From the article page on Kashmir Observer's website, since taken down.

144   "Lock up your daughters." The Economist. April 12, 2007. https://www.economist.com/asia/2007/04/12/lock-up-your-daughters — reprinted with permission.

145   "Asiya Andrabi Played Key Role in Cinemas' Closure in Valley: NIA." Outlook India. Oct 26, 2019. https://www.outlookindia.com/website/story/india-news-asiya-andrabi-played-key-role-in-cinemas-closure-in-valley-nia/341158.

146   Latif, Aamir. "Family of jailed Kashmiri woman leader fears for her safety." Anadolu Agency. July 28, 2020. https://www.aa.com.tr/en/asia-pacific/family-of-jailed-kashmiri-woman-leader-fears-for-her-safety/1924720.

147   Ahmed, Munir. "Family asks for help in release of Kashmir separatist leader." Associated Press. Jan 4, 2021. https://apnews.com/article/kashmir-pakistan-india-united-nations-islamabad-794468b6f1bdabff5ead29fa7b1a9070.

148   "Senate passes unaminous resolution on Yasin Malik, Asiya Andrabi." Kashmir News Service. Jan 18, 2021. https://kmsnews.org/news/2021/01/18/senate-passes-unanimous-resolution-on-aasiya-andrabi-yasin-malik/.

149   Coll, "Back Channel."

150   Ali, Jehangir. "Three Years After Centre's Aug 5 Move, Mirwaiz Umar Farooq Still in Detention." The Wire. Aug 7, 2022. https://thewire.in/rights/three-years-after-centres-august-5-move-mirwaiz-umar-farooq-still-in-detention.

151   "Habba Khatoon poems." Poetryhunter.com. 2012. https://www.poemhunter.com/i/ebooks/pdf/habba_khatoon_2012_7.pdf.

152   Nazir, Aijaz. "Kashmir loses its cinema halls to prolonged conflict." Al
      Jazeera. July 2, 2018. https://www.aljazeera.com/features/2018/7/2/
      kashmir-loses-its-cinema-halls-to-prolonged-conflict.

153   Mogul, Rhea, and Manveena, Suri. "Movie theaters reopen in Indian-
      controlled Kashmir for the first time in more than two decades."
      CNN. Sept 21, 2022. https://edition.cnn.com/2022/09/21/india/india-
      kashmir-cinemas-opening-intl-hnk/index.html

154   "Salman Khan is helping cultural aggression of Kashmir: Asiya
      Andrabi, separatist leader." https://www.firstpost.com/bollywood/
      salman-khan-is-helping-cultural-aggression-of-kashmir-asiya-
      andrabi-separatist-leader-2253364.html.

155   "Kashmir will get its first multiplex today in Srinagar." Live Mint. Sept
      20, 2022. https://www.livemint.com/news/india/kashmir-is-to-get-its-
      first-multiplex-today-in-srinagar-see-photos-11663637869213.html.

156   Bonaparte, Napoleon. Quotepark. https://quotepark.com/
      quotes/2110175-napoleon-i-of-france-anarchy-is-the-stepping-stone-
      to-absolute-power/.

157   Bhat, Sunil. "Zojila Pass on Srinagar-Leh Highway reponed in record
      73 days." India Today. https://www.indiatoday.in/india/story/border-
      roads-organisation-zojila-pass-srinagar-leh-highway-record-73-
      days-1927048-2022-03-19.

158   "The road to Zoji La Pass is a thrilling and scary experience."
      Dangerous Roads. https://www.dangerousroads.org/asia/india/111-
      zoji-la-pass-india.html

159   Gaur, Viraj. "Zoji La Tunnel" All you need to know." The Week. May
      23, 2018. https://www.theweek.in/news/india/2018/05/23/zoji-la-
      tunnel--all-you-need-to-know.html.

160   Kumar, Ravi Prakash, ed. "Construction of Zojila tunnel starts. To
      reduce travel time from 3 hrs to 15 mins." Live Mint. Oct 15, 2020.
      https://www.livemint.com/news/india/construction-of-zojila-tunnel-
      starts-srinagar-to-leh-in-just-15-minutes-11602749456570.html

161   Gul, Ayaz. "China's Investments in Pakistan-Administered Kashmir
      Seen as 'Blow' to India." Voice of America. July 15, 2020. https://
      www.voanews.com/east-asia-pacific/voa-news-china/chinas-
      investments-pakistan-administered-kashmir-seen-blow-india.

162   "China building new road in Gilgit-Baltistan — India hits back in
      Indo-Pacific." Economic Times. Jan 18, 2021. https://economictimes.
      indiatimes.com/news/defence/china-building-new-road-in-gilgit-
      baltistan-india-hits-back-in-indo-pacific/articleshow/80305144.cms

163   "India-China clash: 20 Indian troops killed in Ladakh fighting." BBC.
      June 16, 2020. https://www.bbc.com/news/world-asia-53061476

164   "India's Shutdown Numbers." Internet Shutdowns. https://

internetshutdowns.in/.

165   Naqash, Rayan. "Behind the conspiracy theories: Why Kashmir reels under power cuts every winter." Scroll. Nov 15, 2017. https://scroll.in/article/857433/behind-the-conspiracy-theories-why-kashmir-reels-under-power-cuts-every-winter.

166   I was not using a recording device.

167   Melville, Herman. (1999). Moby Dick. Wordsworth Editions. Chapter 9.

168   Gandhi, Mohandas K. "The Gospel of Truth." Gandhi Research Foundation. https://www.mkgandhi.org/momgandhi/chap09.htm.

169   Moorcroft, Trebeck and Wilson. "Travels."

170   "Jammu and Kashmir: Indian Army Initiates Court Marshall Against Captain Bhoopendra Singh for Alleged Encounter in Shopian District." IANS. Apr 4, 2022. https://www.latestly.com/india/news/jammu-and-kashmir-indian-army-initiates-court-martial-against-captain-bhoopendra-singh-for-alleged-encounter-in-shopian-district-3549433.html.

171   Carroll, Lewis. (2016 edition). Alice's Adventures in Wonderland. Wisehouse Classics.

172   Akhtar, Ayad. (2020). Homeland Elegies. Little, Brown and Company. Kindle Edition. p309.

173   Yasir, Sameer. "Kashmir, Under Siege and Lockdown, Faces a Mental Health Crisis." The New York Times. April 26, 2020. https://www.nytimes.com/2020/04/26/world/asia/kasmir-india-mental-health-coronavirus.html

174   "MSF scientific survey: 45 percent of Kashmiri population experiencing mental distress." Medecins Sans Frontiers. May 18, 2016. https://www.msfindia.in/msf-scientific-survey-45-kashmiri-population-experiencing-mental-distress/.

175   "Memory of Religious Plurality," EFSAS.

176   "One bird, two heads." The Patriot. Nov 29, 2018. http://thepatriot.in/2018/11/29/one-bird-two-heads/.

177   Ibid.

178   "Memory of Religious Plurality," EFSAS.

179   Devadas, David. "Radical Land Reforms Were Key to Sheikh Abdullah's Towering Influence in Kashmir." The Wire. Dec 8, 2017. https://thewire.in/government/radical-land-reforms-key-sheikh-abdullahs-towering-influence-kashmir.

180   "Memory of Religious Plurality," EFSAS.

181   Filkins, "Blood and Soil."

182 Singh, Karan Deep, and Raj, Suhasini. "'Muslims Are Foreigners': Inside India's Campaign to Decide Who Is a Citizen." The New York Times. April 4, 2020. https://www.nytimes.com/2020/04/04/world/asia/india-modi-citizenship-muslims-assam.html.

183   "Bombay HC Says Peaceful CAA Protesters Cannot Be Called Traitors, 'Anti-National'." The Wire. Feb 15, 2020. https://thewire.in/law/bombay-high-court-caa-protests.

184 Halarnkar, Samar. "The mass radicalisation that India does not acknowledge." Scroll. Jan 24, 2021. https://scroll.in/article/984915/the-mass-radicalisation-that-india-does-not-acknowledge.

185 Desai, Shweta. "The 'Love Jihad' Conspiracy Theory." Newlines. Dec 21, 2020. https://newlinesmag.com/reportage/the-love-jihad-conspiracy-theory/

186 Pakistan arrests more than a dozen over Hindu temple attack." Al Jazeera. Dec 31, 2020. https://www.aljazeera.com/news/2020/12/31/pakistan-arrests-14-people-over-demolishing-of-hindu-temple.

187 Chadri, Seshari. "Demand of some Kashmiri Pandits to restore Article 370 is illogical and lacks historical support." The Print. July 5, 2020. https://theprint.in/opinion/demand-of-some-kashmiri-pandits-to-restore-art-370-is-illogical-lacks-historical-support/471677/.

188 "Identiy of Kashmir buried with exodus of Pandits in 1990: PM Modi in Lok Sabha." New Indian Express. Feb 6, 2020. https://www.newindianexpress.com/nation/2020/feb/06/identity-of-kashmir-buried-with-exodus-of-pandits-in-1990-pm-modi-in-lok-sabha-2099933.html

189 Chotiner, Isaac. "What a Disturbing New Film Reveals about Modi's India." The New Yorker. June 21, 2022. https://www.newyorker.com/culture/q-and-a/what-a-disturbing-new-film-reveals-about-modis-india.

190 "India PM Modi lays foundation for Ayodhya Ram temple amid Covid surge." BBC. Aug 5, 2020. https://www.bbc.com/news/world-asia-india-53577942.

191 Chakraborty, Abhrajyoti. "India's Leading Documentary Filmmaker Has a Warning." New York Times Magazine. Dec 1, 2020. https://www.nytimes.com/2020/12/01/magazine/india-documentary-anand-patwardhan.html.

192 Langa, Mahesh. "Gujarat court denies bail to Teesta Setalvad, Sreekumar." The Hindu. July 30, 2022. https://www.thehindu.com/news/national/other-states/gujarat-riots-forgery-case-bail-pleas-of-teesta-setalvad-and-sreekumar-rejected/article65702856.ece

193 Saikia, Arunabh, and Iyer, Aishwarya. "Gujarat court ignored trial court's opinion as board with five BJP members set BilkisBano convicts free." Scroll. Aug 18, 2022. https://scroll.in/article/1030779/

gujarat-ignored-trial-courts-opinion-as-board-with-five-bjp-members-set-bilkis-bano-convicts-free.

194 Singh, Karan Deep, Raj, Suhasini, and Mashal, Mujib. "In India, New Wave of Trauma as 11 Convicted of Rape and Murder Walk Free." The New York Times. Aug 20, 2022. https://www.nytimes.com/2022/08/20/world/asia/india-rape-muslim-hindu.html.

195 Ayyub, Rana. "India just take a dangerous step on disinformation." Washington Post. Jan 26, 2023. https://www.washingtonpost.com/opinions/2023/01/26/india-modi-disinformation-press-freedom/.

196 Suri, Manveena, Sehgal, Kunal, and Mogul, Rhea. "Search of BBC offices by India govt ends after three-day raid." CNN. Feb 16, 2023. https://edition.cnn.com/2023/02/16/media/india-bbc-office-raid-third-day-thursday-intl-hnk/index.html.

197 Thucydides. The Peloponnesian War. https://anastrophe.uchicago.edu/cgi-bin/perseus/citequery3.pl?dbname=GreekNov21&query=Thuc.%203.44.3&getid=2.

198 Timmons, Heather. "In 'The Meadow', a chilling alternate view of the 1995 Kashmiri kidnappings." The New York Times. April 13, 2012. https://india.blogs.nytimes.com/2012/04/13/in-the-meadow-a-chilling-alternate-view-of-the-1995-kashmiri-kidnappings/.

199 Aeschylus. Agamemnon. https://dwkcommentaries.com/2014/02/10/aeschylus-on-suffering-and-wisdom/.

200 Jha, Prashant. "Turkish Prez Erdogan raises Kashmir at UN meet again. There is a difference." Hindustan Times. Sept 21, 2022. https://www.hindustantimes.com/world-news/turkish-prez-erdogan-raises-kashmir-at-un-meet-again-there-is-a-difference-101663781800581.html.

201 Lepeska, David. "The destruction of Sur: Is this historic district a target for gentrification?" The Guardian. Feb 9, 2016. https://www.theguardian.com/cities/2016/feb/09/destruction-sur-turkey-historic-district-gentrification-kurdish.

Advance Praise for the book

At a time when media in the Valley has been pressured to abandon its mission of speaking truth to power, *Desiccated Land* is a reminder of a time when courageous journalism defied militants and the state to bring readers information that helped make sense of the enormous forces shaping their lives. This book is a vital document of the bravery of our colleagues in Kashmir.

— **Naresh Fernandes,** *award-winning journalist and bestselling author of City Adrift*

Since it's no longer possible for most of us to see what we have in Kashmir and what we continue to put Kashmiris through, Indians in particular will benefit from reading David Lepeska's *Desiccated Land.*

— **Aakar Patel,** *Amnesty India chair, author Price of the Modi Years and other books*

Desiccated Land is a fascinating exploration of everything Kashmir. This collection of riveting essays — snapshots of people, politics, rights abuses, religion, culture, and more — presents a rich kaleidoscope of Kashmiri struggles, resilience and everyday life. Lepeska examines locals' ideas and aspirations with honesty and subtlety, eavesdropping into lives, moments, minds, and events.

— **Arunadha Bhasin,** *editor Kashmir Times, author A Dismantled State*

Resonating with love and empathy, *Desiccated Land* weaves a rich tapestry to tell the story of a cursed and enchanted land. As the Modi government makes it impossible to chronicle the present, Desiccated Land presents a powerful record of the tragedy that is Kashmir.

— **Debasish Roy Chowdhury,** *journalist, co-author To Kill A Democracy:*
India's Passage to Despotism

David Lepeska's *Desiccated Land* presents a deeply subjective account of his year reporting for the Kashmir Observer. Yet far from detracting, this approach adds enormous value to a book that features his trenchant views on a range of subjects, including the policies of his homeland, the US. In the end, Lepeska's vast empathy for the Kashmiri people shines through, highlighting what life is really like in the troubled Valley.

— **Manoj Joshi,** *ORF Distinguished Fellow,*
author of Lost Rebellion: Kashmir in the Nineties

This is an extraordinary book.

— **Amitabh Mattoo,** *Padma Shri honoree, JNU professor,*
leading political thinker, author, and columnist

Through a gripping personal account, David Lepeska offers a rare and poignant look at life in Kashmir, seamlessly knitting together the complexities of politics, religion, and identity. Written with raw honesty and emotional depth, *Desiccated Land* is mandatory reading for anyone seeking to understand this tumultuous region and the human experiences within it.

— **Adeel Hussain,** *co-author of Nehru: The Debates that Defined India,*
law professor at New York University Abu Dhabi

Desiccated Land is a thoughtful and thought-provoking book. Its engaging and insightful content -- an American journalist's observations, adventures, interviews and reporting — conveys a deep understanding of ethnic Kashmiris and their struggle to endure an arduous and "seemingly endless" insurgency.

— **Christopher Snedden,** *Australian scholar, author of Independent*
Kashmir: An Incomplete Aspiration

A fine collection of vivid vignettes on the Kashmir conundrum by a keen and informed observer.

— **Sumit Ganguly,** *Rabindranath Tagore Chair at Indiana University, author of The Crisis*
in Kashmir and Conflict Unending: India-Pakistan Tensions since 1947

Desiccated Land is an important and timely book. A unique blend of memoir and reportage, this work offers sharp perspectives on Kashmiri intellectuals and leaders while drawing attention to Kashmiri culture under siege. The insightful introduction critiques US' policies in South Asia and argues that they nurtured insurgency in Kashmir. Lepeska encourages readers to question the rhetoric of American exceptionalism and the US' inability to put ideals of freedom and justice into practice, making clear that America's unwillingness to support Kashmir's freedom struggle has enabled further oppression by India's authoritarian Hindu nationalist government, leading to an exclusion of minorities and an erosion of press freedom and democratic principles. A must-read to understand troubled Kashmir.

— **Shahla Hussain,** *St. John's University professor, author of Kashmir in the Aftermath of Partition*

Desiccated Land is old-school foreign correspondence in its purest form. The love for Kashmir and its people shines through.

— **Mike Giglio,** *journalist, author of Shatter the Nations: ISIS and the War for the Caliphate*

David Lepeska is a gifted writer with a knack for deftly handling emotive issues and a deep understanding of Kashmir and the Muslim world. In *Desiccated Land*, these traits come together wonderfully to contextualise the Kashmir conflict within world dynamics and craft a compelling read for Indian and global audiences.

— **Mohamed Zeeshan**, *foreign affairs columnist, author of Flying Blind: India's Quest for Global Leadership*

David Lepeska's *Desiccated Land* examines the human aspect of the decades-long Kashmir conflict and offers a clear-eyed look into the region's origins and evolution that sheds light on how minor disputes escalate into complex, ravaging wars. Lepeska has written an excellent book. I honestly enjoyed every bit of it.

— **Ammar Habib**, *bestselling author of The Orphans of Kashmir*

Kashmir is a complex political conundrum with seemingly no conceivable solution, so what's needed is to understand the situation objectively, understand the people of Kashmir, their lives, history, mythology, and culture, as well as their traumas. That's exactly what this book delivers, through sharp journalistic encounters with local people, scholars, and even militants. *Desiccated Land* is one of the most objective and insightful accounts I've read of the lives of Kashmiri people suffering for years under various political narratives.

— **Rahman Abbas,** *novelist & recipient of India's Sahitya Akademi Award*

Desiccated Land is a delightful read, albeit on a massive tragedy. Lepeska's intimate and visceral portrayal of daily life in Kashmir powerfully surfaces the essential yet oft-ignored human dimensions of the troubled region. I highly recommend this book to all those looking to know and feel the real Kashmir, beyond the headlines.

— **Saqib Qureshi,** *bestselling author of The Broken Contract*

David Lepeska's writing is imbued with a sense of reflexivity, enabling *Desiccated Land* to grapple with the internal, regional, historical and geostrategic forces that have shaped one of the world's most dangerous nuclear flashpoints. Lepeska's journalistic style makes this an enjoyable and insightful work I highly recommend.

— **Syed Mohammad Ali,** *lecturer at Johns Hopkins University,*
author of Development, Poverty and Power in Pakistan

David Lepeska has written an indispensable account of one of the world's most painful and forgotten conflicts. This book is a must-read for anyone seeking to learn about Kashmir, one of the beautiful yet tragic regions of the world.

— **Murtaza Hussain,** *book critic and The Intercept writer*

Desiccated Land offers not only well-informed historical insights and compelling eyewitness accounts, but empathy as well. Lepeska recognizes the pain of the Kashmiris, the repeated abandonment and denial of their right to determine their own fate, and places their predicament in the broadest context: the 'Kashmirization' of India, and even the world — as nationalism is allowed to run amok. One may disagree with some of his political assessments, but we are in Lepeska's debt for reaching out to the marginalized dwellers of the mountains and giving them a loud and resonant voice.

— **Yo'av Karny,** *Israeli journalist, author of Highlanders: A Journey to the Caucasus*

David Lepeska is not just an insightful journalist, but also a sharp and witty writer. *Desiccated Land* puts a magnifying glass to Kashmir and its people and captures myriad complexities of one of the world's most troubled regions. I loved this brilliant book and recommend it wholeheartedly.

— **Mustafa Akyol,** *New York Times opinion contributor, bestselling*
author Reopening Muslim Minds and other books

Desiccated Land offers a rare portrait of the stunning but troubled region of Kashmir. As one of very few Western reporters for Kashmir Observer, Lepeska is uniquely placed to provide the necessary nuance to understand the often volatile reality. He also details how the US has contributed to Kashmir's destabilisation and delivers an accessible and highly enjoyable read.

— **Jessica Mudditt,** *veteran journalist, author Our Home in Myanmar*